# Three Paths to Profitable Investing

# Three Paths to Profitable Investing

## Using ETFs in Healthcare, Infrastructure, and the Environment to Grow Your Assets

Jeffrey Feldman and Andrew Hyman

Vice President, Publisher: Tim Moore
Associate Publisher and Director of Marketing: Amy Neidlinger
Executive Editor: Jeanne Glasser
Editorial Assistant: Myesha Graham
Development Editor: Russ Hall
Operations Manager: Gina Kanouse
Senior Marketing Manager: Julie Phifer
Publicity Manager: Laura Czaja
Assistant Marketing Manager: Megan Colvin
Cover Designer: Alan Clements
Managing Editor: Kristy Hart
Project Editor: Betsy Harris
Copy Editor: Geneil Breeze
Proofreader: Kathy Ruiz
Indexer: Lisa Stumpf
Compositor: Nonie Ratcliff
Manufacturing Buyer: Dan Uhrig

Published by Pearson Education, Inc.
Publishing as FT Press
Upper Saddle River, New Jersey 07458

**This book is sold with the understanding that neither the author nor the publisher is engaged in rendering legal, accounting, or other professional services or advice by publishing this book. Each individual situation is unique. Thus, if legal or financial advice or other expert assistance is required in a specific situation, the services of a competent professional should be sought to ensure that the situation has been evaluated carefully and appropriately. The author and the publisher disclaim any liability, loss, or risk resulting directly or indirectly, from the use or application of any of the contents of this book.**

FT Press offers excellent discounts on this book when ordered in quantity for bulk purchases or special sales. For more information, please contact U.S. Corporate and Government Sales, 1-800-382-3419, corpsales@pearsontechgroup.com. For sales outside the U.S., please contact International Sales at international@pearson.com.

Company and product names mentioned herein are the trademarks or registered trademarks of their respective owners.

ISBN-10: 0-13-705426-2
ISBN-13: 978-0-13-705426-8

Pearson Education LTD.
Pearson Education Australia PTY, Limited.
Pearson Education Singapore, Pte. Ltd.
Pearson Education North Asia, Ltd.
Pearson Education Canada, Ltd.
Pearson Educatión de Mexico, S.A. de C.V.
Pearson Education—Japan
Pearson Education Malaysia, Pte. Ltd.

Library of Congress Cataloging-in-Publication Data

Feldman, Jeffrey Lee, 1947-
   Three paths to profitable investing : using ETFs in healthcare, infrastructure, and the environment to grow your assets / Jeffrey Feldman, Andrew Hyman. — 1st ed.
     p. cm.
   ISBN 978-0-13-705426-8 (hardcover : alk. paper) 1. Investments. 2. Medical care—Finance. 3. Infrastructure (Economics)—Finance. 4. Business enterprises—Environmental aspects. I. Hyman, Andrew
S. II. Title.
   HG4521.F36 2010
   332.63'27—dc22
                           2010004799

For Naomi, Mia, Maxine, and Jonny
—Jeff

To Julia and Adiel
—Andrew

# Contents

# Acknowledgments

There are hundreds of people I have met during my four decades on Wall Street who have taught and counseled me in more ways than I can count. It would be impossible to recognize all of them. For the past seven years, I have been privileged to be a participant in the Exchange Traded Fund (ETF) revolution that has taken place in the market. ETFs have amassed $1 trillion in assets as of March 2010, up from barely $100 billion just seven years ago. ETFs will be a critical capital market tool from now on, and I wish to thank those who helped put me in a front row seat.

Tony Dudzinski, who cofounded XShares with me, was the first person to teach me about ETFs and to this day I have not met anyone more knowledgeable than him. Sam Katz, my first partner in the business, helped me to formulate many of the concepts presented in this book. Bill Kridel, my great friend, has helped me to understand the changing face of medicine and biology. I am indebted to my colleagues at XShares: David Jaffin, Jim McCluskey and Rich Berenger for their unconditional support. Mike Rosella, who runs the fund practice at Paul Hastings, has not only been a great lawyer and advisor, he is a wonderful friend.

Jeanne Glasser, our editor at Pearson, has guided us expertly and comfortably through the creation of this book. I am deeply indebted to Jeanne for allowing me to become an author at this stage in my career. Betsy Harris has edited expertly, and we are grateful to all the folks at Pearson who participated in this venture.

I have been witness to many things in my 40 years in the business and I have drawn on that experience to write this book. For almost all those years, I have had the good fortune to have a true friend and business partner with me every step of the way. I want to thank Joe Schocken; it wouldn't have been fun without him.

Andrew Hyman, my coauthor, suggested we write this book and I am grateful he did. I certainly could not have completed this task on my own and Andrew, an experienced author, has deftly shown me the ropes. I look forward to collaborating with him again.

My wife Judy has spent as much time organizing, editing, and proofing this book as I have cowriting it. This is nothing new as she has been organizing, editing, and proofing my life for more than 40 years. And fortunately for me, she still has a lot of work to do.

**—Jeff Feldman**


This book could not have been written without the help of many people, although the authors remain responsible for the text. My thanks go to all these people; I have tried to list them all.

Professor Baruch Lev, Philip Bardes Professor of Accounting and Finance at the Leonard Stern School of Business at New York University, discussed the finances of biotech companies with me. His articles on biotech finance, available from his website, http://pages.stern.nyu.edu/~blev/, are most enlightening.

Professor David Dranove, Walter McNerney Distinguished Professor of Health Industry Management at Northwestern University's Kellogg School of Management, helped me understand key economic issues around the healthcare debate. His book, *Code Red: An Economist Explains How to Revive the Healthcare System without Destroying It* (Princeton University Press, 2008) is a must-read for anyone trying to understand the healthcare system and how the U.S. healthcare system evolved.

Burton Weisbrod, John Evans Professor of Economics at Northwestern University, spoke with me about healthcare economics. His article, "The healthcare quadrilemma: an essay on technological change, insurance, quality of care, and cost containment" (*J Econ Lit* 1991, 29:523-552) helped guide our discussion of the relationship between medical technology and costs. His article also needs to be read by those seeking to understand the relationship between how medicine is practiced and costs.

Joshua Bilenker M.D., of Aisling Capital, spent a great deal of time with me giving an overview of happenings in the biotech industry from the point of view of venture capitalists and a medical practitioner. I am grateful for his time and interest in our work.

In the field of green, I was fortunate to spend time with Richard Cook and Bob Fox, of Cook + Fox Architects LLP, the designers of the Bank of America tower in New York City, considered the greenest office building in the United States. They showed me how green and business go together and that sustainability in the environment can also create the profits that sustain businesses. They walk the talk in the offices—applying green principles in the workplace and creating a workplace that enlightens. Thanks to Jared Gilbert of Cook + Fox for arranging this most enlightening meeting.

Jon Levey, Chief Lending Officer, and Steve Sherman, Chief Operating Officer of GreenChoice Bank, a green-focused bank in Chicago, explained the nexus between green and banking and the role of the financial sector in fostering a green economy.

Bruce M. Hannon, Jubilee Professor of the Liberal Arts and Sciences at the University of Illinois at Urbana-Champaign, has always influenced my thinking on environmental matters—and how many projects that have bad environmental credentials also have bad business and economics behind them.

John Sodergreen, founder and Editor-in-Chief of Scudder Publishing (www.scudderpublishing.com) and Publisher of the *Energy Metro Desk* has been a help in the writing of this book, and all my other books, as he is always clued in on what is happening in the energy business and happy to share that information. *Energy Metro Desk* is a must-read for those who want to stay on top of what is happening in energy and green markets.

Richard Asplund has provided me with great insight into the whole ETF business and green investing. He knows the ins and outs of index and fund creation at the highest level. I was grateful for all that I learned from him. Anyone who wants to understand how to invest in green energy needs to read his book, *Profiting from Clean Energy* (Wiley, 2008).

Bill Wolff, Julia Rabinowitz, and Bernard Groveman of First Manhattan graciously arranged a meeting with Richard Asplund and XShares to discuss the future of environmental investing, which helped me better understand how leading investors approach the issues related to green investing.

Dan Gary, a very good friend, has provided a reliable sounding board while writing this book for dealing with many of the big picture issues and understanding health insurance's place in our society and the relationship between healthcare and employment.

George Nassos, the Director of the Center for Sustainable Enterprise at the Stuart School of Business, provided useful feedback on the business of the environment and the importance of sustainability for our economic future. He is tremendously knowledgeable.

Michael Gross, an attorney with the Authors Guild, helped us greatly with our contract negotiations. Any author who is about to sign a book contract needs to join the Authors Guild. At $90, it's a bargain because one of their publishing attorneys will review your contract and provide you with suggestions on how to improve it as part of your membership. This is great for authors without agents.

Robert Hyman, my brother, an MIT-trained engineer, guided me to the sources to understand infrastructure issues.

Thank you also to Daniel Elbaum, Jonathan Levine, Andrew Lowdon, Ted Netzky, Eero Pikat, Tina Rothstein, Emily Soloff, and Julie Vanderlip for all their help.

Michael Hyman pointed me in the direction of drugs such as Gleevec and how they are changing medicine, for which I am grateful.

A number of people reviewed the final manuscript and offered valuable comments that we did our best to incorporate into the manuscript. They helped make the book more coherent and more cohesive. These individuals include Mark Faasse, M.D., of the UIC College of Medicine, Paul Goodman of the Kingfisher Group and Allied District Properties, R. Kymn Harp of Robbins, Salomon, and Patt, Ltd., and Howard Singer. Thanks to Dan Hyman of Millennium Properties for referring me to Mr. Harp and to Craig Niederberger, M.D., for referring me to Dr. Faasse.

Also, thanks to Larry Rosenberg and Neal Weintraub, with whom I wrote *ETF Strategies and Tactics* (McGraw-Hill, 2008). Without them, I would not have met our editor, Jeanne Glasser, then at McGraw-Hill—and had the chance to write this book.

My thanks go to our fabulous team at Pearson that made this happen. First, thanks to our editor, Jeanne Glasser, who immediately recognized the vision Jeff had for the investment world and committed her company's resources to bring it to the public. Jeanne gave us time and attention, and we are grateful for her willingness to work with us to make this book happen. Although I haven't met him, Barry Ritholtz, of "The Big Picture" blog (www.ritholtz.com/blog) alerted me that Jeanne had moved to Pearson when we were looking for a publisher, and I gather I was the second author to call her up. Thank you, Barry. In addition, Geneil Breeze, our copy editor, and Betsy Harris, our project editor, have done a fabulous job of taking our material and editing it to make the manuscript flow and read well.

Without my coauthor, Jeff Feldman, this book would never have happened. He had the vision behind this book and the experience on Wall Street to know we need to change the way things work to empower investors. In addition, he sees the importance of investing in what matters in our lives. It has been great working with him and his wife, Judy, on this book.

My father, Leonard Hyman, read and commented on all the chapters, which has been a great help, given his extensive knowledge of utilities and other infrastructure businesses as well as the green aspects of those businesses. As the author of *America's Electric Utilities* (Public Utilities Reports, 2005), which has gone through eight editions, as well as numerous other books on utilities and privatization, he provided greatly beneficial viewpoints and knowledge.

I am grateful for the forbearance of my wife and daughter in the process of writing this book, especially during the final weeks, which fell during school winter vacation, as writing a book takes time away from family life. Still, my daughter must have absorbed something because she started producing her own illustrated books—and produced them faster than this one.

**—Andrew S. Hyman**

# About the Authors

**Jeffrey Feldman** is the Founder and Chief Executive Officer of XShares, a Registered Investment Advisor that specializes in the creation of Exchange Traded Funds. He is the cocreator of the TDX Independence Target Date ETFs which are operated in partnership with Amerivest, a subsidiary of TD Ameritrade. He serves as the Chairman of the Board of those funds.

Jeff has been on Wall Street for 40 years starting his career as a research analyst and then founded his own brokerage firm. In addition, he has taught economics as an adjunct instructor at several community colleges in New Jersey over the past 35 years.

**Andrew Hyman** is Vice President of Private Sector Advisors, Inc., a private consulting and investing company. He is coauthor of *ETF Strategies and Tactics: Hedge Your Portfolio in a Changing Market* and *Energy Risk Management: A Primer for the Utility Industry*, as well as other books on the utility industry.

# Introduction: Three Paths to a Prosperous Future

The first decade of the twenty-first century has not been kind to investors. On average, stocks lost about 1% per year over the ten-year period or more than 10% for the entire decade. During the decade we saw the collapse of three bubbles: the dot-com boom came to an end in 2000, the meteoric rise in housing prices in the middle years of the decade reversed sharply in 2007, and then in 2008 the massive over-leveraging of the banking system came home to roost, very nearly destroying the economy. The decade saw the emergence of vibrant economies and stock markets in the developing world, particularly in China but also in places such as Russia, Brazil, and India, among others. Investors hungry for the returns they had experienced during the roaring '90s sought to capitalize on the economic opportunity created by these emerging markets. Recognizing that growth requires access to commodities, precious metals, energy, and capital, investors sought to ride those new opportunities for investment gains. At the same time, Wall Street recognized this demand and rushed to create investment vehicles that would give investors the access they desired. Mostly these came in the form of exchange traded vehicles, primarily exchange traded funds (ETFs). ETFs, in addition to allowing investors to buy virtually any subset of stocks (by size, style, sector, or geographical division), for the first time ever also allowed for individuals to own foreign currencies, oil and gas, precious metals, and commodities. Previously only institutional investors could access these markets.

While all of this was going on, the United States was engaged in a war in Iraq that has since morphed into two wars, and in early 2010 we had 130,000 troops in Afghanistan. The expense of these wars, cou-pled with the decline in tax revenues as a result of the recession, has caused our national debt to swell past $10 trillion. The combination of a weakening U.S. economy and strengthening emerging markets caused the U.S. trade deficit to balloon to historic highs. This resulted in a weakening dollar. The political havoc in the Middle East, coupled with increased demand for energy worldwide, drove up the price of oil and gas. We have seen this scenario in the markets before, notably in 1973 after the Arab Oil Embargo drove up the price of oil and eventually the price of gold. But, in 1973, most investors could not access those asset classes. In the past five years, investors have poured tens of billions of dollars into macroeconomic bets on oil, precious metals, interest rates and sub-prime mortgages, currencies, and commodities. At the same time, investors have made huge bets against the dollar, which have become something of a self-fulfilling prophecy. A weaker dollar has some virtue in terms of making U.S. goods more attractive to foreign buyers, but never in history has it been a foundation for a strong econ-omy. So a cycle that was once virtuous has become vicious: We invest more in foreign markets, less in our own, and invest in oil and gold, which essentially are bets that we can make money at the expense of our own economy. It is simply irrational. These investments create no sustainable industry, no jobs, and no permanent wealth. The investor who is buying oil in the belief that it will rise to a level where nobody can afford to buy it is delusional. Expensive oil retards economic growth. The investor buying gold believing that gold will go to $3,000 an ounce (from its $1,100 price in early 2010) will earn profits in gravely weakened dollars whose purchasing power will be seriously dimin-ished. And because all this investment frenzy plays out very publicly on the Internet, on television, and in the newspapers, we eventually draw in too many investors and another bubble will develop and burst. Indi-vidual investors who chased the previous bubbles of this decade for the most part lost money when all was said and done.

We need to get back to basics and fund sustainable businesses that will create jobs, drive productivity, and increase our standard of living. It is this type of investment that is and always has been the only source of permanent wealth.

The bad news is that this type of investing does not appeal to those who have become enamored of "casino capitalism." They will continue to make bets against the American economy so long as it is working.

The good news is that there is a technology-based revolution occurring that rivals, and probably will surpass, the 1982 to 2000 bull market led by the information age and telecommunications companies. In medicine and biotechnology, green technologies and alternative energy, and the rebuilding of the U.S. infrastructure lay the greatest investment opportunities in history. Over the next 25 years, medicine will be revolutionized as we completely change the way we diagnose and treat disease. During that same period, we will break free of our dependence on imported fossil fuels by developing alternatives such as solar, wind, and nuclear. We will utilize new technologies first to reduce carbon emissions and eventually to eliminate them. And we will rebuild our roads and bridges, commercial structures, and transportation and shipping systems and retrofit all our real estate to be energy efficient.

The wealth that will be created in the next 25 years will dwarf that of the Internet era. Thirty years ago, one could have made the statement that most of the companies that would be industry leaders in the ensuing 30 years either did not yet exist or were too small to be known by the public. Microsoft, Cisco, Google, Dell, and Amazon all fit that description. In 1980, nobody had heard of any of them. In 2010, the same statement can be made. The companies that will drive us to prosperity in the next 30 years are busy at work right now, but most of us have never heard of them. The best news is that investors can own these companies today. Using the ETF structure, we do not have to figure out which will succeed and which will fail. We can own all the solar companies in one ETF and all the wind companies in another.

The purpose of this book is to describe the path to prosperity, to demonstrate that we must get out of the casino and back to fundamentals. We must create millions of jobs, drive the productivity of workers, deploy new technologies, and ultimately increase the standard of living for all. ETFs have been created that give investors total access to pharmaceutical, biotechnology, alternative energy, green technology, and infrastructure companies. We describe in detail each of the ETFs in these areas and some of their component companies. Many of these companies are small- to mid-cap in size but have the potential to become large and dominant players in their fields in the years to come. Investors should see this as an opportunity akin to investing in Internet companies in the early 1980s.

Three major forces are shaping an environment that will foster this prosperity:

- The first is a demographic wave of new investors—the Baby Boom Echo generation born between 1974 and 1989—who are now starting to invest heavily in the stock market and whose money has great potential to move the markets just as Baby Boomer money in the early '80s ignited the longest bull market of all time.

- The second force comes in the form of the new and innovative technologies being developed in all these areas—biotechnology, saving the environment, and rebuilding infrastructure—that will solve pressing needs for society.

- The third major factor is the development of ETFs, which allow investors to buy into the biotechnology, environment, and infrastructure fields in a diversified, low-cost manner. ETFs increase an investor's ability to gain exposure to innovative new companies while mitigating the risk of that investment.

# The Way Forward

If we are to be a prosperous nation, we must invest in activities that create real economic utility and promote social welfare. The right investments cannot be discovered sitting at a computer terminal in a windowless room. In fact, they are easily revealed if we simply look out the window. We are dependent on fossil fuels, much of which we get from hostile states. We use that fuel inefficiently and waste a great deal of it. Our healthcare system is collapsing just as the Baby Boom generation (78 million people) is reaching its senior years. Healthcare has gone from 8% of gross domestic product (GDP) in 1980 to 17% of GDP ($2.5 trillion) in 2010 and is expected to rise to 25% of GDP by 2020. Finally our infrastructure is in dire need of repair. From the electrical grid to water mains to the rails, roads, and bridges, we need to make a massive investment in the foundations on which our economy runs.

Fortunately, there is a comprehensive set of ETFs that allow us to invest in these three critical areas of our economy. In each case, the required investment is hundreds of billions of dollars. In each industry—alternative energy and clean technology, healthcare, and infrastructure—we can create thousands of new companies and tens of millions of jobs. The technology in each case is ripe and ready for commercialization. In the 1980s, when we saw an economic boom based in the telecom and computer industries, Wall Street made its money by providing capital to these industries. Today, Wall Street has forsaken its capital formation role for a seat in the casino. But we can and must take matters into our own hands. You can travel these three paths to wealth without Wall Street's involvement. You can buy ETFs as easily as buying any publicly traded stock and build a portfolio that works for you.

Our goal here is to explain the various ETFs that invest in these critical areas. There is no question that the country cannot prosper if we do not create sustainable industries, and these three sectors represent our most pressing needs. No doubt there will be other sectors that flourish in the coming years, but none can thrive if we do not solve the fundamental issues. On the other hand, the businesses that tackle and overcome these problems will create substantial and permanent wealth. With a few clicks of a mouse, you can own these companies right now.

Investing in healthcare, the environment, and infrastructure through ETFs allows you to buy into the next major wave of investment and to help create a better society at the same time. For the investors willing to take control of their investments, the combination of demographic changes, new investment tools, and major societal needs make this a great time to seize investment opportunities. Assigning blame for financial misdeeds helps us feel better but locks us into arguing about the past, which will not rebuild the economy or make you money. Which do you want to do? If you want to make money in a sustainable economy, start reading. If not, return this book. It isn't for you.

# 1

## Understanding ETFs and Why They Beat Mutual Funds

Is there a low-cost, simple, easy to use, investment tool for buying into the trends of the future? Yes. It is the *exchange traded fund*, more popularly known as the *ETF*. An ETF is a security that trades on a stock exchange, made up of a basket of securities that track a particular index, such as the Dow Jones Industrial Average, or the S&P 500.[1] ETFs can track the performance of a particular group of stocks, including those in sectors, such as healthcare, green industry, and infrastructure. These funds allow investors to buy into an industry without the worries of buying a single stock. Unlike mutual funds, ETFs trade continuously throughout the day on an exchange, as does any listed security. In addition, their cost efficiency, compared to other investment strategies, makes them the ideal low-cost tool for an investor who wants to take charge of her portfolio.

## What Is an ETF?

An ETF is a security that tracks the performance of an index by holding, with the same weights as in the index, the securities comprising the index.[2] An investor who buys 100 shares of an ETF based on the S&P 500, will own a basket underlain by the shares of the companies in the S&P 500 in proportion to their weights in the index.

# What Is an Index?

Understanding indices helps investors understand what drives the price of an ETF. An index is a number that reflects the value of a basket of items. One common index is the consumer price index, which reflects the overall price level of a basket of commonly used household items that track price levels and inflation. Stock market indices were created to measure the performance of the overall stock market.

# How Does an Index Work?

To understand how an index works, consider the Three Paths Green Index depicted in Table 1.1, which lists the securities and their weights in the index.[3]

**TABLE 1.1    Components and Weights of the Three Paths Green Index**

| Security | Weight |
| --- | --- |
| Sunny Solar | 50% |
| Windy Windmills | 25% |
| Clean Cars | 25% |
| Total | 100% |

The stocks in the Three Paths Green Index determine the performance of the index in proportion to their weighting. For example, while Sunny Solar makes up only one-third (33.33%) of the total membership of the index, its 50% weighting makes its contribution to the index's performance equal to that of both Windy Windmills and Clean Cars *combined*.

The Three Paths Green Index is used to create the Three Paths Green ETF. Despite owning a fund underlain by those three stocks, the average investor cannot redeem the ETF for individual shares of Sunny Solar, Windy Windmills, or Clean Cars. Only market makers who buy and sell large amounts of securities can create an ETF by depositing the component securities, or redeem an ETF to receive the individual securities that make up the ETF.[4] The average investor will buy or sell the ETF and not exchange it for the individual shares. Still, the shares that make up the ETF will actually determine the price of the ETF.

Consider how the prices of the components affect the value of the Three Paths Green Index. The index's value is determined by multiplying the price of each stock by the weight of each stock in the index and totaling up the value. The fund's value is determined by multiplying the fund's index value by $1.00. Let's see what happens to the index, and the ETF, when the prices change in the shares of the three companies.[5] The weights indicate how much the movement of a stock's price will affect the index and consequently the ETF.[6]

Table 1.2 shows how price changes affect the value of the index and the ETF. The index value changes depending on the price action in each of the securities. On Day 1, each stock in the index has a price of $100, the index has a value of 100, and the fund trades at $100. The value of the index is determined by taking the price of each stock, multiplying it by the respective weighting to determine an index value. The index values for the three stocks are added to obtain an index value of 100 and fund value of $100. On Day 2, Sunny Solar increases in price 50% to $150, while the other two components stay the same. This leads to a 25% increase in the value of the index to 125, and the fund rises to $125. On Day 3, the price of Sunny Solar falls to $100, but the other two components each rise $50. The index remains unmoved from Day 2 staying at 125, and the fund is at $125. On Day 4, the price of Sunny Solar falls to $50, while the other components return to $100, and the index falls to 75 and the fund to $75. On Day 5, Sunny Solar returns to $100, yet the other two components both fall to 50, and the index remains at 75 and the fund at $75. Figure 1.1 shows the effect on the price of the ETF. The impact of each price move is in proportion to its weight in the index. The same applies to larger indices and funds with many components, although there might be some premiums, or discounts, in the value of the fund relative to the index due to a number of factors discussed later in this chapter in the section "Index Risk."

TABLE 1.2  Index Values and Weighting of the Three Paths Green Index (Index Value = Price × Weight)

| Security | Weight | Day 1 Price | Day 1 Index Value | Day 2 Price | Day 2 Index Value | Day 3 Price | Day 3 Index Value | Day 4 Price | Day 4 Index Value | Day 5 Price | Day 5 Index Value |
|---|---|---|---|---|---|---|---|---|---|---|---|
| Sunny Solar | 50% | $100 | 50 | $150 | 75 | $100 | 50 | $50 | 25 | $100 | 50 |
| Windy Windmills | 25% | $100 | 25 | $100 | 25 | $150 | 37.5 | $100 | 25 | $50 | 12.5 |
| Clean Cars | 25% | $100 | 25 | $100 | 25 | $150 | 37.5 | $100 | 25 | $50 | 12.5 |
| Index value | | | 100 | | 125 | | 125 | | 75 | | 75 |
| ETF price | | | $100 | | $125 | | $125 | | $75 | | $75 |

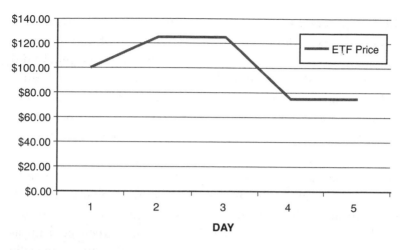

**Figure 1.1   ETF price**

# How Did Indices Change the Fund Management Business?

After indices were developed, investors used them to measure how an investment manager performed compared to the overall market measured by a benchmark such as Standard & Poor's 500 Index, which tracks the performance of 500 of the largest companies listed on U.S. stock exchanges.[7]

In the 1960s, numerous academic studies showed that most investment managers on average failed to outperform the major market indices such as the S&P 500—even before subtracting the fund's expenses from the returns.[8] Factoring in fees made it clear that active mutual fund managers benefited themselves at the expense of investors. Investors would have done better in most cases if they could have just invested in an index. The problem was they couldn't.

However, the birth of the index fund in the 1970s changed all that. The index fund tracks the performance of a market index by holding the same securities that make up the index in the same weights as the index.[9] That way the fund's performance matches the index, aside from minor variations due to the fact that an index incurs no costs, as opposed to a fund.[10] Pension funds and other institutional investors first used indexing. Retail investors then got into the game with the launch of the Vanguard 500 index fund, the first retail fund to track the S&P 500. This proved a cheaper way to invest, because these funds did not require investment managers and research departments—the index did the work for the fund—the fund company simply had to adjust its portfolio to match the index, as opposed to research and buy securities.

The birth of index funds spawned a new business—index manufacturing—that created new indices to benchmark managers in all areas. There are indices based on market capitalization, investing style (value or growth), sectors (such as biotech, green, and infrastructure), and all sorts of other categories. New funds, especially ETFs, have emerged to track these indices.

## Origins of ETFs

ETFs are relatively new. ETF trading on U.S. exchanges started in 1993, when the American Stock Exchange created the Standard & Poor's Depository Receipts, better known as the SPDR, which tracks the S&P 500. That one fund in 1993 spawned the more than 700 funds in existence today. Figure 1.2 depicts the rapid growth in the number of ETFs in the United States.

At the same time, the assets under management have also gone up to more than half a trillion dollars, as shown in Figure 1.3.

## Why Invest with ETFs?

Given their many strengths, it is no surprise that ETFs have grown so rapidly. They are ideal for the self-directed investor. Let's take a look at some of the characteristics of ETFs that make them the investment tool of the future, especially compared with mutual funds.

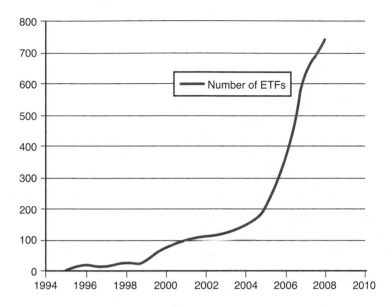

**Figure 1.2    ETFs in the United States by year (Source: Investment Company Institute, www.icifactbook.org)**

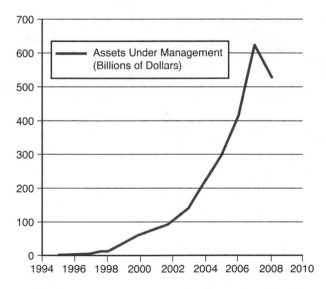

**Figure 1.3    Assets under management (billions of dollars) (Source: Investment Company Institute, www.icifactbook.org)**

## *Liquidity and Tradability*

Liquidity describes the ease with which an investor can buy and sell an investment. Liquid investments are easy to turn into cash. Homes are not particularly liquid, whereas treasury bills, with a deep market, are highly liquid. Mutual funds lie in the middle. They are only valued once a day, after the market closes, which is the only time they can be bought and sold at net asset value. This can create difficulty for investors. What happens if the market is falling and you want to sell your mutual fund during the day to minimize your losses? You can't. You can only sell it at the end of the day, after the market closes. On the other hand, the market may be starting an upward trend and you want to buy into it with a mutual fund. Forget it. Your order will not go in until after trading has ended, so you will buy the fund after prices have gone up, meaning that you will own fewer shares, for the same amount of money, than if you had been able to make your investment in the morning when the rally started.

One advantage of ETFs compared to mutual funds and many other investment products is their high degree of liquidity. Of course this liquidity may vary between ETFs, but on the whole ETFs are relatively liquid instruments. ETFs trade throughout the day, as does any share of stock, making it easier to get in and out of an ETF compared to a mutual fund. Of course, the buyer or seller is not guaranteed of making the sale at a desired price, but the flexibility can benefit the investor. That flexibility extends to the types of orders investors can use to buy and sell ETFs, which are the same as for stocks, including limit, market, and stop loss orders. These orders cannot be used with mutual funds. In addition, traders can sell an ETF short, which cannot be done with a mutual fund, to profit from a falling market. Also, investors can buy ETFs on margin, meaning they can lever their funds to command a larger portfolio, but at the same time face greater risk from an adverse market move.[11]

## *Transparency*

As Bernard Madoff's investors found out the hard way, investors need to know what is in their portfolios. Not knowing what is in one of their funds could lead to people owning something twice—once, for example, as a single stock and again within a mutual fund, which could mean overweighting in particular stocks or sectors. With opaque investments, such as hedge funds, it is highly unlikely investors will know the portfolio's contents, given the secretive nature of hedge fund managers. Even mutual funds are somewhat opaque. A fund may have a mandate to invest in a particular area, but managers are only required to disclose their portfolio every six months, and that information has 60 days to get to investors, so by the time investors receive notification of the fund's holdings, the fund could have turned the portfolio over, adding a totally different group of stocks to the portfolio and making it hard to know what the fund holds at any given time.

ETF owners do not have this problem, because an ETF's components are required to be disclosed, along with their stock prices, every 15 minutes throughout the trading day. An ETF owner, by accessing a website or contacting her broker, can always know what makes up the ETF and what weights are given to each underlying security.

### *Diversification*

Investing all of your resources into a single stock means that if the company goes out of business, you lose all your money. While that is an extreme case, it shows the need to diversify investments, especially when investing in risky fields such as biotech. Investing in a number of companies reduces the risk from putting everything in a single stock, while also damping potential returns. That is the tradeoff between risk and return. What is needed is a way to invest in an industry, yet not have all your money tied to one company. ETFs provide that way to invest, as they enable you to concentrate in a sector, cheaply, yet still have diversification among different companies.[12]

It is important for investors to understand that diversification needs to be considered in the context of the investor's plans and life cycle. An investor needs to concentrate (in a certain investment area) to get rich and diversify to stay rich. When you are seeking to build wealth, that is the time to concentrate. When you are seeking to preserve wealth, that is the time to diversify. Preservation through diversification comes down to taking fewer risks and having investments over a wider field— accepting the tradeoff of potential lower returns for the accompanying lower risk. To concentrate in an investment area, we believe in applying concentrated diversification—choosing to invest in an area, such as biotech, but diversify by investing in a basket of securities in that area, as opposed to pinning your hopes on one or two companies. The natural tool for concentrated diversification is the ETF, allowing investors to access depth and breadth across numerous industries.

ETFs allow investors to put their money into a sector that they believe has the potential for good performance without having the worries of betting on a single stock—the ETF provides a diverse range of companies in that sector. Yes, some may fail, but it is likely that the majority will stick around. Say you want to invest some of your money in biotech, because you believe it can produce significant returns in the future, and you have $10,000 to do so. You decide to put all of that $10,000 into one company, Genepool Biotechnology (a fictional company), that has one drug in FDA trials. After your investment, the drug fails to show any results in treating the intended disease, and the company goes out of business—along with your money and your bet on healthcare. On the other hand, had you put the money into the Better Health Biotech ETF (also fictional), which had 20 companies, 5 of them may have failed, but 15 continued, giving you a way to invest in a sector, without having to worry about the financial health of each individual company. In biotech, where the success of companies depends on the outcomes of drug tests that no one can predict (even biotech experts have trouble picking potential winners from losers), baskets are a sensible way to buy into an industry. True, you may be better off picking the biotech winners, but how many of us can do that, given the uncertainty of drug trials? ETFs allow you to buy an industry in one shot, without your chance riding only on one company.

### Tax Efficiency

ETFs are tax efficient investments. ETFs reduce or eliminate tax burdens associated with actively managed mutual funds.

The first is taxation due to portfolio turnover. Mutual fund managers can easily turn over a fund's entire portfolio in a year—or less. This frequent, often short-term trading means capital gains taxes—and often the more onerous short-term capital gains taxes. An investor can buy a mutual fund, hold it, and wind up with a large tax bill, even though she hasn't sold her shares. To a lesser extent, this can also affect index mutual funds. Whenever an index is adjusted, the fund needs to sell those stocks that are going out of the index and buy those that are coming in, which often means that fund shareholders need to pay capital gains taxes, even if they don't sell their funds. This rarely happens with ETFs because the creation and redemption system minimizes tax liabilities.

If shareholders decide to redeem their shares and the mutual fund does not have enough cash on hand to pay them, then the fund sells shares to raise the cash, yet the remaining shareholders have to foot the tax bill if there are any capital gains. So, once again, mutual fund shareholders wind up paying taxes when they have simply held onto their investments and taken no action of their own to incur taxes. Even index mutual funds have this problem. ETF holders do not have this problem because when other ETF investors sell their shares, they sell to another investor, not the fund company. The only capital gain is incurred by the investor who sells their shares—not the investor who holds onto their shares. This is another reason to consider ETFs, as they give investors more control over when they incur taxes as opposed to getting a tax bill because of the actions of others.

### Low Cost

Not only do ETFs save investors money on taxes compared to mutual funds, their low-cost structure may also help them outperform mutual funds. Since ETFs simply track the performance of a particular index, don't need to make investment decisions, and don't have major infrastructure, they do not have the high management and administrative costs of a mutual fund.

Choosing an ETF because it is the cheaper way to invest is a natural outgrowth of everyday consumer behavior. When people shop, they compare based on price and quality. Consider two bakeries that sell the exact same bread—same ingredients, same baking process, and so on. La Panaderia is a small, family-owned bakery with low overhead because it does not advertise and keeps expenses down. Ye Olde Bread Shoppe is part of a national chain that advertises heavily and has a fancy store in addition to having its employees dress in medieval English costumes, which adds to costs. The two bakeries are located on the same block, equidistant from shopper Jane's house, and they have the same business hours (see Figure 1.4). However, there is a difference: La Panaderia sells wheat bread for $1.00 per loaf, and Ye Olde Bread Shoppe sells the exact same bread for $2.00 per loaf. Jane, after making a comparison and deciding she does not need to buy bread from people dressed up like Maid Marian or Robin Hood, goes to La Panaderia because her money goes further at La Panaderia.

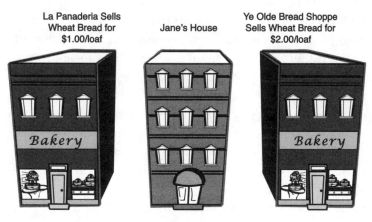

**Figure 1.4    Same bread, different price**

If we can comparison shop and save money when buying bread, why not do the same when buying investment products? After all, that's what we do when we invest; we buy a vehicle that we hope will perform well at the lowest possible entry cost. Now that Jane has bought her weekly bread supply, and saved money by going to La Panaderia, she now wants to invest some of those savings. Jane wants to invest in healthcare. She looks at both a mutual fund and an exchange traded fund. The mutual fund is the Morgan Stanley Health Sciences B (HCRBX), and the other is the iShares Dow Jones U.S. Pharmaceuticals Index Fund (IHE). Table 1.3 shows the top ten constituents of each list. There are a lot of commonalities.

Examine their contents—really they are not that different; their top ten lists share six companies, although the mutual fund is much more heavily weighted to the top two companies—Johnson & Johnson and Pfizer. So, as with the bread, buyers are getting the same goods. Where the difference lies is in the costs, seen in Table 1.4. The mutual fund is five times the price—for inferior returns.

**TABLE 1.3    Top Ten Constituents of Morgan Stanley Health Sciences B (HCRBX) and iShares Dow Jones U.S. Pharmaceuticals Index Fund (IHE)**

| Morgan Stanley Health Sciences B (HCRBX) | | iShares Dow Jones U.S. Pharmaceuticals Index Fund (IHE) | |
|---|---|---|---|
| Security | % of Fund | Security | % of Fund |
| Johnson & Johnson | 10.82 | Johnson & Johnson | 8.69 |
| Pfizer | 10.07 | Pfizer | 9.88 |
| Abbott Labs | 4.75 | Abbott Labs | 7.39 |
| Bristol-Myers Squibb | 4.50 | Bristol-Myers Squibb | 6.09 |
| Merck | 4.38 | Merck | 10.09 |
| Eli Lilly | 3.17 | Eli Lilly | 5.53 |
| Wyeth | 5.06 | Allergan | 4.44 |
| Gilead Sciences | 4.48 | Hospira | 3.66 |
| Medtronic | 3.34 | Forest Labs | 3.41 |
| Schering Plough | 4.02 | Mylan | 3.21 |

**TABLE 1.4    Comparative Fund Data**

| Fund | HCRBX | IHE |
|---|---|---|
| Expense Ratio | 2.40% | 0.48% |
| 1 Year Return | 33.27% | 51.41% |
| 3 Year Annualized Return | -0.24% | 2.71% |
| Standard Deviation | 17.2 | 17.98 |
| Sharpe Ratio | -.10 | -.05 |
| Annual Rate of Return after expenses assuming 6% return for market | 3.6% | 5.52% |
| Return after 25 years on initial investment of $10,000 with reinvestment of returns | $24,210 | $35,514 |

When dealing with two similar investments, lower costs usually make the ETF the better performer for investors looking for diversified instruments.

It's highly unlikely that a mutual fund will beat the index—once costs are factored in, that probability falls even closer to 0. The low-cost investment is the safer wager. The main reason the ETF costs less is because the mutual fund investor pays for a lot of infrastructure. Those costs add up, while the ETF investor only pays a brokerage fee and a modest management fee.

ETF investors avoid all these fees that reduce returns for mutual fund shareowners:

- Front end loads of up to 8.75% when they buy a fund
- 12b-1 fees, whereby an investor pays for the manager to recruit new investors to the fund
- Shareholder service fees to pay for the investors' support infrastructure of the fund
- Account fees for small accounts
- Management fees that can easily be ten times as much as an ETF's management fee
- Sales charges when they sell their funds
- Redemption fees of up to 2% to sell their shares back to the fund

Consider the investors in the funds listed in Table 1.3, assuming a 6% per year return.

The investor in IHE will receive a return of 5.52% per year (6% – .48%), while the investor in HCRBX will receive a return of 3.6%, as seen in Table 1.4. Over 25 years, the investor in the low-cost fund has over 50% more than the investor in the high-cost fund before taxes.

# Risks of Investing with ETFs

Despite their advantages, ETFs are not risk free. No investment is. However, understanding the risks that are particular to ETFs helps investors prepare for unforeseen events and build their portfolios.

### Index Risk[13]

As discussed previously, ETFs are designed to match an index, and are passive investments.[14] In contrast to a mutual fund, they are not actively managed, which provides many benefits, as seen earlier. However, because an ETF is not actively managed, it will not sell a security if the security's issuer is in financial trouble—unless the security is removed from the index. This means that the fund will move up and down with the index and the fund manager will not take defensive positions, or sell losing positions, in a market downturn. This also means that the manager won't increase exposure to positions that it anticipates increasing in value, either. This lack of management means that investors are placing their money with an index, not a manager, and their fortunes are related to the performance of the index.[15] The best way for an investor to deal with index risk is to understand what is in the index and the rules governing what goes into, or out of the index, as covered in the fund's documentation.

### *Tracking Error*[16]

In addition to the risk of their investment being exposed to the movements of the index, investors also are at risk when the fund does not match the performance of the index, a situation known as *tracking error.*

Tracking error represents the difference between the performance, or return, of the fund's portfolio and the underlying index. Tracking error occurs for a number of reasons. The first is that a fund has expenses that an index does not have, because it incurs costs when it buys and sells securities.[17] The frequency of these transactions, such as how often a fund rebalances its portfolio, can increase the costs that increase tracking error and diminish a fund's performance.

Another reason for tracking error occurs when a fund holds cash, which will earn a different rate of return than funds invested in the portfolio and cause a deviation in returns between the index and the fund. (At some times the cash may perform better than the fund.) With ETFs, however, the amount of cash held tends to be small— maybe some 0.1% to 0.2% of the total assets under management.

Certain ETFs may exhibit tracking error because the weights of the securities in their portfolios do not match those in the fund. When the weights are based on market capitalization, this will not be much of a problem, because the weights are tied to the capitalization of the stocks, and if a stock moves up in price in the index, that will be captured in the fund. The difficulty arises when a fund assigns weights by another means, such as equal weighting or some arbitrary method of weighting. In these cases, changes in the values of the securities in the index may not show up in the fund until the fund is rebalanced, where the fund's securities are adjusted to match those in the index. This lag can induce tracking error.

Another source of tracking error comes from the fact that many funds do not hold all the securities that make up the index. There are two ways for a fund to track an index. The first is replication, whereby the fund holds all the securities in an index in the same proportions as in the index. The second is by representative sampling, whereby the fund uses a sampling methodology to select securities that it believes will provide the same performance as the entire portfolio. This methodology usually produces larger tracking errors than if the fund bought the whole index. The amount varies depending on the quality of the sampling process.

Recently, a major problem has arisen with certain types of ETFs that exhibit significant tracking error—*leveraged ETFs* and *inverse ETFs*. Leveraged ETFs, also called *ultra funds*, are intended to multiply the performance of the index or benchmark they track. For example the Proshares Ultra S&P 500 (SSO) is intended to deliver twice the *daily* performance of the S&P 500. Inverse ETFs, also called *short funds*, intend to deliver the opposite performance of the index they follow. For example, if the S&P 500 goes up 10% in one day, the ProShares Short S&P 500 (SH) is supposed to fall 10%. Investors can use inverse ETFs to profit in a falling market without having to engage in the stock borrowing process that is traditionally used to short an ETF. Leveraged and inverse ETFs do this by using derivatives to trade that market.

In addition, *leveraged inverse funds* are intended to provide a leveraged return that moves in the opposite direction to the underlying market's daily move.

Note the use of the word "daily" in describing the returns of the funds. Many investors have mistakenly thought that the multiples also apply over the long term. These funds do not work that way, however. Over the long run, fund performance can significantly deviate from the index, showing great tracking error. The SEC cites two recent examples of how these funds have gone off track:

- "Between December 1, 2008, and April 30, 2009, a particular index gained 2 percent. However, a leveraged ETF seeking to deliver twice that index's daily return fell by 6 percent—and an inverse ETF seeking to deliver twice the inverse of the index's daily return fell by 25 percent.

- "During that same period, an ETF seeking to deliver three times the daily return of a different index fell 53 percent, while the underlying index actually gained around 8 percent. An ETF seeking to deliver three times the inverse of the index's daily return declined by 90 percent over the same period."[18]

Here's how that can happen:

"Let's say that on Day 1, an index starts with a value of 100 and a leveraged ETF that seeks to double the return of the index starts at $100. If the index drops by 10 points on Day 1, it has a 10 percent loss and a resulting value of 90. Assuming it achieved its stated objective, the leveraged ETF would therefore drop 20 percent on that day and have an ending value of $80. On Day 2, if the index rises 10 percent, the index value increases to 99. For the ETF, its value for Day 2 would rise by 20 percent, which means the ETF would have a value of $96. On both days, the leveraged ETF did exactly what it was supposed to do—it produced daily returns that were two times the daily index returns. But let's look at the results over the two-day period: the index lost 1 percent (it fell from 100 to 99) while the 2x leveraged ETF lost 4 percent (it fell from $100 to $96). That means that over the two day period, the ETF's negative returns were 4 times as much as the two-day return of the index instead of 2 times the return."[19]

### Leveraged and Inverse ETFs Are Not for Long-Term Buy and Hold Investors

At the moment, with their system whereby they reset daily, leveraged and inverse ETFs are not suitable for long-term buy and hold investors. These ETFs are designed as short-term trading vehicles. The moment an investor holds them beyond one day, she exposes herself to significant tracking error. Because these ETFs reset each day, as shown in the previous example, it is possible for someone who buys one of these ETFs to undergo a major loss, even if the underlying index shows a gain.[20]

### Tax Problems with Leveraged and Inverse ETFs

ETFs have been praised for their tax efficiency. However, leveraged and inverse ETFs, because of their daily resets, can cause an ETF to realize significant short-term capital gains that may not be offset by capital losses.[21]

## Credit Risk

Investors in one form of exchange traded vehicle, the exchange traded note (ETN), need to be aware of credit risk if they buy ETNs. ETNs are senior unsecured debt obligations that are designed to track the total return of an index after subtracting fees. They are not equities or index funds, although they have similarities to those funds. They trade on an exchange, and investors can short them. Their return is linked to the return of a particular index. ETNs provide exposure to sectors and asset classes that can be hard to access cheaply with other types of investments and can be used as a hedging tool.

Whereas ETFs own securities, ETNs own nothing.[22] The repayment of the principal and any interest, and payment of any returns at maturity or upon redemption, depends on the ability of the issuer of the ETN to pay. This means, if something happens to the ETN issuer—notably going bankrupt—the investors in an ETN line up with all the other unsecured creditors. Investors who choose to put their money into ETNs need to pay attention to the credit ratings of the issuers, although as the credit crisis of 2008 showed, credit ratings may not be worth much. Remember, the issuers of the ETNs *pay* the ratings agency to get rated.

## Changing Tax Laws

Changes in U.S. tax laws could affect the tax status of ETFs, which could help or hurt investors in a particular ETF, depending on how the tax change affected the fund in question. One area that could be of concern is change in how dividends are taxed. *Dividends* are distributions of money, stock, or other property that a corporation pays to owners of its stock.

Dividends are classified as either *ordinary dividends* or *qualified dividends*. Ordinary dividends, the most common form of distributions, are taxed as ordinary income at an investor's marginal tax rate. Ordinary dividends are paid out of a corporation's earnings and profits and are taxable as ordinary income, not as capital gains.[23]

Qualified dividends are ordinary dividends that receive the same tax treatment as capital gains—a 0% or 15% maximum tax rate, depending on the investor's tax bracket. The 0% rate applies to investors whose tax bracket is less than 25%, and the 15% rate applies to those whose tax bracket is 25% or higher. To qualify for the 0% or 15% maximum rates, all of the following requirements must be met:

- The dividends must have been paid by a U.S. corporation or a qualified foreign corporation.[24]
- The dividends do not fall under the IRS's list of dividends that are not qualified dividends.[25]
- The investor has held the securities for a minimum holding period.[26]

Repealing or failing to extend the current tax treatment of qualified dividend income could decrease demand for dividend paying securities, which may affect funds based on dividend paying stocks.[27] This is scheduled to happen in 2011, when dividends are again subject to being taxed as ordinary income at the investor's highest marginal tax rate.

While the Three Paths investing approach is not built around dividends, certain companies, such as large pharmaceutical companies (featured in some healthcare funds) and utilities (featured in many infrastructure funds), tend to pay decent dividends, so a change in tax law could affect the prices of ETFs holding those stocks.[28]

### Market Capitalization Risk

Many of the companies in both the green and biotech funds have market capitalizations that range from small ($200 million to $1 billion) to medium ($1 billion to $5 billion) in size. By virtue of investing in small- to mid-cap companies, the funds subject themselves to risks associated with these companies. These companies may be startups with little revenue, narrow product lines, inexperienced management, few financial resources, and less stability than larger, more established companies.

These stocks often have more price volatility, lower trading volumes, and less liquidity than larger companies, which could mean that the funds also acquire those characteristics.

## Concentration Risk[29]

One risk from investing in the three paths comes from concentrating your investments in three areas: healthcare, green, and infrastructure. While we do this concentration in a diversified manner, using ETFs to reduce single stock risk, there is still risk from focusing on a particular sector. By concentrating in a particular sector, a fund makes itself susceptible to economic, political, or regulatory events affecting only that particular industry, which may not move the whole market. For example, changes in FDA drug approval processes could affect the fates of healthcare companies, but would have a lesser impact on the stock market as a whole.

## Geographic Risk

One variant of concentration risk is geographic risk. Some ETFs are composed of companies in one country or geographic area. This exposes the investor to risks particular to that country or region. For example, in the European Union, many economies are not only tightly interwoven in trading but also share a common currency, the Euro, and its accompanying European Central Bank. Economic problems in one country can quickly spread to others, and because Eurozone countries no longer have control of their currencies and interest rates, they have a more difficult time adjusting their monetary policies in tough times.[30]

Geographic risk can also arise from environmental factors. Consider the Netherlands, a large part of which lies underwater. If a major storm overwhelmed Dutch flood control structures, there could be major damage to the whole Dutch economy, hurting the performance of an ETF based on Dutch companies.

The geographic risk could also apply to a particular industry in a certain area. For example, much of the U.S. oil and gas industry has its fortunes tied to wells in the Gulf of Mexico. A hurricane could damage a large number of offshore platforms and hurt the stocks of companies in the oil and gas production sector. However, at the same time, the need to repair the platforms could also lead to increased growth in the offshore oil services sector. Risk can play both ways.

### Foreign Security Risk[31]

Investors who venture outside the United States bear risks beyond those associated with investments in U.S. securities. This doesn't mean that you should not diversify geographically, because there may be benefits from exposure to other currencies in reducing overall portfolio risk. Just understand the risks before you take the trip. It's your money after all.

Some of the risks may include greater market volatility (depending on the market), less reliable financial information (depending on the market), higher transaction and custody costs, foreign taxation, and less liquid markets.[32] Political instability may make it difficult for a fund to invest in certain countries or repatriate the proceeds of its investments back to the United States.

Many ETFs may be focused on companies based outside the investor's home country. In this case, those companies may have earnings or a stock that is priced in a currency that differs from the investor's home country. This exposes the investor to the risk that currency moves could affect the investor's holdings—advantageously or harmfully.

## Conclusion

ETFs are the natural tool for the Three Paths investor because they allow investors to take charge of their finances and invest without the middleman. ETFs provide low-cost ways to access investment themes without all the fees of a mutual fund and are transparent and easy to use. Investors can get in and out of them easily. With this knowledge, individuals can use ETFs to navigate along the Three Paths of healthcare, green, and infrastructure, because each path has a number of ETFs available to the investor. Later in the book, we'll look at how to invest in each of the Three Paths areas using ETFs.

# Notes

[1] There are hundreds of other indices, too.

[2] Funds that do not hold securities are not legally known as ETFs in the United States. However, there does not seem to be common agreement on what to call these funds. Some call them exchange traded portfolios (ETPs) or exchange traded vehicles (ETVs).

[3] This is a hypothetical index, and investors will not find an ETF in the United States that has only three stocks in it because it is insufficiently diversified.

[4] This creation and redemption mechanism allows ETFs to be more tax efficient relative to mutual funds, as highlighted in the "Tax Efficiency" section of this chapter.

[5] This example has been simplified for ease of explanation. It assumes that the value of the fund will be equal to the net asset value (NAV) of the component shares. The NAV of a fund is calculated by this formula:

$$\text{Net Asset Value} = \frac{\text{Current Market Value of Assets} - \text{Liabilities of Fund}}{\text{Shares Outstanding}}$$

In reality, an ETF's price is determined in the open market. However, due to the ability of the ETF to be redeemed for its underlying basket of stocks, and for the ability to use the underlying basket of stocks to create an ETF, there is usually very little difference between the NAV of the ETF and the market price, especially for the highly liquid ETFs. For some of the more thinly traded ETFs, or those with foreign securities, there may be more of a divergence. An ETF's prospectus usually contains material describing the magnitude and frequency of these divergences between the NAV and the ETF's price in the market.

[6] The weights here are given for ease of example. The values of the weights in the index can be set in any number of ways. The weights could be assigned by price, assigned by the market capitalization of the stocks in the index, equally weighted, or based on any of a number of methodologies. An ETF's documentation explains the methodology.

[7] This process, known as *benchmarking*, shows how an investment manager performs relative to a particular market. If a manager did better than the market, then the manager was considered to have outperformed the market. If the manager did

worse than the market, then the manager was considered to have underperformed the market.

The comparison is somewhat oversimplified. First, a benchmark needs to be relevant to measure a manager's performance. That raises the question of what is the market to be benchmarked. Indices reflect the biases of their makers. For example, the constituents of both the Dow Jones and the S&P 500 are selected by committees with great discretion to decide what to include. These indices are not really passive investment instruments but actually the results of active decisions of what to add, or subtract, based on a committee's decision of what represents the stock market or the economy. Isn't that active management?

Even so-called rules-based indices derive from rules based on someone's conception of what belongs in an index. Those rules could be based on market capitalization, or volume of trading, or some other criteria that may appear scientific because it is quantitative but in reality is the result of a human decision of where to set a cutoff for inclusion in an index. Is it always easy to classify a company? What is GE, for example? Is it a financial company, a manufacturing company, a media company? The answer is it is all of those. Placing a company into a sector, or industry, is not always so simple.

Also, what is the appropriate benchmark? It is not appropriate to benchmark a biotech fund manager who manages a fund with small capitalization companies that are not profitable against the S&P 500, a broad market index that contains established companies with large capitalizations across many industries. The S&P tends to be less risky than a biotech fund, because it is more diversified, and the companies are larger and tend to be profitable, whereas many biotech companies may never turn a profit.

Another difficulty using benchmarks is that a simple comparison of a fund with a benchmark does not account for risk. If a fund underperforms a benchmark, but the fund is much less risky, then did the fund really underperform? If the funds are compared based upon returns that account for the risk of the investment, then it is easier to compare.

Here is a way that investors can think about risk. This reasoning is the same that Harry Markowitz used to develop Modern Portfolio Theory.

- If two portfolios have the same return, the one with less risk is superior.
- If two portfolios have equal risk, then the one with the better returns is superior.

Looking at risk-adjusted returns may be a better way to compare a fund with a benchmark. A number of measures can be used to do this, including the Sharpe ratio, Treynor ratio, or Jensen's measure. Each of these measures compares the return of the portfolio in question with that of a risk free instrument—usually the return on treasury bills over a three year period.

$$Sharpe\ Ratio = \frac{(\text{Portfolio return} - \text{Risk-free return})}{\text{Standard deviation of portfolio return}}$$

The Sharpe ratio measures the amount of return per unit of risk. A higher Sharpe ratio means a higher risk adjusted return.

$$Treynor\ Ratio = \frac{(\text{Portfolio return} - \text{Risk-free return})}{\text{Portfolio's beta}}$$

The Treynor ratio measures the amount of return per unit of risk, with the unit in this case being beta, which compares how much the portfolio in question moves relative to the market as a whole. A higher Treynor ratio implies a more efficient use of risk.

*Jensen's Measure* = Portfolio return – Risk-free return – Portfolio beta × (Benchmark return – Risk-free return)

Jensen's measure is used to compare a money manager with a market index and determine whether the risk is balanced by the reward. Although it requires more calculation than the other measures, it does provide more information about the performance of a fund relative to a benchmark. If the investor then factors in costs, it provides more information about the cost effectiveness of investing with a particular fund.

Using risk adjusted returns helps hold fund managers to account, as they may take risky bets in order to match a benchmark—with potentially harmful consequences for the investors. A fund that underperforms a benchmark, with greater risk, could reveal a predilection toward risky bets by the fund manager. Managers who attempt to beat the benchmark may take excessive risks, but these do not show up in the simplistic benchmark comparisons that are widely used in advertisements for funds or in press coverage.

[8] For a discussion of the whole move toward indexing and its academic basis, readers will benefit from reading Burton Malkiel's *A Random Walk Down Wall Street: The Time-Tested Strategy for Successful Investing* (New York: W.W. Norton & Company, 2007). Malkiel holds the Chemical Bank Chairman's Professorship in Economics at Princeton University and is a former member of the President's Council of Economic Advisors.

[9] Originally the portfolio of an index fund was designed to replicate, or copy, the index it tracked. A fund that replicates an index has all the stocks that are in the index in the same weights as the index. Today, funds may either replicate the index or use a representative sample of stocks in the index to track the index. A fund that samples an index has most of the stocks in weights that approximate those in the index, but not the complete match of a fund that replicates an index. Funds that use a representative sample of the index have the potential for larger tracking error than funds that replicate an index, as discussed in footnote 10.

[10] This difference in performance between the index and the fund is known as tracking error and is discussed in this chapter in the section "Tracking Error."

[11] Buying on margin creates a double-edged sword—it can magnify gains and losses. If the market drops quickly and a speculator fails to meet his margin requirement, the broker can liquidate his position to meet the requirements.

[12] Theoretically an investor could invest in an industry by buying a number of companies in that industry, but that could get expensive due to commissions and may prove complicated when it comes to managing an industry portfolio. ETFs allow you to get in and out of an industry by buying or selling in one shot. Also, for certain industries that have a strong overseas component—such as green technology—it

may be difficult for U.S. investors to buy the overseas securities directly, whereas they can access those securities easily through an ETF, which does trade on a U.S. exchange. The ETF operator handles the foreign transactions for the investor.

[13] Also known as passive investment risk and replication management risk.

[14] There are a few actively managed ETFs, but their numbers are miniscule and the assets under management even more inconsequential. According to the Investment Company Institute, at the end of 2008, there were 12 actively managed ETFs, with less than $250 million in assets in the United States out of a total of 728 ETFs with total assets of $531 billion.

[15] This risk can be considered a subset of market risk, which is the risk that the shares a fund owns can fall in value for any number of reasons. That risk can't be escaped.

[16] Also known as noncorrelation risk, index tracking risk, and management risk.

[17] First Trust Exchange-Traded Fund, *Prospectus*, May 1, 2009, 4.

[18] U.S. Securities and Exchange Commission, Leveraged and Inverse ETFs: Specialized Products with Extra Risks for Buy-and-Hold Investors, http://www.sec.gov/investor/pubs/leveragedetfs-alert.htm, last modified 8/18/09.

[19] Ibid.

[20] Ibid.

[21] Ibid.

[22] ETNs are not investment funds and are not registered under the Investment Company Act of 1940.

[23] Unless a payer notifies you otherwise, dividends should be assumed to be ordinary dividends. Ordinary dividends are found in box 1a of any Form 1099-DIV that an investor receives. Source: IRS Publication 550.

[24] The IRS defines Qualified Foreign Corporation as follows in Publication 550:

**"Qualified foreign corporation.** A foreign corporation is a qualified foreign corporation if it meets any of the following conditions.

1. The corporation is incorporated in a U.S. possession.

2. The corporation is eligible for the benefits of a comprehensive income tax treaty with the United States that the Treasury Department determines is satisfactory for this purpose and that includes an exchange of information program. For a list of those treaties, see Table 1-3.

3. The corporation does not meet (1) or (2) above, but the stock for which the dividend is paid is readily tradable on an established securities market in the United States. See *Readily tradable stock*, later.

**Exception.** A corporation is not a qualified foreign corporation if it is a passive foreign investment company during its tax year in which the dividends are paid or during its previous tax year.

**Controlled foreign corporation (CFC).** Dividends paid out of a CFC's earnings and profits that were not previously taxed are qualified dividends if the CFC is otherwise a qualified foreign corporation and the other requirements in this discussion are met. Certain dividends paid by a CFC that would be treated as a passive foreign investment company but for section 1297(d) of the Internal Revenue Code may be treated as qualified dividends. For more information, see Notice 2004-70, which can be found at www.irs.gov/irb/2004-44_IRB/ar09.html.

***Readily tradable stock.*** Any stock (such as common, ordinary, or preferred stock), or an American depositary receipt in respect of that stock, is considered to satisfy requirement (3) if it is listed on one of the following securities markets: the New York Stock Exchange, the NASDAQ Stock Market, the American Stock Exchange, the Boston Stock Exchange, the Cincinnati Stock Exchange, the Chicago Stock Exchange, the Philadelphia Stock Exchange, or the Pacific Exchange, Inc.

**TABLE 1-3    Income Tax Treaties**

**Income tax treaties that the United States has with the following countries satisfy requirement (2) under *Qualified foreign corporation*.**

| | | |
|---|---|---|
| Australia | Indonesia | Portugal |
| Austria | Ireland | Romania |
| Bangladesh[1] | Israel | Russian Federation |
| Barbados[2] | Italy | Slovak Republic |
| Belgium | Jamaica | Slovenia |
| Canada | Japan | South Africa |
| China | Kazakhstan | Spain |
| Cyprus | Korea | Sri Lanka[3] |
| Czech Republic | Latvia | Sweden |
| Denmark | Lithuania | Switzerland |
| Egypt | Luxembourg | Thailand |
| Estonia | Mexico | Trinidad and Tobago |
| Finland | Morocco | Tunisia |
| France | Netherlands | Turkey |
| Germany | New Zealand | Ukraine |
| Greece | Norway | United Kingdom |
| Hungary | Pakistan | Venezuela |
| Iceland | Philippines | |
| India | Poland | |

[1]  Effective for dividends paid after August 6, 2006.

[2]  Effective for dividends paid after December 19, 2004.

[3]  Effective for dividends paid after July 11, 2004."

[25] This is the list of nonqualified dividends from IRS Publication 550:

"The following dividends are not qualified dividends. They are not qualified dividends even if they are shown in box 1b of Form 1099-DIV.

- Capital gain distributions.

- Dividends paid on deposits with mutual savings banks, cooperative banks, credit unions, U.S. building and loan associations, U.S. savings and loan associations, federal savings and loan associations, and similar financial institutions. (Report these amounts as interest income.)

- Dividends from a corporation that is a tax-exempt organization or farmer's cooperative during the corporation's tax year in which the dividends were paid or during the corporation's previous tax year.

- Dividends paid by a corporation on employer securities which are held on the date of record by an employee stock ownership plan (ESOP) maintained by that corporation.

- Dividends on any share of stock to the extent that you are obligated (whether under a short sale or otherwise) to make related payments for positions in substantially similar or related property.

- Payments in lieu of dividends, but only if you know or have reason to know that the payments are not qualified dividends.

- Payments shown in Form 1099-DIV, box 1b, from a foreign corporation to the extent you know or have reason to know the payments are not qualified dividends."

[26] According to IRS Publication 550, the minimum holding period is as follows:

"You must have held the stock for more than 60 days during the 121-day period that begins 60 days before the ex-dividend date. The ex-dividend date is the first date following the declaration of a dividend on which the buyer of a stock will not receive the next dividend payment. When counting the number of days you held the stock, include the day you disposed of the stock, but not the day you acquired it....

***Exception for preferred stock.*** In the case of preferred stock, you must have held the stock more than 90 days during the 181-day period that begins 90 days before the ex-dividend date if the dividends are due to periods totaling more than 366 days. If the preferred dividends are due to periods totaling less than 367 days, the holding period in the preceding paragraph applies....

***Holding period reduced where risk of loss is diminished.*** When determining whether you met the minimum holding period discussed earlier, you cannot count any day during which you meet any of the following conditions.

1. You had an option to sell, were under a contractual obligation to sell, or had made (and not closed) a short sale of substantially identical stock or securities.

2. You were grantor (writer) of an option to buy substantially identical stock or securities.

3. Your risk of loss is diminished by holding one or more other positions in substantially similar or related property."

[27]  Wisdom Tree, International Sector Funds, *Prospectus*, 4.

[28]  Many of the funds of Wisdom Tree are built around dividend paying companies, so investors in their funds may want to pay attention to the status of taxes on dividends.

[29]  Also known as sector risk or nondiversification risk.

[30]  Interest rates in the Eurozone are set by the European central bank. Individual members of the Eurozone cannot arbitrarily adjust their rates or alter the value of their currencies to adjust to changing economic conditions. Those decisions are made centrally.

[31]  Also known, for U.S. investors, as non U.S. security risk.

[32]  U.S. investors may qualify for a foreign tax credit when investing in global funds, provided that more than 50% of the index is made up of non-U.S. companies. Otherwise, investors only qualify for a tax deduction, which in all likelihood means they pay more taxes on their overseas investments.

# 2

## Get Rid of the Middleman, Take Charge of Your Portfolio, and Invest in the Future with ETFs

Our current investment system does not work for the typical investor. We have created a system full of financial middlemen and women who make sure they get their cut, even if you lose money! Still, profitable investing is possible. Understanding our investment infrastructure and the accidents that created it will help investors take the next steps to cut out the middleman, understand how to best use financial professionals, and take control of their own portfolios to make more, and keep more, for themselves by investing in the future with ETFs.

## Who Are All These Middlemen?

A middleman is a person who gets between the buyer and seller of a good. As you can imagine, they are not there for charitable purposes but expect to be paid. Usually, the buyer pays the middleman's fee, or cut.

Clearly, a knowledgeable buyer who can choose her purchase wisely and avoid the middleman saves money and keeps more of her wealth. The investment business is full of middlemen who stand between the buyer of an investment and the seller. These middlemen consist of brokers, mutual fund salespeople, mutual fund managers, and the whole investment infrastructure, such as the fund company's bureaucracy (which does nothing to improve the investor's return).

The hallmark of these middlemen in the financial services industry is that they get paid. And they get paid well. In 2007, these intermediaries took in more than $400 billion. They are paid regardless of whether the investor makes money or loses money. That is not a system that bodes well for investors.

### What Is Their Record?

This doesn't mean there may not be a role for financial professionals. The question that needs asking is: Are their services effective? In many cases, the answer is no. Tens of thousands of mutual fund salespeople call on millions of investors every year with the promise of a better return on their money than they can get elsewhere. Mutual fund managers want us to believe that they, like the children of Lake Wobegon, are all above average. And, incredibly, we believe them. But simple logic tells us this cannot be true. In fact, 75% of money managers do not outperform their benchmark (the index to which they choose to have their performance compared). Some great money managers do exist, but they are a minority.

Unfortunately, there has been a total disconnect between the desires of investors and the motivations of those on Wall Street who are supposed to provide the tools and strategies to fulfill those desires.

## Why Have We Turned Our Money Over to Others?

Our money is something we work hard to obtain and seek to safeguard. So why do we turn our money over to others to invest? Will they treat our money the same way they treat their own? Why do we invest this way?

We have always turned our money over to our brokers and advisors because, until recently, we had no other choice. Most individual investors feel inadequate dealing with the factors that go into building a portfolio. We believe that the folks who live *in* the financial markets must know more about them. After all, we don't do our own brain surgery; we rely on doctors. We then apply that logic to those in finance. They are professionals; the rest of us are amateurs. The problem lies in that chasm of training and experience separating a medical professional from the do-it-yourself brain surgeon compared to the not so big gap between many investment professionals and the serious do-it-yourself investor. The truth is that these investment "professionals," especially mutual fund managers, have not done well for investors at all, and, in fact, have done much better for themselves. Consider a simple example: Most investors over the past 30 years have put their money into mutual funds. In almost every case, investors would have made a better return buying the shares of the mutual fund management company than they did owning the funds. The money managers themselves create most of their own wealth in the stock of their management company, so investing in that company creates more commonality with them than one gets from having them manage the portfolio.

We are certain that we cannot manage our money, yet we want to be equally certain that someone else has the expertise to do it for us. Why do we do that? One reason is that, until the past ten years, it was difficult for the do-it-yourself investor to gain complete access to the market. Sure, investors could easily buy stocks, mutual funds, and to a lesser extent bonds, but it was hard for the individual investor to buy commodities, precious metals, and real estate investments, and extremely difficult to navigate the futures markets (and still is). Hedge fund strategies such as long/short, 130/30, option buy-write programs, and inverse investing were simply unattainable, not to mention incomprehensible.[1] Even investors who believed themselves competent to build and understand their own portfolios found it preferable to retain the services of a broker or financial advisor. The number of financial intermediaries grew dramatically to meet the rapidly increasing demand, as 80 million new investors came to the stock market between 1980 and 2000.

Fortunately, the rise of the exchange traded fund (ETF) means that investors no longer have to pay high fees to mutual fund managers for subpar performance and high tax bills. Instead, they can embrace the future by investing today with the tool of tomorrow—the tax efficient, low-cost, ETF that trades with the ease of a share of stock. Just as the money market fund met the needs of the inflationary 1970s, the ETF meets the needs of the thrifty, tax conscious, take control investor of today. With ETFs, investors can buy baskets of the public companies that are creating new technologies in healthcare, the environment, and infrastructure. These funds eliminate single stock risk, are liquid, and provide access to innovation with mitigation of risk (diversified concentration). ETFs are in general a superior investment vehicle to mutual funds.

ETFs allow the masses to get into new investment areas sooner than ever before, with less risk, which is timely as demographics point to more people coming into the market.

# Why Do We Have Our Current Investment Infrastructure with All These Middlemen?

If investment managers don't do a great job, why do we have them? Today's investment system arose from fearful reactions to a 1974 federal pension law, the Employee Retirement Income Security Act (ERISA), that said if a pension plan's investments were not enough to pay benefits, the sponsor (company) had to make up the difference from its earnings. This caused many employers to eliminate their defined benefit pension plans (and hire advisors for the ones that kept these plans) or introduce defined contribution plans, such as 401(k)s, where employees choose the investments. These new plans were overwhelming to many investors, so they sought professional help, such as financial advisors or fund rating services. Still, no advisor or service promises that the funds they recommend will perform better than those they don't. Nonetheless, advisors have proliferated. The timing here is significant. If ERISA had passed in 1999 instead of 1974, every pensioner would be able to access index funds from his home computer; there would be no reason to pay the burden of administering pension plans, hiring consultants, and otherwise building this huge infrastructure to buy simple index funds.

# What to Do About the Financial Professionals in Your Life

All this raises questions about the role of financial professionals in your life. What should you do?

### *Proper Role*

First and foremost, you have to get involved in making your financial decisions. You have to get involved in the process. The amount you do so is up to you, but this decision cannot be simply handed off to others with no consideration. That is how middlemen get rich. When assessing where your investment dollars go, you want them to go to individuals, or tools, that help your money grow. Ask yourself if mutual fund marketers, mutual fund bureaucracies, or high-priced salesmen help your investment grow? They all take a cut, for sure, but what do they provide? Think about that when you choose an investment instrument.

Professional investment advisors can serve a purpose for individual investors. First and foremost, they can help an investor assess her investment time frame and risk appetite and guide her to a strategy that may be appropriate, including the proper asset allocation and types of areas to invest in. They can also assist in dealing with insurance and special financial needs. In addition, they can help with advice on tax matters related to investment strategies and tax advantaged investment options, such as saving for college and for retirement. A good advisor can help an investor avoid making what John Bogle considers dumb mistakes such as chasing past performance or trying to time when to get in and out of the market.[2]

Investment advisors who help guide their clients toward low-cost funds and reduce costly turnover in their portfolios can certainly help investors gain better returns than those who guide their clients toward expensive funds, which is a sure road to underperformance. Investors who know how their advisors are compensated and understand the incentives that their advisors or brokers have to invest in a certain manner are better able to assess their advisor's performance and whether the fit is right for them.

### *Consider ETFs instead of Mutual Funds for New Investments*

For the investments you already hold, selling a mutual fund could mean incurring taxes. You will need to decide if this is the right decision for you.

However, for new investments, when choosing between ETFs and mutual funds, it really behooves you to consider the ETF, especially when investing in the same sort of instrument, simply because the ETF cuts out most of the middlemen and allows you to access the market directly for a small fee—a brokerage commission—rather than employing all the resources of hiring a manager in the form of a mutual fund or other expense laden investment scheme.

## What about the Advisors You Can't Seem to Get Rid of?

While it may be easy to select, or discharge, an advisor for your own financial accounts, it's harder when you are dealing with financial plans that you may participate in but don't control, most notably your retirement funds, when they are handled by your employer. What can you do? It all depends on what kind of retirement plan you have and what say you have in its direction.

### Defined Contribution Plans

For many people today, at least in the private sector, the defined contribution plan is the only plan offered. In this plan, the employee contributes funds that are deducted from her salary and contributed to an account, where they can grow free of taxes, until they are withdrawn from the account. The contribution may be matched by an employer's contribution. In these plans, the employee gains two tax advantages. The first is the contribution to the plan is not taxed, lowering the employee's income tax, and the contributions accumulate free of tax. The downside is the typical plan doesn't have a great range of investment options. Typically, the employee is given a few choices of mutual funds to purchase, with little or no advice from the employer, and very little information on the costs of the fund to guide her decision. Ideally, it would be better for employees to have more choices, especially to invest with ETFs to lower the costs of the investments and to access more investment opportunities.

The question is how to get these choices. It's not easy. You can try to communicate your wishes and interest to your corporate plan manager, usually your Human Resources department. Don't expect much however, as HR folks will probably be reluctant to change because they fear new plans may create problems—after all they aren't managed funds—although this doesn't stop companies from offering their employees badly managed expensive funds. However, more and more companies are going this route—pointing out examples may help. In addition, it may help to lobby your Congressperson to enact changes into law to require these choices in 401(k) plans. Still, don't expect much in the short term—there are a lot of entrenched interests—notably mutual fund companies that like things the way they are.

In reality, if your fund doesn't have ETFs, you probably won't get them in the near future. However, you may be able to roll over some of your 401(k) money into a tax-free account at a brokerage house, such as an IRA. Then you can invest those funds as you choose—into ETFs or other index-based investments.

### Pension Funds

What if you are one of those (fewer and fewer) with a defined benefit pension plan? What can you do about the layers of advisors that your plan undoubtedly uses—and which may very well reduce your returns? Well, the first thing is to look at the annual report of your fund. What are the fund's goals—what benchmark does it seek to match? Look at the performance of the fund relative to the benchmark. If the fund underperforms or matches the performance of the benchmark, it may be time for the fund to look into using more index-based investments. In addition, find out the costs of the fund's investment strategy—the fund's managers, the advisors it hires, and the consultants—and subtract that from the returns to figure out the real returns after expenses. Then compare the costs an ETF could have incurred for the fund. If the ETF, or some similar strategy, would have been cheaper, then it may pay for the fund to look at a different investment strategy. Although you may not be able to get much traction, at least let the trustees of your fund know what you think. Vote for candidates who will pay attention to the costs of the fund's management and embrace new investment instruments. It may not work at first, but together with fellow pensioners, you may be able to lobby for a less costly investment process. Remember, the same returns with lower expenses mean more returns for beneficiaries or lower risks that a fund will not be able to pay its beneficiaries. It's worth a try, but it will probably take time to get managers or trustees to wake up to the need for change. Many managers would rather fail doing what everyone else does than to succeed by trying a new approach—especially when few tread that new ground.

# A Look Ahead

Despite the plague of the middlemen and the poorly designed investment infrastructure, do not despair. Opportunities exist to invest in the future.

### Innovative Opportunities Are Available

Retail investors are not currently investing in innovation. But the opportunities are hiding in plain sight. Healthcare, the environment, and infrastructure are getting most of the venture capital money now. We mapped the human genome five years ago, and that is starting to spin out exciting new treatments. New technologies will make us more energy efficient and less dependent on oil. And the infrastructure, from roads to hospitals to schools to water systems and telecommunications systems, must be overhauled. Great new technologies are ready to be commercialized right now. The wealth potential of these developments far exceeds that of the Internet (at the peak of the bubble in technology in 2000, we had created $8 trillion of wealth). The markets will overreact again, but much of the wealth generated in the 1990s stuck, and the same will be the case now.

# Why Healthcare, Green, and Infrastructure Represent the Innovative Places to Put Your Money

ETFs provide the investment tool that helps eliminate the middlemen and answers the question of how to invest. The next question is, "Where to invest?" The answer is in industries that will grow and sustain our world and our economy. Those are healthcare, the environment, and infrastructure.

## Medicine and Biotechnology

The biggest fiscal issue facing the United States today is the cost of healthcare. The numbers are staggering as both Medicare and Medicaid already face unfunded liabilities measured in the tens of trillions of dollars. Frighteningly, the "baby boom generation" is still quite young from a healthcare perspective. Baby Boomers, 78 million of them, were born between 1946 and 1964. In 2010, the oldest are turning 64 while those born in 1964 will be 46. In 2010, about 40 million people in the United States will be over the age of 65. On average, people over 65 spend 17% of their income on health-related matters while people under 65 spend about 6%. In 2009, total healthcare expenditures in the United States totaled $2.5 trillion (about 16% of GDP). By 2020, when the number of people over 65 grows to about 55 million, total expenditures are expected to reach $5 trillion, which will represent 25% of GDP. It is interesting to note that we think of healthcare in terms of what it costs and not in terms of the benefits that are provided. Those benefits are substantial. Economists figure a year of life for the average citizen is worth about $100,000 to the economy. Consider this fact: U.S. GDP in 1900 (measured in 2008 dollars) was $320 billion. In 2000 it was more than $12 trillion (2008 dollars) or 40 times as much. Life expectancy for the average American in 1900 was 46. In 2000 it was 78.

During the entire twentieth century, we also saw the development of a cure for one major disease—polio.[3] Also, because of antibiotics, blood pressure medicines, statins, better hygiene, and diet, we saw life expectancy increase by more than 30 years. Two-thirds of the increase in GDP is attributable to the longer life spans—all those billions of man years of economic participation valued at $100,000 each. The point is that society gets a great economic benefit from healthcare expenditures, not to mention the fact that it creates commerce, has the potential to create millions of jobs, and the therapies and treatments could represent hundreds of billions of dollars of exportable products. To top it off, the technologies being developed in medicine today are more exciting than at any time in human history.

And yet, many are reluctant to invest in the sector. The combination of a long time to realize a return and the high risk of not realizing any return makes the sector unattractive, particularly when compared to an instant gratification investment in precious metals or commodities.

One reason for the risk is that the Food and Drug Administration (FDA) process for approving a new product is long and expensive. It can cost $1 billion to get a new drug approved, and the trials can take ten years or more. Many products fail to show substantial benefit and never make it to market.

But two factors are very different at the dawn of the twenty-first century.

The first factor is that the existence of ETFs means that an investor no longer has to incur single stock risk when investing in medicine and biotechnology. Each ETF, reviewed in detail in Chapter 6, "Investing in Healthcare ETFs," has at least 25 component companies and on average has more than 50 companies in the portfolio. This gives the investor exposure to innovation with mitigation of risk. Also, a basket of several dozen companies will not be drastically impacted by a failure of a product in any one of them.

The second, and more significant factor, is that we are at a major turning point in the way we treat disease. The pharmaceutical industry markets some wonderful medicines for the various maladies that confront human beings. These medicines control the effects of these diseases. That is, they treat the symptoms of disease. Blood pressure medication brings one's blood pressure reading into a normal range, but it will not affect the underlying condition that causes the pressure to be high in the first place. Statins reduce high cholesterol but do not stop the body from manufacturing it. In short, today's medications treat the symptoms of disease, not the underlying condition. The business model of the pharmaceutical industry is to provide patients with drugs that treat them on a chronic basis. But today, more than 100 million people in the United States have at least one chronic condition. And with the Boomers aging rapidly, millions more will join their ranks. This is why the cost of care is rising so rapidly.

As a nation, we can no longer afford to treat the symptoms of disease. We must move toward prevention and cure. As it turns out, the medical and biotechnology industries are developing a myriad of products and drugs that will allow us to do just that. A number of ETFs hold stock in the companies that will completely change the face of medicine.

To get an idea of the changes in store, we will highlight three companies that have the potential to make revolutionary contributions to medicine. (Even more companies and technologies are discussed in Chapter 4, "The Biotech Revolution Is Changing the Face of Healthcare: What It Means for Medicine and Investors.") They are Myriad Genetics (MYGN), Isis Pharmaceuticals (ISIS), and Intuitive Surgical (ISRG). All three of these companies are owned by several different healthcare sector ETFs. They represent the kinds of companies one will find in these portfolios.

Myriad develops diagnostic tests for specific diseases such as the BRAC test for the risk of breast cancer and COLARIS which predicts the risk of colon cancer. One of the major changes in medicine is the move from diagnosis to prognosis, and Myriad's test is predictive. Historically, the purpose of a blood test was to determine whether an abnormality (symptom) had developed. We are moving to a system in which many perfectly healthy people will be tested to determine whether they have a predisposition to a certain illness. The BRAC test looks for mutations in certain genes that are known to be associated with breast cancer. Finding a disease early has always been vital in prolonging and saving lives. Now tests can identify a disease years before it occurs. Myriad and several other companies are developing hundreds of such tests that will predict most potential illnesses before there are any symptoms. The benefits of this are incalculable. Prevention and early intervention are much less expensive and produce far superior outcomes.

Diagnosing a disease early and taking appropriate actions to adjust things like lifestyle and diet will benefit society. But medicine is ready to move beyond that. Several years ago, scientists mapped the entire human genome, and now there are companies mapping the genomes of all the major diseases. Eventually, perhaps within ten years, we will know the genetic makeup of many diseases. There are modalities in development today that will allow therapies to actually interfere with the genetic process that leads to a disease. Several such modalities are in development, and one of the leading companies is Isis Pharmaceuticals. Isis is developing drugs based upon a technology known as antisense. Antisense drugs target individual genes that are responsible for various illnesses. Isis has several drugs in development targeting cardiovascular diseases, various cancers, neurodegenerative disease, and inflammatory conditions. This technology has great potential but is, so far, largely unproven. An investment in Isis alone would be risky, but as one of a few dozen innovative companies in an ETF, it makes a great deal of sense. This company has enormous potential as it holds more than 1,600 patents.

Intuitive Surgical is the manufacturer and distributor of the daVinci Surgical System, a revolutionary new robotic surgical device. The robot can perform minimally invasive surgery for a wide variety of conditions with enhanced results for the patient. The precision and dependability of the robot means less trauma and blood loss, less infection, shorter hospital stays, and faster recovery.

Myriad, Isis, and Intuitive have had a great deal of success in their businesses, but they are still relatively small companies. Myriad's market cap is $2 billion, Isis has a market cap just over $1 billion, and Intuitive is at $10 billion. All three companies have enormous growth potential but with significant risk. Now consider that there are dozens more companies just like them that can be accessed through a few ETFs. All of these companies are equally involved in game-changing developments of medical devices and therapies. A revolution is underway in medicine that will ultimately create more wealth than was created in the development of the Internet.

## Green Technologies and Alternative Energy

There has been much debate about whether we are experiencing global warming and general climate change. There is substantial evidence that we have polluted the environment, and matters are only getting worse. While there are strong voices on both sides of this argument, it cannot be denied that U.S. dependence on imported oil is a politically undesirable situation that must be corrected.

Just as the pharmaceutical industry has been a strong oligopoly deterring innovation in medicine, so too, the oil and gas industry dominates the energy picture in the United States. But as with medicine, dozens of new technologies are in development that can reduce our dependence on oil. At the same time, many other devices and tools are being developed that will allow us to meet our energy demands far more efficiently and cleanly than today's technology.

Many of the companies engaged in these activities are relatively new and still developing. An investment in any one of them would be very risky. But once again, these companies have been packaged into ETFs so that investors can get access to the innovations without having to incur the risk of single stock ownership. There are ETFs for solar power, nuclear power, clean technologies, clean water, energy efficiency, and electric power generation. There are also ETFs that combine companies from each of these sectors.

It is important to remember that these technologies are in the early stage of development. There will be breakthroughs and failures. Some stocks will soar while other companies will go out of business. Historically, when a technology experiences a rapid change, coupled with a rapid increase in demand (think computers, telecommunications, and the Internet), this creates enormous wealth.

ETFs did not exist during the growth of personal computing and networking. Despite the fact that more than $8 trillion of wealth was created in the stock market from 1990 until 2000, many investors managed to make little or no profits. They invested in single companies and if they chose wrong, the results were disastrous. For example, there were many investors whose only telephone stock was WorldCom. It turned out that the once high-flying company had been cooking its books and was engaged in a massive fraud. Investors in WorldCom were wiped out. If there had been an ETF of wireless telecom companies, investors would have been able to own all the competitors in the industry. The customers of WorldCom simply became customers of the other carriers when WorldCom folded. The investor in this hypothetical ETF would have lost the WorldCom investment but would have seen corresponding offsets in other component companies.

Had it existed, a telecom ETF, would have allowed investors to participate in the explosive growth of the industry without any concern for which competitors would ultimately prevail. The Claymore Global Solar Energy ETF (TAN), for example, owns a number of solar panel and solar battery companies. It is unlikely that all of these companies will survive. But if one fails, the other competitors will benefit. If a new company enters the space, the ETF will adjust its portfolio to include that company. The investor gets comprehensive exposure to innovation with as much mitigation of risk as is possible.

Combined with the need to reduce emissions, if we accept the premise that one day we will run out of oil, it makes sense not to wait for that day to seek alternatives. The price of oil is now at a level where other forms of energy are economically competitive and these alternatives are commercially feasible. While we do not know which forms of energy will succeed, it does make sense that, we as a nation, start to invest in several of those that have a chance. In Chapter 8, "Green ETFs: Overview and Analysis," we discuss the green and alternative energy ETFs in detail.

## Infrastructure

For most of the twentieth century, the first impression of a U.S. citizen traveling in Europe or Asia was to note how much more modern the U.S. was when compared with the rest of the world. That began to change in the late twentieth century. Today, we travel overseas and are jealous of how well the trains run, of the modern hotel amenities, and of the wireless phone system reliability. This modernity affects not only quality of life but also productivity. In the United States, our infrastructure is dangerously old and needs repair. Water mains burst, bridges collapse, and blackouts occur due to age and lack of maintenance. These failures, as well as everyday problems (think airports), create a tremendous drag on our personal and industrial productivity at every turn.

We must invest in our infrastructure. It would normally be the case that much of this investment would come from the government. But already facing huge deficits stemming from war and recession, the government simply does not have the funds to make these crucial investments. We must recognize that, if we are to have a future at all, we need to invest in the modernization of the United States. Our roads and rails must be improved. We are the only major economic power that does not have nationwide high-speed train service.

Investing in infrastructure involves several different industries. A major component is real estate, which is currently a very depressed business. But as the economy recovers, so will the real estate market. There are several real estate ETFs whose major components are Real Estate Investment Trusts (REITs). A major component of infrastructure replacement and renewal will be industrial metals, led by copper. There are both ETFs and ETNs that provide investors access to the copper market. Other basic materials used in construction can be accessed by investors through basic materials ETFs. These ETFs own our major industrial and chemical companies including DuPont, Dow, and Alcoa. A complete analysis of infrastructure ETFs is available in Chapter 10, "Infrastructure ETFs: Overview and Analysis."

We must recognize that the future will not happen if we don't create it. While the bankers and advisors who control our investment dollars are busily engaged in casino capitalism, they are arrogantly ignoring this obligation. Even if they could create satisfactory returns (they cannot) through short-term trading strategies, that wealth would quickly dissipate unless we have a sustainable economy that can compete on the world stage. We have before us an opportunity to create a golden age of innovation in the United States. This process will likely take 20 to 30 years in total. But during that time, we have the potential to create more wealth than has been created in our entire history put together. At the same time, the quality of life improvements we can achieve are breathtaking. The medical breakthroughs in the laboratory today cannot only extend life significantly, but also can help millions to overcome illnesses and live symptom free for many more years.

We have the tools available to reduce our dependence on foreign oil, clean up the environment, and substantially decrease our energy costs. At the same time, we can modernize America and improve our quality of life. All of the innovations that will bring about this revolution require capital. They are all sustainable businesses, which means they will provide a real return on that capital. Many new businesses will succeed; most will fail. By owning ETFs, we are ensured of owning the successes that will more than pay for the failures. And we do not need to pay any middleman to make these investments for us. The ETFs are transparent, liquid, and easy to trade. And, purchased in a portfolio, they give an investor comprehensive ownership of a new and exciting economy.

In 1981, we saw the introduction of the personal computer, and for the next 20 years, we watched the information age unfold. Those companies became the driver of our economic prosperity. We invested in those new technologies through mutual funds. In 2010, we are witnessing the emergence of exciting new technologies in medicine, clean technologies, and infrastructure. We will invest in these companies through Exchange Traded Funds. These companies will become the drivers of our new prosperity.

## Conclusion

The bottom line is individuals should take control of their own money and invest in healthcare, green industry, and infrastructure to catch the wave as it builds, because the tremendous needs in those areas will drive innovations that could create a boom similar to that from the technology breakthroughs of the 1980s and 1990s. As more investors see the appeal, more money will flow into those sectors, driving up prices and benefiting those investors who understand the waves of history and invest before those waves hit.

We need to drive productivity, which will improve our standard of living. Financial middlemen have greatly improved their standard of living, but the same is not true for investors. We do not need financial engineering or mathematics to be successful investors. In fact, all we need to do is look out the window. If we do, we can see that we need to clean up the air, reduce our dependence on fossil fuel, make healthcare affordable, and rebuild our nation's infrastructure. Whoever owns the factors of production in these sectors will become wealthy. While in the past it was hard to build an appropriate portfolio without an advisor, ETFs allow us with a few clicks of the mouse to build a portfolio that gives us access to all of the innovation that will drive our personal and societal prosperity.

# Notes

[1] In a long short strategy, a speculator both buys (goes long) certain securities or commodities and sells (goes short) others in an attempt to profit from movements in the two legs of a particular strategy and make investments that are not determined by the performance of the overall market, also known as being *market neutral, whereby the payoff, if any, comes from the changing relationship between the two investments—widening or narrowing.* In a 130/30 strategy, the investor goes short for up to 30% of a portfolio's value and then uses the proceeds from the short sale to buy more shares. This way up to 130% of a portfolio can be used to buy securities. A buy write strategy consists of writing options on a security you already own to generate income. Inverse investing is buying a security that will increase in value if its underlying index falls in value. This enables speculators to go short on a security without having to buy it, as if they sold it short.

[2] John Bogle, *The Little Book of Common Sense Investing* (Hoboken, NJ: John Wiley, 2007), 101.

[3] It is likely that the twenty-first century will see the cure of at least one and possibly two major diseases. A cure for diabetes would increase life expectancy an average of five years.

# 3

## The Healthcare Crisis in America— How We Got to Where We Are

Who wants to die? Or be sick? Or see their child suffer? Nobody. People want to live forever and be healthy, driving demand for medical services and technology. And that demand isn't going away. In fact it's growing every day as the U.S. population over 65 grows to record size. A growing, aging population and the increased spending our nation will put into healthcare make this field a major element of the three paths to wealth, because aging Baby Boomers will create a significant market for the medical breakthroughs of the biotech age.

## Demographics Drive the Case for Investing in Healthcare

One of the major factors driving the case for investing in healthcare is the aging of the U.S. population. Healthcare needs and costs increase with age. Consider that 78.2 million Baby Boomers began turning 60 in 2006, and another 15,000 turn 60 every day. Take a look at Table 3.1 and Figure 3.1, which show the growth in the over 65 and over 85 populations in the United States from the year 1900 and project their growth through 2050. The U.S. population age 65 and over is expected to double in the next 25 years. By 2030 some 72 million people will be 65 or older, and by 2050 some 20% of all Americans are projected to be over age 65.

**TABLE 3.1   Number of People Age 65 and Over and 85 and Over, Selected Years 1900-2006 and Projected 2010-2050**

| Year | Estimates in Millions | | Percent of Population | |
|------|-------------|-------------|-------------|-------------|
|      | 65 and Over | 85 and Over | 65 and Over | 85 and Over |
| 1900 | 3.1  | 0.1  | 4.1  | 0.2 |
| 1910 | 3.9  | 0.2  | 4.3  | 0.2 |
| 1920 | 4.9  | 0.2  | 4.7  | 0.2 |
| 1930 | 6.6  | 0.3  | 5.4  | 0.2 |
| 1940 | 9    | 0.4  | 6.8  | 0.3 |
| 1950 | 12.3 | 0.6  | 8.1  | 0.4 |
| 1960 | 16.2 | 0.9  | 9    | 0.5 |
| 1970 | 20.1 | 1.5  | 9.9  | 0.7 |
| 1980 | 25.5 | 2.2  | 11.3 | 1 |
| 1990 | 31.2 | 3.1  | 12.6 | 1.2 |
| 2000 | 35   | 4.2  | 12.4 | 1.5 |
| 2005 | 36.8 | 5.1  | 12.4 | 1.7 |
| 2006 | 37.3 | 5.3  | 12.4 | 1.8 |
| 2010 | 40.2 | 6.1  | 13   | 2 |
| 2020 | 54.6 | 7.3  | 16.3 | 2.2 |
| 2030 | 71.5 | 9.6  | 19.6 | 2.6 |
| 2040 | 80   | 15.4 | 20.4 | 3.9 |
| 2050 | 86.7 | 20.9 | 20.6 | 5 |

Federal Interagency Forum on Aging-Related Statistics. Older Americans 2008: Key Indicators of Well-Being. Federal Interagency Forum on Aging-Related Statistics, Washington, DC: U.S. Government Printing Office. March 2008.

Number of people age 65 and over and 85 and over, by age group, selected years 1900-2006 and projected 2010–2050

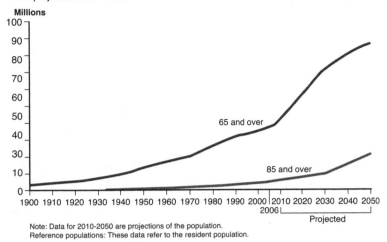

Note: Data for 2010-2050 are projections of the population.
Reference populations: These data refer to the resident population.

**Figure 3.1    Number of people age 65 and over and 85 and over, by age group, selected years 1900-2006 and projected 2010-2050 (Source: U.S. Census Bureau, Decennial Census, Population Estimates and Projections)**

When faced with that aging cohort, many people ask, "How can we continue paying for such an aging population?"—especially when they see that the per capita healthcare expenditures of those over 65 are about three times that of the overall population in 2004 (see Table 3.2). Those over 65 account for about 34% of U.S. healthcare spending while making up about 12% of the population. However, taking a look at the bottom of Table 3.3, the reader will see that the proportion of spending by each age group has not changed dramatically since the late 1980s. Instead, all health spending has soared.

**TABLE 3.2    Per Capita Healthcare Spending in the United States by Age Group in 2004**

| Per Capita (in dollars) Age Group | Total |
|---|---|
| Total | $5,276 |
| 0-18 | $2,650 |
| 19-44 | $3,370 |
| 45-54 | $5,210 |
| 55-64 | $7,787 |
| 65-74 | $10,778 |
| 75-84 | $16,389 |
| 85+ | $25,691 |
| **0-18** | **$2,650** |
| **19-64** | **$4,511** |
| **65+** | **$14,797** |

Source:  http://www.cms.hhs.gov/NationalHealthExpendData/downloads/
2004-age-tables.pdf

**TABLE 3.3    Total Personal Health Care Spending by Age Group, Calendar Years, 1987, 1996, 1999, 2002, 2004**

Total Personal Health Care (PHC) Expenditures (in millions)

|  | 1987 | 1996 | 1999 | 2002 | 2004 |
|---|---|---|---|---|---|
| Total PHC | $442,771 | $910,273 | $1,068,313 | $1,341,226 | $1,551,255 |
| 0-18 | $58,965 | $120,985 | $142,964 | $184,240 | $206,025 |
| 19-44 | $126,042 | $239,112 | $276,130 | $337,645 | $368,734 |
| 45-54 | $42,045 | $106,287 | $136,085 | $179,670 | $217,242 |
| 55-64 | $58,214 | $106,435 | $133,626 | $174,669 | $227,792 |
| 65-74 | $69,667 | $133,678 | $146,608 | $173,000 | $197,108 |
| 75-84 | $56,282 | $127,513 | $144,893 | $182,575 | $208,909 |
| 85+ | $31,557 | $76,263 | $88,007 | $109,427 | $125,443 |
| 0-18 | $58,965 | $120,985 | $142,964 | $184,240 | $206,025 |
| 19-64 | $226,302 | $451,834 | $545,841 | $691,984 | $813,768 |
| 65+ | $157,506 | $337,454 | $379,508 | $465,003 | $531,460 |

**TABLE 3.3   Total Personal Health Care Spending by Age Group, Calendar Years, 1987, 1996, 1999, 2002, 2004 (cont.)**

### Total PHC Average Annual Growth

|          | 1987-96 | 1996-99 | 1999-02 | 2002-04 | 1987-04 |
|----------|---------|---------|---------|---------|---------|
| Total PHC | 8.3%   | 5.5%    | 7.9%    | 7.5%    | 7.7%    |
| 0-18     | 8.3%    | 5.7%    | 8.8%    | 5.7%    | 7.6%    |
| 19-44    | 7.4%    | 4.9%    | 6.9%    | 4.5%    | 6.5%    |
| 45-54    | 10.9%   | 8.6%    | 9.7%    | 10.0%   | 10.1%   |
| 55-64    | 6.9%    | 7.9%    | 9.3%    | 14.2%   | 8.4%    |
| 65-74    | 7.5%    | 3.1%    | 5.7%    | 6.7%    | 6.3%    |
| 75-84    | 9.5%    | 4.4%    | 8.0%    | 7.0%    | 8.0%    |
| 85+      | 10.3%   | 4.9%    | 7.5%    | 7.1%    | 8.5%    |
| 0-18     | 8.3%    | 5.7%    | 8.8%    | 5.7%    | 7.6%    |
| 19-64    | 8.0%    | 6.5%    | 8.2%    | 8.4%    | 7.8%    |
| 65+      | 8.8%    | 4.0%    | 7.0%    | 6.9%    | 7.4%    |

### Total PHC Distribution by Age

|          | 1987   | 1996   | 1999   | 2002   | 2004   |
|----------|--------|--------|--------|--------|--------|
| Total PHC | 100.0% | 100.0% | 100.0% | 100.0% | 100.0% |
| 0-18     | 13.3%  | 13.3%  | 13.4%  | 13.7%  | 13.3%  |
| 19-44    | 28.5%  | 26.3%  | 25.8%  | 25.2%  | 23.8%  |
| 45-54    | 9.5%   | 11.7%  | 12.7%  | 13.4%  | 14.0%  |
| 55-64    | 13.1%  | 11.7%  | 12.5%  | 13.0%  | 14.7%  |
| 65-74    | 15.7%  | 14.7%  | 13.7%  | 12.9%  | 12.7%  |
| 75-84    | 12.7%  | 14.0%  | 13.6%  | 13.6%  | 13.5%  |
| 85+      | 7.1%   | 8.4%   | 8.2%   | 8.2%   | 8.1%   |
| 0-18     | 13.3%  | 13.3%  | 13.4%  | 13.7%  | 13.3%  |
| 19-64    | 51.1%  | 49.6%  | 51.1%  | 51.6%  | 52.5%  |
| 65+      | 35.6%  | 37.1%  | 35.5%  | 34.7%  | 34.3%  |

Source: http://www.cms.hhs.gov/NationalHealthExpendData/downloads/
2004-age-tables.pdf

While that question of how can we keep paying is certainly valid, it needs to be considered in the context of the whole healthcare system, where policymakers consider access, cost, and quality as key measures of how well a healthcare system serves its users. Access is the ability of users to get into the healthcare system, cost reflects the economic resources committed, and quality measures the results of treatments.[1] While costs have gone up considerably in recent years, that is not the whole picture. One reason those costs have increased is because medicine is able to do so much more than it did in previous years. Diseases that used to be fatal, such as high blood pressure, can be treated effectively with medicines—creating better quality of care. So, yes costs are up, but they are up because we can treat diseases we couldn't treat before. This fact needs to be understood when thinking about costs in our healthcare system.

In trying to understand the healthcare system, let's take a look at where we spend our healthcare dollars and who does the spending. Table 3.4 shows where our current healthcare dollars are spent by age group, and Table 3.5 shows who pays.

The top recipients of spending are hospitals, medical providers, and, then manufacturers and providers of prescription drugs. One area that may see considerable growth is provision of nursing home services. Table 3.5 is very useful to consider when we talk about how we can afford to pay for an aging population, because payments for medical care for the elderly primarily come from Medicare and Medicaid. Medicare is healthcare for U.S. residents over age 65, and Medicaid is for poor people. Medicare is funded by federal taxes, and Medicaid is funded by the federal as well as state governments. Table 3.6 combines the projected over 65 population with current per capita spending for people over 65 to give a conservative projection of healthcare costs for people over 65. Spending on people over 65 in 2004 totaled 1,551 billion dollars. By 2050 the spending on the over 65 set will come close to the *total* healthcare bill for all ages today.

**TABLE 3.4   Personal Healthcare Expenditures in 2004**

| Total Services (in millions) Age Group | Total PHC | Hospital Care | Physician and Clinical Services | Other Professional Services | Dental Services | Other Personal Health Care | Home Health | Nursing Home Care | Prescription Drugs | Durable Medical Equipment | Other Non-durable Medical Products |
|---|---|---|---|---|---|---|---|---|---|---|---|
| Total | $1,551,255 | $566,886 | $393,713 | $52,636 | $81,476 | $53,278 | $42,710 | $115,015 | $189,651 | $23,128 | $32,761 |
| 0-18 | $206,025 | $77,779 | $58,505 | $5,419 | $24,803 | $13,887 | $4,909 | $1,414 | $16,298 | $1,618 | $1,393 |
| 19-44 | $368,734 | $143,414 | $105,028 | $15,987 | $25,092 | $14,652 | $6,386 | $7,868 | $40,258 | $4,389 | $5,660 |
| 45-54 | $217,242 | $71,120 | $60,997 | $9,888 | $12,836 | $6,161 | $4,507 | $7,024 | $36,108 | $3,619 | $4,980 |
| 55-64 | $227,792 | $80,521 | $60,552 | $8,030 | $10,388 | $6,572 | $3,214 | $7,963 | $41,320 | $3,474 | $5,758 |
| 65-74 | $197,108 | $76,646 | $49,662 | $6,041 | $4,887 | $3,908 | $5,214 | $14,801 | $25,214 | $4,180 | $6,554 |
| 75-84 | $208,909 | $78,756 | $44,140 | $5,282 | $2,897 | $4,393 | $9,352 | $33,432 | $20,782 | $4,097 | $5,777 |
| 85+ | $125,443 | $38,651 | $14,830 | $1,988 | $573 | $3,704 | $9,127 | $42,511 | $9,669 | $1,750 | $2,640 |
| 0-18 | $206,025 | $77,779 | $58,505 | $5,419 | $24,803 | $13,887 | $4,909 | $1,414 | $16,298 | $1,618 | $1,393 |
| 19-64 | $813,768 | $295,055 | $226,576 | $33,905 | $48,316 | $27,385 | $14,108 | $22,856 | $117,686 | $11,482 | $16,398 |
| 65+ | $531,460 | $194,053 | $108,632 | $13,311 | $8,358 | $12,006 | $23,693 | $90,744 | $55,666 | $10,027 | $14,971 |

**TABLE 3.4   Personal Healthcare Expenditures in 2004 (cont.)**

| Service Distribution by Age Group | Total PHC | Hospital Care | Physician and Clinical Services | Other Professional Services | Dental Services | Other Personal Health Care | Home Health | Nursing Home Care | Prescription Drugs | Durable Medical Equipment | Other Non-durable Medical Products |
|---|---|---|---|---|---|---|---|---|---|---|---|
| Total | 100% | 37% | 25% | 3% | 5% | 3% | 3% | 7% | 12% | 1% | 2% |
| 0-18 | 100% | 38% | 28% | 3% | 12% | 7% | 2% | 1% | 8% | 1% | 1% |
| 19-44 | 100% | 39% | 28% | 4% | 7% | 4% | 2% | 2% | 11% | 1% | 2% |
| 45-54 | 100% | 33% | 28% | 5% | 6% | 3% | 2% | 3% | 17% | 2% | 2% |
| 55-64 | 100% | 35% | 27% | 4% | 5% | 3% | 1% | 3% | 18% | 2% | 3% |
| 65-74 | 100% | 39% | 25% | 3% | 2% | 2% | 3% | 8% | 13% | 2% | 3% |
| 75-84 | 100% | 38% | 21% | 3% | 1% | 2% | 4% | 16% | 10% | 2% | 3% |
| 85+ | 100% | 31% | 12% | 2% | 0% | 3% | 7% | 34% | 8% | 1% | 2% |
| **0-18** | **100%** | **38%** | **28%** | **3%** | **12%** | **7%** | **2%** | **1%** | **8%** | **1%** | **1%** |
| **19-64** | **100%** | **36%** | **28%** | **4%** | **6%** | **3%** | **2%** | **3%** | **14%** | **1%** | **2%** |
| **65+** | **100%** | **37%** | **20%** | **3%** | **2%** | **2%** | **4%** | **17%** | **10%** | **2%** | **3%** |

Source: http://www.cms.hhs.gov/NationalHealthExpendData/downloads/2004-age-tables.pdf

**TABLE 3.5  Healthcare Spending in the United States by Age Group in 2004**

| Per Capita (in dollars) Age Group | Total | Total Private | PHI | OOP | Other Private | Total Public | Medicare | Medicaid | Other Public |
|---|---|---|---|---|---|---|---|---|---|
| Total | $5,276 | $2,921 | $1,898 | $802 | $221 | $2,355 | $1,032 | $918 | $405 |
| 0-18 | $2,650 | $1,558 | $1,096 | $338 | $124 | $1,092 | $2 | $819 | $271 |
| 19-44 | $3,370 | $2,269 | $1,559 | $520 | $190 | $1,100 | $87 | $662 | $351 |
| 45-54 | $5,210 | $3,760 | $2,570 | $899 | $290 | $1,451 | $310 | $737 | $403 |
| 55-64 | $7,787 | $5,371 | $3,784 | $1,225 | $363 | $2,415 | $706 | $1,026 | $683 |
| 65-74 | $10,778 | $3,851 | $2,174 | $1,437 | $241 | $6,927 | $5,242 | $1,112 | $573 |
| 75-84 | $16,389 | $5,066 | $2,428 | $2,281 | $358 | $11,323 | $8,675 | $2,058 | $590 |
| 85+ | $25,691 | $8,304 | $2,817 | $4,886 | $601 | $17,387 | $10,993 | $5,424 | $970 |
| **0-18** | **$2,650** | **$1,558** | **$1,096** | **$338** | **$124** | **$1,092** | **$2** | **$819** | **$271** |
| **19-64** | **$4,511** | **$3,117** | **$2,154** | **$722** | **$241** | **$1,395** | **$239** | **$738** | **$417** |
| **65+** | **$14,797** | **$4,888** | **$2,351** | **$2,205** | **$331** | **$9,909** | **$7,242** | **$2,034** | **$633** |

Note: PHI: Private Health Insurance, OOP: out of pocket

Source: http://www.cms.hhs.gov/NationalHealthExpendData/downloads/2004-age-tables.pdf

**TABLE 3.6   Cost of Medical Care for Those Over 65 Projected 2010–2050**

**Spending on All Healthcare in USA in 2004: $1,551 billion**

| Projections | Population Over 65 in Millions | Cost of Healthcare per Capita (2004 Rates) | Projected Cost in 2004 Dollars (Billions) |
|---|---|---|---|
| 2010 | 40.2 | $14,797 | $595 |
| 2020 | 54.6 | $14,797 | $808 |
| 2030 | 71.5 | $14,797 | $1,058 |
| 2040 | 80 | $14,797 | $1,184 |
| 2050 | 86.7 | $14,797 | $1,283 |

Source: Federal Interagency Forum on Aging-Related Statistics. Older Americans 2008: Key Indicators of Well-Being. Federal Interagency Forum on Aging-Related Statistics, Washington, DC: U.S. Government Printing Office. March 2008.

The fact that taxes are the main source of healthcare funding for the elderly makes spending in these areas a political issue, especially for Medicare, which covers all elderly regardless of income. Are we going to stop seeking cures for disease purely because of potential cost implications, especially when an aging population makes up a significant voting bloc that influences the political system? The question that investors may want to ask, is, do they want to live in a society that isn't going to pay those costs?

It goes without saying that everyone will benefit from making the healthcare system more efficient. How can we improve outcomes (quality) and cut costs? One way to do this is to change the way we treat disease by focusing on curing diseases—not managing symptoms.

Curing disease is the best outcome (think polio) and certainly would appear to be the most cost-effective solution.

# Looking at the Medical System through the Inverted U

Medical systems that focus on treating disease rather than curing it are expensive and do not deliver the most desired quality—a cure. Lewis Thomas, the noted physician and author, described three stages of technology in medicine. The first stage, or "nontechnology," consists of reassuring patients and providing hospitalization, because in reality not much can be done for the disease since the disease is poorly understood.[2] The second stage, or "halfway technology," deals with the effects of the disease on the body.[3] The third stage, "high technology," such as immunization, comes about after an understanding of the disease mechanism and is often the most inexpensive treatment—while at the same time being the most effective.[4]

Graphically, the stages can be considered as an inverted U-Curve (see Figure 3.2), which shows the interconnection between the stages and the course of costs in the transition between the stages.[5] This interrelationship can help us assess the potential of a treatment by seeing where it fits along the treatment continuum and can provide insight into the potential impact of a new technology, *relative to the current treatments.*

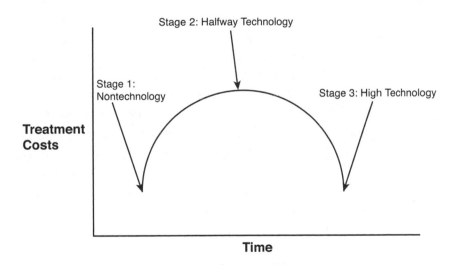

**Figure 3.2   The inverted U-Curve of disease treatment costs**

The treatment of polio provides a good illustration of progression along the inverted U-Curve, according to Weisbrod. In the early 1900s, polio treatment was in the nontechnology stage.[6] Many victims died from the disease.[7] Although the medical effects were a disaster for the patient, the healthcare costs were small.[8]

Later in the century, the development of a halfway technology, in the form of the iron lung, allowed the victims of the disease to live, but at a high monetary cost.[9] (Iron lungs are machines that enable people to breathe when they have lost normal muscle control over breathing, or they do not have enough ability to actually do the work that breathing entails.) Some of these polio victims spent their whole lives in these machines, at risk of death from power failures.

The third stage in the treatment of polio, came through the "high technology" breakthrough of the Salk and Sabin polio vaccines. These innovations practically eliminated polio in the United States. Polio vaccines wiped out a debilitating disease at modest cost. The polio vaccine has proven to be one of the great public health success stories and stands as the gold standard of cost-effective medicine.[10]

This inverted U analysis provides a lens to view treatments for diseases and assess their potential to improve both treatment quality and cost effectiveness. Let's use that inverted U analysis and apply it to one of the major medical problems of our time—the treatment of high cholesterol. At one time, people who had high cholesterol either did not know they had this condition, due to lack of tests, or if their doctors knew they had the condition, tried to treat it via diet or exercise. In this case, the cost of treatment was quite inexpensive because people either died from a heart attack or made modifications in their diet.

Through the development of statin drugs, we have advanced along the inverted U to some point between Stages 2 and 3. Statins cause the liver to increase production of an enzyme that digests cholesterol. They have been shown to reduce heart disease significantly. More than 45 million Americans take them. We are able to treat the condition and keep people alive but at a significant cost. Statins do not cure high cholesterol—when patients stop taking statins, high cholesterol returns. They reduce it and make it into a chronic, manageable condition. However, it is still treating symptoms—not curing disease. Don't forget, statin drugs are expensive and have to be taken for life.

With a young and healthy populace, society can afford to treat symptoms this way—at Stage 2 of the inverted U. However, the United States has 120 million people with chronic diseases such as high blood pressure, high cholesterol, diabetes, heart disease, cancer, and metabolic and endocrine problems. Combining the existence of those conditions with the fact that most Baby Boomers are still relatively young, makes the outlook for the current model of treating disease not very good from the cost and quality point of view—remember Stage 2 is expensive and symbolizes the lack of a *cure*.

Baby Boomers are aging into a system everybody knows is broken. But one reason it's broken is because society can't afford to continue treating symptoms. Fixing the system requires changing the course of disease from a genetic perspective, while also engaging in preventative measures. This will bring us to the third phase of the inverted U for treating high cholesterol and other diseases, the high technology breakthrough—where quality of care and cost containment are maximized.

# Healthcare Is Expensive and Not Getting Cheaper

Healthcare in America is not cheap. In 2007, Americans spent $7,600 per capita on healthcare—more than they spent on food. These expenditures are not evenly distributed by age. The over 65 population consumes about $12,300 of healthcare per year, while those under 65 use about $2,800 per year. If the healthcare system continues treating symptoms, rather than curing disease, those costs will skyrocket simply because of the aging population, as shown in Table 3.6.

History shows that healthcare costs rise steadily. In 1980, healthcare accounted for 8% of U.S. Gross Domestic Product (GDP). Healthcare spending currently totals $2 trillion, making up 16% of GDP. And those costs and percentages are not predicted to go down. The National Institutes of Health (NIH) predicts that healthcare spending will total four trillion dollars and account for 20% of GDP by 2016.

Healthcare costs are growing faster than prices in the overall economy. In 2007, national health expenditures rose 6.9%—two times the rate of inflation. If this pace keeps up, it means healthcare costs will double every ten years while prices in the overall economy double every 20 years.

## Relying on the Current Pharmaceutical Industry Won't Cut Costs

Wherein lies the solution? At the moment some 12% of the U.S. healthcare budget goes to prescription drugs. The problem with the pharmaceutical industry is that it treats symptoms but does not cure disease. Its profit model rests on chronic disease, which means selling condition-specific drugs over a person's lifetime. Consider the statins discussed earlier. What if a one-time cost-effective treatment could cure high cholesterol? The economics of the disease would change dramatically—not only reducing the need for drugs but also other related medical care that deals with treatment of chronic illness.

Essentially, the pharmaceutical industry is an example of the worst aspects of oligopolies. An oligopoly exists when a few manufacturers dominate an industry. As oligopolies mature, their focus turns more toward protecting their profit margins on existing products at the expense of innovations which might be superior. The longer this goes on, the more they become vulnerable to outside influences such as technological advances and regulatory changes.

The strongest oligopoly in the United States in the 1960s was steel. The import laws changed, allowing cheaper foreign imports, and the major steelmakers went bankrupt. In the early 1970s the auto industry was the dominant oligopoly in the United States. In 1973, American auto companies were in the business of making big, gas-guzzling cars when the energy crisis hit. They were unable to adjust to the new demand for smaller, gas-efficient cars and, despite government intervention in terms of "voluntary" import quotas, Japanese car companies now dominate the U.S. market. In 2009, GM went bankrupt and only survived thanks to government intervention.

In the early 1980s the only way to make a phone call was on a landline. AT&T had a monopoly on long-distance telephone service and the Bell Companies controlled local service. They were all wire-based carriers. When the wireless technology was introduced, the entrenched phone companies were stuck with their massive land line infrastructure. The wireless companies moved in, took market share and revolutionized the industry.

In the late 1980s and early 1990s, the major airlines included TWA, Pan Am, United, and Delta, which operated large airplanes in hub and spoke models. TWA and Pan Am no longer exist. United and Delta have entered, and emerged, from bankruptcy. In the spring of 2010, the largest airline in the United States, by market capitalization, was Southwest, which doesn't operate on a hub and spoke model but uses small planes for short hauls. Again, the existing oligopoly could not adjust to the new model.

Now the pharmaceutical industry, the dominant oligopoly of today, finds itself in a similar situation. Pharmaceuticals treat symptoms; biologic drugs treat disease. The process of developing biologics is very different from that used to develop conventional drugs, and again the dominant industry is unable to make the adjustment. Further, just like every other oligopoly, the pharmaceutical companies have been busy protecting their existing products at the expense of innovation. The typical patent for a drug lasts 17 years; it is interesting to note that drug companies never replace a drug before the patent expires even if a better product is available.

From an investor perspective, there is a great opportunity to create wealth during the breakup of an oligopoly. In the 1970s, investors should have sold General Motors and bought Toyota. In the 1980s, the right trade was to sell the landline phone companies and buy stock in one of the wireless carriers. In the 1990s, investors should have switched from long-haul airline carriers to short-haul ones. Today, investors need to own more of the biotech industry and less of the pharmaceutical companies. Look at the stock prices of the major pharmaceutical companies over the past five years. They have declined dramatically.

# Pharma Can Be a Risky Investment— Or the Savior of Biotech

While investing in the pharmaceutical industry may have more of an imprimatur of respectability than investing in the biotech industry, it still is risky. To better understand this, take a look at Table 3.7, which shows the five largest selling drugs in the United States, what percent of revenue those drugs provide for their manufacturers, and when they go off patent. In each case, one drug is a significant source of revenue for the major global drug companies—very risky from an investor's point of view. If anything happens to any one of these drugs, such as the discovery of major side effects, or discovery of a lack of efficacy, then these companies' earnings could suffer badly. Also, many of these drugs will lose patent protection in the coming years, meaning that they will be open to generic competition.

**TABLE 3.7   Best-Selling Drugs and Manufacturers**

| Rank | Drug | Sales ($Billion) | Company | Disease | Patent Expiration | % of Revenues |
|------|------|------------------|---------|---------|-------------------|---------------|
| 1 | Lipitor | 12.7 | Pfizer (PFE) | Cholesterol | 2010 | 26% |
| 2 | Advair | 7.0 | Glaxo Smith Kline (GSK) | Asthma | 2010 | 15% |
| 3 | Enbrel | 5.3 | Amgen (AMGN); Wyeth (WYE) | Arthritis, psoriasis | 2013 | 22% of Amgen's revenues; 8.9% of Wyeth's revenues |
| 4 | Nexium | 5.2 | AstraZeneca (AZN) | Heartburn | 2015 | 18% |
| 5 | Plavix | 4.8 | Bristol Myers Squibb (BMY) | Blood clots | 2011 | 25% |

Source: Wikipedia and 2007 10-Ks of respective companies. The sales are for the lead manufacturer. Sometimes drugs are distributed by different companies around the world, so sales may be larger, but they are split among different companies.

However, the most important thing about these drugs is that *none of them prevent or cure a disease*. Each simply treats *symptoms*. Basically they allow people who are sick to continue living and functioning—and that's good—but none provides a cure for the underlying condition, which is not good.

However, if pharma awakens to the need to cure diseases, as well as shore up their pipelines of new drugs, the pharmaceutical companies may choose to license biotech discoveries, or simply take over biotech companies outright to access their patents and talent pools.

The possibility of takeover by a large pharmaceutical company could further make biotech companies attractive investments.

In addition, increasing healthcare spending, and the fact that much of the medical care for the elderly is paid for by Medicare, a federal program, could push the federal government to increase spending on biotechnology in the future. The promise of biologics is their ability to interfere with the development of a disease or even to cure it, which could substantially reduce the overall cost of healthcare for society.[11]

# Conclusion

Facing the medical needs of an aging population and unsustainable costs of healthcare delivery, the time is ripe for a paradigm shift from treating symptoms to preventing disease. Traditional pharmaceutical companies develop chemical-based drugs that treat symptoms, but do not cure disease.[12] In contrast, the genetic drugs that biotech companies develop prevent cells mutating as the result of a disease or may kill cells that spawn disease.[13] This does not mean that chemically based drugs are bad. Conditions that used to kill people, such as high blood pressure and high cholesterol, can be successfully managed with drugs. That is good. But there is no reason treatments can't be more cost effective and higher quality, in terms of outcomes. The focus needs to be on curing disease, not managing symptoms. As can be seen from the previous discussion, the paradigm shift will not come from the pharmaceutical industry. The solution will come from the biotech revolution—the subject of Chapter 4, "The Biotech Revolution Is Changing the Face of Healthcare: What It Means for Medicine and Investors."

# Notes

[1] This healthcare triad of access, quality, and cost comes from David Dranove's book, *Code Red: An Economist Explains How to Revive the Healthcare System without Destroying It* (Princeton: Princeton University Press, 2008). *Code Red* is a concise and easy-to-read explanation system of how the U.S. healthcare system works, where it falls short, how it has evolved, and suggestions on how to improve the system. If you read one book about problems in the U.S. healthcare system, this should be the book.

[2]  Burton Weisbrod, "The Health Care Quadrilemma: An Essay on Technological Change, Insurance, Quality of Care, and Cost Containment," *Journal of Economic Literature*, Vol. XXIX (June 1991), 533.

[3]  Ibid.

[4]  Ibid.

[5]  The inverted U-Curve concept is from Weisbrod.

[6]  Ibid.

[7]  Ibid.

[8]  Ibid.

[9]  Ibid.

[10]  Interview with David Dranove, 9 December 2008.

[11]  Tom Taulli, *Investing in IPOs: New Paths to Profit with Initial Public Offerings* (Princeton: Bloomberg Press, 1999), 121.

[12]  Ibid.

[13]  Ibid.

# 4

## The Biotech Revolution Is Changing the Face of Healthcare: What It Means for Medicine and Investors

As seen in Chapter 3, "The Healthcare Crisis in America—How We Got to Where We Are," the pharmaceutical industry has taken us far in terms of improving health in this country and around the world. Still, that doesn't mean there isn't room to improve. The question is how can we go from treating diseases to curing them? The answer lies in moving away from treating symptoms by taking drugs to curing diseases through biotechnology.

## How We Have Produced Drugs in the Past

For most of history, the pharmaceutical industry has operated by finding a substance in nature, such as tree bark, that appeared to have an effect on disease and then chemically isolating the substance that appeared to produce the cure and packaging that substance into a pill.[1] This pill was then tested in the clinical trials process to obtain approval to be sold to the public, a process itself that can often take ten years or more.

What if the process could be speeded up at the outset of research by predicting what substances may work on the human body? By understanding the genetic nature of disease, rather than waiting for chance discoveries, perhaps we could improve outcomes faster. This understanding would make it possible to design cures that attack a particular disease and not have to wait for serendipity to provide a cure. This can accelerate the pace of medical innovation and simultaneously lead to medicines that zoom in on a particular disease while minimizing side effects.

In contrast with traditional drugs that treat symptoms but do not cure disease, drugs from the biotech industry, based on genetic principles, are designed to keep cells from mutating and becoming diseased, or to kill the cells that create the disease.[2]

Consider some examples of how biotech-based medicines actually work.

## Molecular Targeting to Reduce Cancer Treatment Side Effects

One hardship for patients undergoing cancer treatment comes from drug side effects. Because many chemotherapy drugs destroy more than just the cancer cells, they often create adverse effects throughout the whole body. A new wave of drugs practice "molecular targeting," because they focus on disrupting the specific protein that causes a particular cancer. This specificity allows the drug to be strong, yet to spare other enzymes, which can mean reduced side effects and better chances of surviving cancer.[3]

One example of molecular targeting is the drug Gleevec that is marketed by Novartis (NVS). This drug treats a form of leukemia known as chronic myeloid leukemia (CML). This disease affects about 20,000 people in the United States and is fatal within three to five years of inception if not treated. Gleevec works by targeting, and then turning off, particular proteins in cancer cells that induce the cancer cells to grow and multiply.[4] Gleevec does not treat the symptoms but halts the underlying disease.

But, wait, you say. Novartis is a big drug company. That is true, but although Novartis had the compound that underlies Gleevec under patent, it is based on work originally done at the University of Pennsylvania. Later, Professor Brian Druker at the Oregon Health Sciences University came up with the idea of trying to use the drug against CML and ran the first drug trials.[5] In fact, Novartis was originally reluctant to use the compound to treat CML.[6] What this means is that pharmaceutical companies will embrace biotech when they see profit potential as Novartis did. In fact, the company came under scrutiny for charging about $25,000 a year for the treatment—a treatment for which it initially showed little interest.[7]

# Helping the Body Make Up for Failure to Produce Needed Blood Cells

Certain individuals are afflicted with a disease known as myelodysplastic syndrome (MDS), whereby the bone marrow does not function properly and fails to produce enough normal blood cells. The disease may lead to leukemia. People who suffer from MDS have bone marrow that makes fewer cells than normal, and the cells that are produced do not always work as intended. Celgene (CELG) produces a drug called Vidaza that helps bone marrow make healthy red blood cells, white blood cells, and platelets, as well as kills unhealthy cells in the bone marrow that reproduce abnormally.[8] Here is an example of a direct biotech cure—where no other treatment exists. The medicine does not treat the symptoms but changes the process within the bone marrow that causes underproduction of blood cells and makes the marrow function normally again. The medicine treats the underlying disease and fixes the bodily mechanism that has failed.

# RNA Interference Regulates Genetic Activity to Stop Diseases

Human genes provide cells with instructions for producing proteins that perform vital functions. Inappropriate activity of particular genes producing unwanted proteins causes many diseases. Stopping this unwanted expression of proteins could provide a new way to treat many diseases.[9]

One technique that can be used to silence and regulate the expression of genes is RNA interference. (RNA stands for ribonucleic acid. Messenger RNA takes the genetic information encoded in DNA and translates that information into a protein.[10]) RNA interference (RNAi) targets disease by silencing messenger RNAs that would otherwise lead to the manufacture of disease-causing proteins. RNAi was first discovered in plants and worms, and two of the scientists who made the discovery, Drs. Andrew Fire and Craig Mello, received the Nobel Prize for Physiology or Medicine in 2006.[11]

RNAi may provide a way to manage cholesterol without using statin drugs for treating hypercholesterolemia, which is a high level of LDL cholesterol, one of the major risk factors for coronary artery disease, the leading cause of death in the United States.[12] Hypercholesterolemia therapies based on existing treatments, including statins, do not work well for many patients. In the United States some 500,000 patients have high cholesterol that is not controlled by current therapies for lowering lipids, including statins.[13] Also, about 5% of statin users have to stop treatments because of side effects, leaving them with few options.[14]

One biotech company, Alnylam (ALNY), is applying RNAi to treat high cholesterol. The human liver determines cholesterol levels by absorbing it from the bloodstream. A protein known as pro-protein convertase subtilisn/kexin 9 (PCSK9) reduces the liver's ability to absorb cholesterol. Reducing the level of PCSK9 activity may improve the liver's ability to absorb more cholesterol.[15] This knowledge comes from observing that individuals with genetic mutations that lower PCSK9 activity have increased absorption of cholesterol, lower blood cholesterol levels, and dramatically decreased risk of coronary artery disease and heart attacks. RNAi techniques may be able to bring the benefits of this natural cholesterol lowering process to people with high cholesterol and potentially reduce the risk of heart attack.

# Enabling Technologies for Diagnostics and Therapeutics

New enabling technologies allow low-cost providers to perform procedures that were not previously possible outside major medical centers. Procedures previously performed only in hospitals could be performed in clinics, doctors' offices, or mobile clinics that could improve access to healthcare in rural areas. Primary care physicians will use new diagnostic and therapeutic technologies to perform many of the services previously referred to hospitals and specialists. A move toward more services performed in doctors' offices, rather than hospitals, could create competition for hospitals and perhaps reduce healthcare costs and improve access to testing. The tests alert people to potential risks in their future, so they can take the necessary steps to be prepared, such as undergoing regular screenings for a particular disease as well as modifying their behavior and diet to reduce their chances of getting sick.

Consider one example from Myriad Genetics (MYGN), which has developed a molecular diagnostic product for breast and ovarian cancer, known as BRACAnalysis®. This test is a comprehensive analysis of genes that assesses a woman's risk for coming down with breast and ovarian cancer. According to Myriad Genetics, "A woman who tests positive with the BRACAnalysis test has an 82% risk of developing breast cancer during her lifetime and up to a 54% risk of developing ovarian cancer."[16] The company believes that BRACAnalysis provides patients with information that allows them to make "better informed lifestyle, surveillance, preventive medication and treatment decisions."[17] The company makes these projections based on research in various journals, which show that individuals who are genetically predisposed to breast cancer and ovarian cancer can significantly reduce their chances of having these diseases by using appropriate preventive therapies.[18]

# Regenerative Medicine

Regenerative medicine is an area of research that could lead to the regeneration of damaged tissues and organs in vivo (in the living body) by repair techniques that allow organs to heal themselves.[19] In addition, regenerative medicine techniques, including stem cells, allow scientists to grow tissues and organs in vitro (in the laboratory) and then implant them into the body, when self-healing is not possible.[20] Regenerative medicine could lead to cures for diabetes, osteoporosis, and spinal cord injuries among other maladies, as well as diseases arising from poorly functioning or damaged tissues.[21]

One company doing work in the regenerative field is Integra Life Sciences (IART). When people undergo severe third-degree burns, they need skin grafts; however, they may not have enough skin to move from other parts of the body.[22] To promote healing, Integra developed the Integra Template, a regenerative skin product. It is a skin replacement that imitates the function of human skin. It closes the wound and regenerates the skin under it, so when it is removed, skin has grown in over the wound. This means that patients will have less scarring and less need to graft skin from other parts of the body.

# Nanomedicine

Nanomedicine is the medical use of molecular-sized particles to deliver drugs, heat, light, or other substances to specific cells in the human body. Engineering particles to be used in this way allows detection and/or treatment of diseases or injuries within the targeted cells, minimizing damage to healthy cells. Nanomedicine has shown promise in delivering drugs to places they heretofore could not reach.[23] For example, nanomedical systems allow the body to absorb previously unabsorbable drugs.[24] New delivery systems allow drugs to penetrate previously impermeable cell membranes, allowing drugs to reach new targets inside cells.[25]

Arrowhead Research Corporation (ARWR) is developing drug delivery systems to overcome these cellular barriers.[26] One technology is designed to improve the effectiveness of RNAi treatments discussed previously. Ineffective delivery systems hamper use of RNAi, because the form of RNA necessary to deliver the message, siRNA, can be degraded or destroyed while in the bloodstream.[27] Arrowhead's delivery system binds and protects the RNA to prevent it from being degraded in the bloodstream. This enables it to be delivered to a particular cell, absorbed by that cell, and then released inside the cell—permitting effective delivery of the drug, which was not possible without nanomedicine.

# Pharmacogenomics Can Improve Treatments and Reduce Side Effects

There will be a move away from wide spectrum blockbuster drugs to individually tailored treatments. This shift could dramatically improve treatments, because genetic makeup influences how patients respond to drugs. Companies are now developing genetic tests to predict drug response for individuals, based on their genetic profiles. These developments underlie the field known as pharmacogenomics, which is "the science that examines the inherited variations in genes that dictate drug response and explores the ways these variations can be used to predict whether a patient will have a good response to a drug, a bad response to a drug, or no response at all."[28]

Pharmacogenomics can also help reduce side effects, or adverse drug reactions, which create more than patient discomfort. In 1994, there were more than 2.2 million cases of adverse drug reactions which lead to more than 100,000 deaths, making adverse drug reactions one of the leading causes of hospitalization and death in the United States.[29] Pharmacogenomics helps doctors find alternatives to medicines that don't work for particular patients or cause bad side effects. For example, after testing a patient's DNA, a doctor would take that information into account when prescribing a medicine, because it may predict an adverse reaction to one drug, but then show that the patient will be greatly helped by another drug or therapy. By using pharmacogenomics in conjunction with diagnosis, the physician has cut the chance of side effects and improved the chance of prescribing effective drugs.

One company doing work in pharmacogenomics is Gen-Probe Incorporated (GPRO). Gen-Probe develops pharmacogenomic tests based on the relationship between a patient's genetics and her reactions to particular drugs. Its genetic tests, known as nucleic acid assays, screen patients for a genetic variation known as single nucleotide polymorphism (SNP). Individuals with SNP in a gene responsible for drug metabolism may not respond to a drug, or may have severe side effects, because the body does not metabolize the drug normally. These tests help physicians design better treatments for patients and help them avoid costly—or fatal—side effects, lowering treatment costs and improving quality of care.

# Theranostics

Theranostics is a strategy, related to pharmacogenomics, for treating patients by first identifying patients who are likely to be helped, or harmed, by a new medication and then targeting treatment based on the test results.[30] Theranostic solutions play an increasingly important role in pharmaceutical research and development—increasing safety, speeding up clinical development, and facilitating regulatory acceptance. One example of a theranostics company is Amorfix Life Sciences Ltd. (TSX: AMF). Amorfix is developing therapeutic products and diagnostic devices that target brain-wasting diseases, such as amyotrophic lateral sclerosis (ALS), also known as Lou Gehrig's disease, Alzheimer's disease, Parkinson's disease, and variant Creutzfeldt-Jakob disease (vCJD).[31] One of its tests may permit doctors to diagnose Alzheimer's disease in living patients, as opposed to through autopsies, which could improve their early and ongoing treatment.

# The Case for Investing in Biotechnology

The case for investing in biotechnology and innovative healthcare comes down to simple addition. Take the huge cohort of aging baby boomers with deteriorating physical conditions, add the dramatic medical advances of the biotech revolution, and the sum is a major investment opportunity. As author Tom Abate writes in his book *The Biotech Investor*, "Here in a nutshell is the central rationale for biotech investment. You'll need to memorize and repeat it when short-term market fluctuations make you question your sanity. An aging population has arisen at just the time when an increasingly sophisticated biotech industry has aimed itself at unmet medical needs."[32]

# Conclusion

Combine biomedical breakthroughs with an aging population, and healthcare emerges as one of the three paths to wealth. In 2007, the accounting firm of Ernst & Young (E&Y) reported that the revenues of global, publicly traded, biotech companies rose by 8%, reaching record revenues of $80 billion.[33] Had big pharma not acquired many of the leading biotech companies, revenues would have increased by 17% over 2006, which is closer to the historical annual compound growth rate of the biotech industry.[34] Although the global biotech industry is not profitable, as a whole, losses are falling—dropping from $7.4 billion in 2006 to $2.7 billion in 2007.[35] E&Y reports that the U.S. industry came closer to profitability in 2007 than any other year.[36] In 2007, global pharmaceutical sales totaled $712 billion, an increase of 6.4% over 2006.[37] The size of the pharmaceutical industry, relative to the size of the biotech industry, indicates potential for the biotech industry to grow by providing new products to replace conventional pharmaceutical drugs.

We won't live forever, but we can live better with biotechnology—and better ourselves financially through investing in those areas.

# Notes

[1] Tom Abate, *The Biotech Investor: How to Profit from the Coming Boom in Biotechnology* (New York: Times Books, 2003), 9.

[2] Tom Taulli, *Investing in IPOs: New Paths to Profit with Initial Public Offerings* (Princeton: Bloomberg Press, 1999), 121.

[3] PhRMA, "Glcevec, 2004," http://www.phrma.org/node/223.

[4] Gleevec, "About Gleevec," http://www.gleevec.com/info/ag/index.jsp.

[5] Arnold S. Relman and Marcia Angell, "America's Other Drug Problem: How the drug industry distorts medicine and politics," *The New Republic*, December 16, 2002, 32.

[6] Ibid.

[7] Ibid.

[8] Vidaza, "Understanding Vidaza," http://www.vidaza.com/patient/understanding-vidaza.aspx.

[9] Alnylam Pharmaceuticals, Inc., Annual Report on Form 10-K For the Year Ended December 31, 2007, 2.

[10] Entries for DNA and RNA, *Hutchinson Pocket Encyclopedia* (London: Hutchinson, 1987), 405, 407.

[11] Alnylam Pharmaceuticals, Inc., Annual Report, 3.

[12] Ibid., 9.

[13] Ibid.

[14]  Ibid.

[15]  Ibid.

[16]  Myriad Genetics, Inc., Annual Report on Form 10-K for the fiscal year ended June 30, 2008, 3-4.

[17]  Ibid.

[18]  Ibid., 4.

[19]  U.S. Department of Health and Human Services, "A New Vision—A Future for Regenerative Medicine," http://www.hhs.gov/reference/newfuture.shtml.

[20]  Ibid.

[21]  Ibid.

[22]  Integra Life Sciences, "Integra Dermal Regeneration Template. Information for Patients and their Families," http://www.integra-ls.com/PDFs/03.176_IDRTPT-NTBRO_121003.pdf.

[23]  Arrowhead Research Corporation, Annual Report on Form 10-K for the fiscal year ended September 30, 2008, 4.

[24]  Ibid.

[25]  Ibid.

[26]  The case of Arrowhead Research Corporation also points out the need to invest in baskets of stocks. Throughout 2009, Arrowhead constantly faced the threat of being delisted from the NASDAQ because the bid price for its stock fell below $1.00 for more than 30 days. Delisting would make the stock harder to sell.

[27]  Arrowhead Research, Annual Report, 8-9.

[28]  National Center for Biotechnology Information, "Just the Facts: A Basic Introduction to the Science Underlying NCBI Resources," http://www.ncbi.nlm.nih.gov/About/primer/pharm.html.

[29]  Ibid.

[30]  Susan Warner, "Diagnostics + Therapy = Theranostics," The Scientist, 2004, 18(16):38, published 30 August 2004, http://www.thescientist.com/2004/8/30/38/1/.

[31]  Amorfix, "About Us," http://www.amorfix.com/about.html.

[32]  Tom Abate, The Biotech Investor: How to Profit from the Coming Boom in Biotechnology (New York: Times Books, 2003), 26.

[33]  Ernst & Young, "Record venture capital and heated deal environment propel global biotechnology industry forward in 2007," http://www.altassets.com/private-equity-knowledge-bank/industry-focus/healthcareandlifesciences/article/nz13430.html

[34]  Ibid.

[35]  Ibid.

[36]  Ibid.

[37]  IMS Health, Inc., "Global Pharmaceutical Sales 2000-2007, http://www.
imshealth.com/deployedfiles/imshealth/Global/Content/StaticFile/
Top_Line_Data/GlobalSales.pdf.

# 5

# Understanding the Risks of Healthcare Investing

Biotech investing is hard and risky. Most biotech companies fail. Biotech stocks are notoriously volatile. They are not for the risk averse and certainly not a place to invest money you need in the near future.[1] It is hard to predict which biotech companies will succeed. Within this tough investing environment, investors benefit from understanding the drug development and approval process and other factors that affect the value of the stocks of publicly traded biotech companies and their chances of success. To access this market and minimize the great risks, investors need to invest in baskets of biotech stocks—and ETFs make it easy to do. (The various ETFs are covered in Chapter 6, "Investing in Healthcare ETFs.")

## Drug Approval Process Makes Biotech Investing Risky

Biotech investors don't have to be pharmacologists, but they need to understand how drugs are approved and to appreciate the risks they face. Selling a drug in the United States requires approval from the Food and Drug Administration (FDA), which requires extensive testing to ensure the drug is safe and effective. Other countries have similar, though less arduous, approval processes. Drugs do not come to market overnight—both development and approval take a long time. It can take from 10 to 15 years for drugs to make it from the research lab to treating patients.[2] Some companies may have no revenue during the approval process. Delays in drug approval push those expected revenues further into the future—if they ever happen—decreasing the chance of a company profiting from the drug.[3] Companies may announce positive results in early stage drug testing, providing a short-term bump up in the price of their stocks, and then the drug fails in further tests, and the companies fade into obscurity or go out of business.

## Novacea Had Ups and Downs During the Approval Process

Consider Novacea, a company that had an IPO on May 11, 2006, at a price of $6.65. On May 30, 2007, Schering Plough, a large pharmaceutical company, now part of Merck, announced an alliance with Novacea, whereby Schering Plough provided $60 million to develop and commercialize Asentar, a prostate cancer drug. When the alliance was announced, Novacea's stock nearly doubled in price from $8 to $15 that very day. You can imagine that Schering Plough did significant due diligence on the company, and Asentar, before making a substantial investment in Novacea. Without a doubt, it had its scientists review the drug's potential carefully.

It must have been quite a surprise then, on November 5, 2007, about five months after Schering Plough made its investment, when Novacea announced it was ending trials due to a high death rate among patients. The stock dropped to $2.89 from $7.19 the previous day. By January 30, 2008, Novacea's stock dropped further to 90 cents. On that day it underwent a reverse merger with a private company called Transcept Pharmaceuticals (TSPT). Holders of Novacea's stock received one share of the new company for each five shares they held of Novacea. On November 30, 2009, Transcept's stock traded at $6.53 (equivalent to $1.31 a share for the old Novacea).

This story should make clear the significant risks that come from investing in a single biotech stock and further emphasizes the need to buy these stocks in baskets. If Schering Plough with teams of pharmacologists, physicians, and other scientists could not anticipate the problems with Asentar before the company ploughed $60 million into Novacea, what chance does the small investor have? Not much. Better to invest in a biotech basket, knowing that some companies will fail, some will do okay, and others will perform well. And those companies that really perform well can provide major returns for investors.

# Understand the Time Frame and Risks

To better navigate the choppy seas of biotech investing, investors need to understand the drug approval process that governs the fate of these companies whose success depends on getting their products approved. No FDA approval, no drug sales, no revenues.[4] For many companies, their valuations are based on hopes investors have for drugs or other products in the development pipeline. Consequently, investors react dramatically to milestones in the drug approval process, creating great volatility in biotech stocks. These reactions are exacerbated by the fact that these companies usually lack sales, let alone income or dividends, to cushion the shock for investors of a drug's failure in trials.

## Biotech Is Long-Term Investing

Trials take a long time to complete, and investors need to consider that time frame when investing. This time frame needs to be matched to the investor's time frame. Investors should recognize that any funds invested directly in a biotech company are unlikely to bear fruit in less than five years. It is likely that the stock may trade at a discount to the company's intrinsic value at times of declines in the overall stock market. In other words, an investor cannot rely on the liquidity of her investment in any individual biotech company. In an ETF, which owns dozens of positions, the liquidity of the entire basket will be unaffected by events at any one of the component companies.

## Understanding Stages Helps Investors Avoid Hype

At the very least, understanding the drug development and approval process helps investors interpret the hype that companies build around results at certain stages in testing. Table 5.1 outlines the stages of drug testing, along with the probability of success and average duration of testing.

**TABLE 5.1   Stages of Drug Development and Testing**

| | Identification and Preclinical Testing | Clinical Trials | | | Post Clinical Trials | |
| --- | --- | --- | --- | --- | --- | --- |
| | | *Phase I* | *Phase II* | *Phase III* | *New Drug Application* | *FDA Approval* |
| What Happens | • Screening of compounds to identify ones suitable for preclinical testing<br><br>• Laboratory/preclinical testing to assess the safety of the compounds and their effects on animals and animal cells<br><br>• Investigational New Drug Application (IND) filed with Food & Drug Administration (FDA) | Determines safe dosage and how to give the treatment | Evaluates effectiveness and looks for side effects | Determines whether the new treatment, or new use of treatment, is better than the current standard treatment | | Drug is approved and enters market. |
| Average duration | 4.4 years | 1.8 years (22 months) | 2.8 years (34 months) | 3.8 years (45 months) | | |
| Probability of moving to next stage | 5% | 81% | 58% | 57% | Around 75% | N/A |

Source: http://plan2004.cancer.gov/discovery/drug.htm; Rosa M. Abrantes-Metz, Christopher P. Adams, and Albert D. Metz, "Pharmaceutical Development Phases: A Duration Analysis," Working Paper No. 274. Bureau of Economics. Federal Trade Commission. October 2004.

# The Drug Approval Process

Consider a hypothetical biotech company, Salud Biopharmaceuticals, that has done research on a hypothetical preventive treatment for melanoma called AntiSolar. The drug is designed to help prevent melanoma in fair-skinned people whose genetics and family history put them at high risk for developing the disease. Based on its research, the company's scientists believe the treatment, which increases patients' melanin levels, could dramatically reduce the occurrence of melanoma in these susceptible groups, and further, there is no comparable treatment, meaning little competition. The company decides to take the steps to bring the drug to market.

## Preclinical Trials

The first thing that Salud will do is start preclinical testing of AntiSolar. Preclinical testing happens before any tests on people, to determine if AntiSolar (or any drug or treatment) is safe for testing on humans. Salud will test AntiSolar on animal cells, or animals first.

It is important to understand that preclinical testing is simply the first step on the way to getting drug approval. Many drugs that complete preclinical testing never make it to the market, because they don't work on people. So the next time you read about a drug that has successfully completed preclinical testing, remember that drug is years away from approval.

Upon completing preclinical testing, Salud receives test results indicating that AntiSolar is safe for testing on people. It then files an Investigative New Drug Application (IND) with the FDA to obtain permission to test the drug on people. It is performing its clinical trials at a major medical school. The school and clinic where the tests are done have set up, as required by the FDA, an Institutional Review Board (IRB) to approve the clinical trial protocols. These protocols describe the type of people who can participate in the trials, the tests and procedures, the medication and dosages that will be studied, the length of the study, its objectives, and other aspects of the research. These boards ensure that the study is acceptable according to law and medical ethics, that participants have given consent to participate and are fully informed of the risks, and that the researchers take the necessary steps to protect patients from harm.[5]

## IND Approval

AntiSolar's IND becomes effective when the FDA decides not to disapprove it within 30 days of its receipt. Investors should not get too excited, because about 85% of applications receive approval. All the IND shows is that the FDA believes, based on review of data provided by the drug company, that the drug, in this case, AntiSolar, is safe for clinical testing.

## Phase I

Now that it has its approval, Salud proceeds to clinical trials. Fortunately, Salud's management has carefully hoarded its cash from its initial public offering (IPO), so it has the resources to make it through the whole process without extra funding, barring any major surprises.[6]

Phase I testing represents the first time that AntiSolar is tested on human beings. These tests determine safe dosages of the drug and the best route to administer it. Patients in Phase I tests usually consist of paid volunteers who may be terminally ill patients or prisoners.[7] These populations are usually small because the drug's toxicity is unknown, and the goal is to minimize potential harm to patients. Phase I trials take on average about 22 months and about 81% of the drugs succeed.[8] (Successful drugs make it through in 20 months on average, while unsuccessful drugs take about 32 months to fail.)

Given that their focus is on determining toxicity, not on effectiveness against a disease, Phase I trials do not offer much information that investors can use to assess the chances of a drug's success.[9] If a drug makes it through Phase I, and the FDA does not stop the study for reasons of safety, then the trials move to Phase II.[10]

After extensive testing lasting 20 months (the average for a successful Phase I trial), AntiSolar passes muster and proceeds to Phase II.[11]

## Phase II

In Phase II, AntiSolar is tested in varying doses, helping determine how much medicine to administer and the effects of the varying doses on the course of the disease.[12] Phase II is more complex, time consuming, and costlier than Phase I. One reason Phase II tests cost more is that the trial's patient population is much larger than Phase I, typically between 100 to 1,000 people.[13] Researchers evaluate the safety and effectiveness of the treatment and learn how the drug works in the body. Investigators also check for side effects. Phase II may be the most critical part of the approval process, because the drug is first tested against the disease.[14] This phase weeds out more drugs than Phase I, with on average 58% of the drugs surviving Phase II and the trials lasting an average of 34 months.[15] (Successful drugs take about 30 months to get through Phase II, while unsuccessful drugs take longer before they fail—about 40 months.)[16]

When knowledgeable investors analyze Phase II trials, they look for dramatic outcomes in the trials, especially if treatments already exist. They do this because, if the drug later completes Phase III trials, the FDA wants to see exceptional performance relative to current drugs before it approves a new drug. Drugs coming up against already proven treatments face higher hurdles than drugs for a disease with no treatment. On the other hand, if no drug is available to treat that disease, the FDA may look more favorably upon that application. Consequently, companies entering a field with a lot of competitors—or available treatments—face a harder time, because of the greater regulatory hurdles that arise from adding another drug to a crowded field.[17]

AntiSolar completed its trials in 30 months and moves into Phase III. The drug appears to have dramatic results in reducing incidence of melanoma in the Phase II trial population.

## Phase III

Phase III is the final stage of drug testing and the most involved. The goal of Phase III trials is to see how well the drug works in a large population over a long time period, usually close to four years, and to observe any side effects.[18] Typically thousands of people are tested in double blind studies. Patients are randomly assigned to receive either the drug or a placebo. A *placebo* is a preparation containing no active ingredients that is given to a patient in a clinical trial to provide a baseline against which to assess the performance of the actual drug. This is because people often seem to improve from the psychological effect of receiving some sort of treatment. Comparing the drug to a placebo allows researchers to see how the drug under investigation performs relative to no treatment. The purpose of Phase III trials is to see if medication under review performs better than a placebo at a level considered statistically significant—that is, not due to chance. Neither the patient, nor the examining doctor, knows whether the patient has received the placebo—only the administrators of the study know.

Moving to Phase III is a positive signal, because a company needs much money and manpower to set up and administer Phase III trials. It would not commence trials unless it thought the drug had a good chance of success.[19] Phase III trials are about more than testing whether or not a drug is effective. They are needed to show that a drug is more effective and safer than other treatments that may be in the marketplace.

Now, Salud Pharmaceuticals has never run any Phase III trials before. It has reached Phase III with $45 million in cash and no debt. Based on past statistics, it knows it will take about four years to get through its trials. It anticipates spending about $10 million as the trial goes forward. To this point the company has spent about $5 million per year. This creates a risky situation because it will spend most of its capital on the trials—which have about a 60% chance of being successful.[20] Unfortunately, Phase III brings some problems for Salud. (These are based on events that have happened in Phase III trials.) In an effort to find more people for the study and speed up the process, the company and medical school decided to recruit people and monitor them in three satellite clinics. The total population to be studied at the medical school and the three clinics was to be 1,000 people. However, the staff in these clinics was not highly trained in administering medical trials. There was some pressure to get things done quickly. In this haste, they made big mistakes.

At clinic one, the patients were administered both the placebo and the medicine due to poor investigative controls. This meant that the data from that clinic became invalid. This also meant that the data from these patients could not be used in the study, and the sample size was shrunk. At the second satellite clinic, it was discovered that the actual medicine was not properly refrigerated at the clinic site and became ineffective. At the third satellite site, the nurses who prepared the drugs for administration also were the ones giving the drugs, so they knew which were placebos and which weren't, so the study was not blind. Because of these problems in the protocols, at the end of its Phase III trials, Salud did not have adequate data to submit to the FDA for approval.

It was faced with trying to raise more capital—but how many investors would want to put money into a company that was not well managed? Salud wound up selling the compound for $5 million to a major drug company that then ran its own trials, got the drug approved, and earned $10 million a year from the drug.

## Marketing Approval and Follow-Up

If the Phase III trials are successful, the drug is sent to the FDA for approval known as a New Drug Approval (NDA). If a drug passes Phase III, the manufacturer can apply for marketing approval, which can take up to one year to obtain. After receiving marketing approval, the drug can be sold to the public. Even though a drug has been approved, that doesn't mean it can't be removed from the market if complications arise later. Passing through the FDA process does not always guarantee patients that drugs are safe. Stories about drugs being removed from the market after they appeared to cause dangerous side effects in users are often in the news. Often drug companies are sued when a drug appears to cause complications. These lawsuits can prove very expensive—and point out another risk of being in the drug development business. Peruse the annual report of any major drug company and there will be a section devoted to lawsuits, along with the results of the cases and the reserves the company sets aside to pay any claims.

## Some Observations on the Drug Approval Process

Considering the long time frames for drug development, it is useful to consider a company's cash position in evaluating its prospects for success. The combination of long development and testing timetables and no revenues until a drug is approved can make companies that are dependent on a single drug very risky.

If a company has no revenues, and little chance of revenues in the next few years, then, unless it goes to the capital markets, it will finance its activities from its cash and related assets. Investors can get an idea of how much longer a company can function by dividing its cash on hand by its annual losses to get a rough idea of how much longer the company can function. This provides an estimate of a company's financial viability.

Consider the case of a company with $100 million in cash and $50 million a year in losses that has been in business for ten years but has yet to produce income. It has drugs that are in Phase I trials and will take about five years to come to market. This company has cash that will allow it to go on for two years, but it has no hope of revenues until five years down the road. This company is not in a strong position, limiting its options. It may be able to go to the capital markets to raise new funds. But it may not get a favorable reception because it has not yet produced income—any potential revenues may be years down the road.

The early investors probably would have done better putting their money in treasury bonds. The IPO investors, if they held on, have probably lost large amounts of money.

So, if the new financing option doesn't work, the company may try to sell itself to another company or set up an alliance with a pharmaceutical company. In exchange for an alliance, or rights to the drugs, the pharmaceutical company will inject cash into the operation. But who has the stronger hand in the negotiations, the cash strapped biotech startup or the cash rich pharmaceutical company that has lots of options on where to spend its cash? That's right: The pharmaceutical company has the upper hand that it will use to its advantage in negotiating the alliance or rights agreement. The other option for the startup is to go bankrupt.

## Healthcare Reform and Biotech Investing

One question on the mind of biotech investors is, "How will healthcare reform affect biotech investments?" We don't know exactly how reform will affect each company or fund. As the authors were writing this book, healthcare reform had not been enacted, so it is hard to pinpoint the precise effects. However, we perceive some general benefits for the biotech sector coming from healthcare reform.

One of the goals of healthcare reform is to reduce the costs of healthcare. As we discussed in the inverted U discussion in Chapter 4, "The Biotech Revolution Is Changing the Face of Healthcare: What It Means for Medicine and Investors," the best way to cut costs is to cure diseases with inexpensive, highly effective treatments, such as the polio vaccine. The biotechnology industry offers the potential to provide those cures.

Perhaps the most important point for the sector is that if healthcare reform is enacted, more people who need healthcare will have insurance. This could create tens of millions of people who could afford more healthcare—and more medicines. Consequently, more people with an ability to pay could mean larger markets—a larger pie for all the healthcare companies to divvy up. So, for investors in the medical technologies of the future, healthcare reform that means more access to care could be a good thing.

## Conclusion

Biotech investing offers enormous potential with considerable risk. That risk is mitigated by buying these stocks in baskets. As the population ages and more of us develop chronic diseases, it becomes increasingly expensive, and eventually unaffordable, to treat the symptoms of illness. We must prevent and cure disease both for our own well-being as well as that of society. The increasing demand for such products means that investors have a unique opportunity to catch the wave of what will be one of the most important wealth-building sectors in our history.

## Notes

[1] If you cannot afford to lose the money you want to invest in biotech stocks, then stay away from biotech investing (or any form of equity investing).

[2] Pharmaceutical Research and Manufacturers of America, "The Drug Discovery, Development and Approval Process," 16, http://www.phrma.org/files/attachments/ApprovingNewMedicines.pdf.

[3] Drugs only receive patent protection for a limited period of time. If a drug is not approved in time, the drug may go off patent, which means the owner of the patent no longer has the exclusive rights to that compound, and it may face competition from other manufacturers that can also produce the product.

[4] Tom Taulli, *Investing in IPOs: New Paths to Profit with Initial Public Offerings* (Princeton: Bloomberg Press, 1999), 125.

[5] U.S. Food and Drug Administration, www.fda.gov.

[6] Other companies are not so fortunate. One of Salud's competitors, Pequeno Biopharmaceuticals, ran out of money in the midst of its trials for a drug to combat bedbug infestations—AntiCama—and was only able to continue thanks to a cash infusion from Grande Pharma. Of course Grande did not do this for nothing; it took the rights to AntiCama and agreed to pay Pequeno a modest annual licensing fee, if the drug was approved. Pequeno lost out on the upside from AntiCama because it did not have much negotiating room due to its precarious financial situation. Although this case is fictional, such things do happen, and small biotech companies often do not have much leverage when they need funds.

[7] Taulli, *Investing in IPOs*, 125.

[8] Rosa M. Abrantes-Metz, Christopher P. Adams, and Albert D. Metz, "Pharmaceutical Development Phases: A Duration Analysis," Working Paper No. 274, Bureau of Economics, Federal Trade Commission, October 2004, 8.

[9] George Wolff, *The Biotech Investor's Bible* (New York: John Wiley & Sons, 2001), 55.

[10] The FDA can stop a study at any point for safety reasons.

[11] Abrantes-Metz et al., "Pharmaceutical Development Phases," 9.

[12] Taulli, *Investing in IPOs*, 125.

[13] Ibid.

[14] Ibid.

[15] Abrantes-Metz et al., "Pharmaceutical Development Phases," 9.

[16] Ibid., 9-10.

[17] Wolff, *Biotech Investor's Bible*, 55.

[18] Ibid., 56.

[19] Ibid.

[20] U.S. Food and Drug Administration, http://www.fda.gov/ICECI/Enforcement Actions/WarningLetters/ucm177398.htm.

# 6

## Investing in Healthcare ETFs

In 2010, annual healthcare expenditures in the United States will reach $2.5 trillion, or more than 17% of the Gross Domestic Product (GDP). Nearly one of every five dollars we spend goes to health-related expenditures. That ratio was only 8% in 1980, just 30 years ago. With Baby Boomers now turning 60 at an unprecedented rate that will continue for another 15 years, that ratio is expected to grow to 25% by 2020. Despite this rapid growth, most investors have underweighted healthcare in their portfolios. There are 13 healthcare exchange traded funds (ETFs) currently trading in the United States with total invested assets of about $7 billion. This is an astonishingly small amount of ETF participation in an enormous sector of the economy. Contrast that $7 billion with the $50 billion invested in the four gold ETFs, for example.

The ten largest pharmaceutical companies have a total market cap (as of December 31, 2009) of approximately $1 trillion. Table 6.1 lists them.

The five largest biotech companies represent another $150 billion of market capitalization seen in Table 6.2.

And the major device and instrument manufacturers represent another $200 billion of market cap as seen in Table 6.3.

**TABLE 6.1    Ten Largest Pharmaceutical Companies as of December 31, 2009**

| Company | Market Cap in $ Billions |
| --- | --- |
| Johnson & Johnson (JNJ) | 180 |
| Pfizer (PFE) | 150 |
| Novartis (NVS) | 125 |
| GlaxoSmithKline (GSK) | 110 |
| Sanofi (SNY) | 100 |
| Abbott (ABT) | 85 |
| Merck (MRK) | 80 |
| AstraZeneca (AZN) | 65 |
| Bristol-Myers Squibb (BMY) | 50 |
| Eli Lilly (LLY) | 40 |

**TABLE 6.2    Five Largest Biotech Companies by Market Capitalization as of December 31, 2009**

| Company | Market Cap in $ Billions |
| --- | --- |
| Amgen (AMGN) | 57 |
| Gilead (GILD) | 41 |
| Celgene (CELG) | 25 |
| Biogen Idec (BIIB) | 14 |
| Genzyme (GENZ) | 13 |

**TABLE 6.3    Six Largest Medical Device Companies by Market Capitalization as of December 31, 2009**

| Company | Market Cap in $ Billions |
| --- | --- |
| Medtronic (MDT) | 50 |
| Alcon (ALC) | 50 |
| Baxter (BAX) | 36 |
| Covidien (COV) | 24 |
| Stryker (SYK) | 20 |
| Becton Dickinson (BDX) | 18 |

The three preceding tables list a total of 21 companies with a cumulative market cap of $1.3 trillion. There are a few hundred additional companies with a total market cap of more than $500 billion in other areas of healthcare including generic drugs, contract research organizations (CROs), hospitals and nursing homes, and health insurers and HMOs.[1] All these sectors appear in the ETFs we discuss in this chapter. Yet currently, though healthcare is unquestionably the fastest growing segment of the economy, only $7 billion is invested in the industry's ETFs. Compare this with the $43 billion invested in the single largest gold ETF (GLD) or the $36 billion invested in the emerging market index (EEM). One reason investors shy away from healthcare is that many feel it is difficult to understand the science and technology involved. Yet it is undoubtedly true that most investors know very little about the emerging markets represented in EEM and even less about the specific companies in that portfolio. Another reason investors avoid healthcare investments is that the process for bringing new products to market is long and expensive. Contrast that with the instant gratification afforded from an investment in gold at a time of great volatility in the economy.

The long-term benefits to the U.S. economy from investing in the healthcare industry far exceed those that can come from investing in gold or emerging markets. Investors may profit from the latter two investments, but they may just as easily lose a great deal of money. On the other hand, healthcare is a growing industry that has the potential to create several million jobs in the next five years and vastly improve the quality of life for billions of people around the world. The industry has more than 10,000 products in clinical trials and development, many of which are revolutionary in their potential. Healthcare should be a significant part of investors' portfolios, and they should be enthusiastic about the prospects. But, for a number of reasons, that is not the case.

As 2009 came to a close, Congress was embroiled in a heated debate about healthcare reform. These political considerations create substantial uncertainty, which always drives off investors. There is an ongoing debate in this country about whether healthcare is a right or a privilege. As a practical matter, investors need to view healthcare as a business. Some argue that an industry that sustains health should not be a for-profit enterprise. But the agriculture industry provides us the food we need to survive, and the construction industry provides us with shelter. Those businesses work because they are subject to free market competition. Healthcare is heavily regulated, and there are many impediments preventing it from being a free market. As different presidential administrations come and go, there is an ever-shifting philosophy about regulating healthcare.

Beyond political considerations, there is the issue of the impending expiration of patents that protect the industry's most popular drugs. Drugs representing more than $140 billion of industry sales will come off patent (and therefore be subject to copy and sale by generic manufacturers at much lower prices) by 2014. These drugs must be replaced, and this represents an unprecedented opportunity for the biotech industry. On the other hand, the FDA process for approval of new drugs is long, expensive, and uncertain. It is easy to see why investors have avoided this sector of the economy, despite its size. There is strong reason to believe that dynamic may change now, and we are likely at the beginning of what will become a boom in healthcare investing. The Baby Boom generation, 78 million strong, is now 46 to 64 years of age. Increasingly this group, which is the predominant investor cohort, is concerned about good health and the cost of maintaining it. Websites like WebMD have become very popular as Boomers confront their mortality and try to maintain and extend their lives. As they do, they are discovering the myriad of investment opportunities that present themselves in the healthcare and biotech space.

The following is a review of the larger healthcare ETFs (greater than $100 million in market capitalization) currently available in the marketplace. Table 6.4 provides an overview of these funds. Complete listings of the components of each fund, and their weights, are found in Appendix A, "Healthcare and Biotech ETFs."

The healthcare funds fall into four major categories: the pharmaceutical industry, overall healthcare funds, biotechnology, and medical devices.

**TABLE 6.4   Healthcare ETFs with Market Cap over $100 Million**

| Industry Category | Fund Company | Fund Name | Ticker Symbol | Total Expense Ratio |
|---|---|---|---|---|
| *Biotech* | | | | |
| | BlackRock | iShares Nasdaq Biotech Index Fund | IBB | 0.48% |
| | Invesco Power-Shares Capital Mgmt LLC | PowerShares Dynamic Biotechnology & Genome Portfolio | PBE | 0.63% |
| | State Street Bank & Trust Company | SPDR S&P Biotech ETF | XBI | 0.35% |
| *Healthcare* | | | | |
| | BlackRock | iShares Dow Jones U.S. Healthcare Sector Index Fund | IYH | 0.48% |
| | State Street Bank & Trust Company | Health Care Select Sector Fund | XLV | 0.22% |
| | Vanguard Group Inc. | Vanguard Health Care ETF | VHT | 0.25% |
| *Medical Devices* | | | | |
| | BlackRock | iShares Dow Jones U.S. Medical Devices Index Fund | IHI | 0.48% |
| *Pharmaceuticals* | | | | |
| | BlackRock | iShares Dow Jones U.S. Pharmaceuticals Index Fund | IHE | 0.48% |
| | BlackRock | iShares S&P Global Healthcare Sector Index Fund | IXJ | 0.48% |

# Pharmaceutical ETFs

Pharmaceutical companies engage in the research, development, and production of pharmaceuticals, including veterinary drugs. The pharmaceutical companies dominate the industry and in one way or

another will continue to play a major role. While many of their important drugs will come off patent in the next five years, we have already
seen a fair amount of takeover activity as these companies attempt to
refill their shelves. Also, the cost of distributing a drug is prohibitively
expensive, so biotech companies look to partner with the major pharmaceutical companies for that purpose. While the growth in the
industry will be driven by the biotech and medical device sectors,
steady earnings will be generated by the major pharmaceutical companies. There are two ETFs that own these companies: the iShares
S&P Global Healthcare Fund (IXJ) (see Table 6.5) and the iShares
Dow Jones U.S. Pharmaceutical Fund (IHE) (see Table 6.6). IXJ
owns the major pharmaceutical companies regardless of where they
are headquartered, and the IHE owns only U.S. companies. Holdings
in Abbott Labs, Merck, Johnson & Johnson, Bristol Myers, and Pfizer
represent nearly 50% of IHE, which had total assets of $180 million
at the end of 2009. These same companies represent about 30% of
the $550 million portfolio of IXJ. International giants Novartis,
Roche, GlaxoSmithKline, AstraZeneca, and Bayer represent another
30% of the total holdings. IXJ is a larger fund portfolio (80 components compared to 32 for IHE) and includes all the world's major
drug companies. It is interesting to note that IHE outperformed IXJ

**TABLE 6.5    iShares S&P Global Healthcare Sector Index Fund (IXJ)
Expense Ratio (0.48%)    Top 10 Holdings (30 November 2009)**

| Ticker Symbol | Name | Weight | Sector |
|---|---|---|---|
| JNJ | Johnson & Johnson | 8.48% | Pharmaceuticals |
| NOVN | Novartis AG-REG | 7.19% | Pharmaceuticals |
| PFE | Pfizer Inc. | 7.18% | Pharmaceuticals |
| ROG | Roche Holding AG-Genusschein | 5.63% | Pharmaceuticals |
| MRK | Merck & Co. Inc. | 5.41% | Pharmaceuticals |
| GSK | GlaxoSmithKline PLC | 5.25% | Pharmaceuticals |
| ABT | Abbott Laboratories | 4.13% | Pharmaceuticals |
| SAN | Sanofi-Aventis | 3.96% | Pharmaceuticals |
| AZN | AstraZeneca PLC | 3.17% | Pharmaceuticals |
| BAYN | Bayer AG | 3.1% | Pharmaceuticals |

**TABLE 6.6   iShares Dow Jones U.S. Pharmaceuticals Index Fund (IHE)
Expense Ratio (0.48%)   Top 10 Holdings (30 November 2009)**

| Ticker Symbol | Name | Weight | Sector |
|---|---|---|---|
| MRK | Merck & Co. Inc. | 10.33% | Pharmaceuticals |
| PFE | Pfizer Inc. | 9.77% | Pharmaceuticals |
| JNJ | Johnson & Johnson | 8.67% | Pharmaceuticals |
| ABT | Abbott Laboratories | 7.49% | Pharmaceuticals |
| BMY | Bristol-Myers Squibb Co | 6.22% | Pharmaceuticals |
| LLY | Eli Lilly & Co. | 5.55% | Pharmaceuticals |
| AGN | Allergan Inc. | 4.25% | Pharmaceuticals |
| HSP | Hospira Inc. | 3.57% | Pharmaceuticals |
| FRX | Forest Laboratories Inc. | 3.55% | Pharmaceuticals |
| MYL | Mylan Inc. | 3.22% | Pharmaceuticals |

by about 10% in 2009 as investors anticipated the passage of health-care reform. American pharmaceutical companies spent more than $200 million lobbying on behalf of the legislation. A conservative investor need only own IXJ to get total exposure to pharmaceutical companies worldwide.

Those who believe that U.S. companies will derive a benefit from reform may wish to divide their investment between the two funds.

# Healthcare ETFs

Healthcare ETFs cover the gamut of all elements of the healthcare business. They are usually dominated by pharmaceutical companies.

There are three broadly diversified healthcare ETFs: Vanguard Health Care (VHT) (see Table 6.7), the Health Care Select SPDR (XLV) (see Table 6.8), and the iShares Dow Jones Healthcare (IYH) (see Table 6.9). XLV has about $2.5 billion in assets while the other two each have about $500 million. The holdings are similar, and the returns are highly correlated. The Vanguard fund tracks the MSCI Investable Market Health Care Index, which includes all the stocks in the U.S. healthcare universe. It also has a low expense load of 25 basis points. The XLV tracks the healthcare sector of the S&P 500 and has a similar load of 22 basis points. The IYH has a 48 basis point load and tracks the Dow Jones U.S. Healthcare Index. Over the last several years the performance of all three funds has been similar. The Vanguard fund offers broader diversification while the XLV offers a slightly lower fee. An investor building an ETF portfolio in healthcare need only own one of these funds, and they are all perfectly acceptable.

**TABLE 6.7   Vanguard Healthcare ETF (VHT)**
**Expense Ratio (0.25%)   Top 10 Holdings (30 September 2009)**

| Ticker Symbol | Name | Weight | Sector |
|---|---|---|---|
| JNJ | Johnson & Johnson | 11.3% | Pharmaceuticals |
| PFE | Pfizer Inc. | 7.5% | Pharmaceuticals |
| ABT | Abbott Laboratories | 5.2% | Pharmaceuticals |
| MRK | Merck & Co. Inc. | 4.5% | Pharmaceuticals |
| | Wyeth (Now part of Pfizer) | 4.4% | Pharmaceuticals |
| AMGN | Amgen Inc. | 4.1% | Biotechnology |
| | Schering-Plough Corp.(Now part of Merck) | 3.1% | Pharmaceuticals |
| BMY | Bristol-Myers Squibb Co. | 3.0% | Pharmaceuticals |
| GILD | Gilead Sciences Inc. | 2.8% | Biotechnology |
| MDT | Medtronic Inc. | 2.8% | Medical Equipment |

**TABLE 6.8   Healthcare Select Sector SPDR Fund (XLV)**
**Expense Ratio (0.22%)   Top 10 Holdings (18 December 2009)**

| Ticker Symbol | Name | Weight | Sector |
|---|---|---|---|
| JNJ | Johnson & Johnson | 14.16% | Pharmaceuticals |
| PFE | Pfizer Inc | 11.77% | Pharmaceuticals |
| MRK | Merck & Co Inc./NJ | 9.11% | Pharmaceuticals |
| ABT | Abbott Labs | 5.58% | Pharmaceuticals |
| AMGN | Amgen Inc. | 4.5% | Biotechnology |
| MDT | Medtronic Inc. | 3.83% | Medical Equipment |
| BMY | Bristol-Myers Squibb Co. | 3.59% | Pharmaceuticals |

**TABLE 6.8   Healthcare Select Sector SPDR Fund (XLV)**
**Expense Ratio (0.22%)   Top 10 Holdings (18 December 2009) (cont.)**

| Ticker Symbol | Name | Weight | Sector |
|---|---|---|---|
| GILD | Gilead Sciences Inc. | 3.07% | Biotechnology |
| UNH | UnitedHealth Group | 2.95% | Health Insurance |
| LLY | Eli Lilly & Co. | 2.88% | Pharmaceuticals |

**TABLE 6.9   iShares Dow Jones US Healthcare Sector Index Fund (IYH)**
**Expense Ratio (0.48%)   Top 10 Holdings (30 November 2009)**

| Ticker Symbol | Name | Weight | Sector |
|---|---|---|---|
| JNJ | Johnson & Johnson | 12.54% | Pharmaceuticals |
| PFE | Pfizer Inc. | 10.56% | Pharmaceuticals |
| MRK | Merck&Co. Inc. | 7.96% | Pharmaceuticals |
| ABT | Abbott Labs | 6.05% | Pharmaceuticals |
| AMGN | Amgen Inc. | 4.11% | Biotechnology |
| BMY | Bristol-Myers Squibb Co. | 3.59% | Pharmaceuticals |
| MDT | Medtronic Inc. | 3.4% | Medical Equipment |
| GILD | Gilead Sciences Inc. | 3.02% | Biotechnology |
| LLY | Eli Lilly & Co. | 2.6% | Pharmaceuticals & Biotechnology |
| UNH | UnitedHealth Group | 2.4% | Health Insurance |

# Biotechnology

Because healthcare expenditures will grow faster than the rate of inflation for the foreseeable future and healthcare as an industry will grow faster than the rest of the economy, any one of the healthcare funds discussed previously represents a good long-term holding. But there will be explosive growth in certain subsectors of healthcare, especially in biotech. While the previously described broadly diversified funds should be core holdings, there is significant upside potential (with increased risk of course) in focusing on this sector. There are three biotech ETFs to consider.

The iShares Nasdaq Biotech Index Fund (IBB), at $1.6 billion in assets, is by far the largest biotech ETF (see Table 6.10). The SPDR S&P Biotech ETF (XBI), shown in Table 6.11, has $390 million, and the PowerShares Dynamic Biotechnology & Genome Portfolio (PBE) (see Table 6.12) has about $200 million.

**TABLE 6.10    iShares Nasdaq Biotech Index Fund (IBB)**
**Expense Ratio (0.48%)    Top 10 Holdings (30 November 2009)**

| Ticker Symbol | Name | Weight | Sector |
|---|---|---|---|
| AMGN | Amgen Inc. | 10.58% | Biotechnology |
| GILD | Gilead Sciences Inc. | 8.48% | Biotechnology |
| TEVA | Teva Pharmaceutical-Sp ADR | 7.78% | Pharmaceuticals |
| CELG | Celgene Corp. | 6.52% | Biotechnology |
| VRTX | Vertex Pharmaceuticals Inc. | 3.96% | Biotechnology |
| BIIB | Biogen Idec Inc. | 3.08% | Biotechnology |
| GENZ | Genzyme Corp. | 2.78% | Biotechnology |
| ALXN | Alexion Pharmaceuticals Inc. | 2.48% | Biotechnology |
| MYL | Mylan Inc. | 2.28% | Pharmaceuticals |
| WCRX | Warner Chilcott Plc-Class A | 2.27% | Therapeutics |

**TABLE 6.11    SPDR S&P Biotech ETF (XBI)**
**Expense Ratio (0.35%)    Top 10 Holdings (18 December 2009)**

| Ticker Symbol | Name | Weight | Sector |
|---|---|---|---|
| REGN | Regeneron Pharmaceuticals | 4.22% | Biotechnology |
| UTHR | United Therapeutics Corp. | 4.17% | Biotechnology |
| INCY | Incyte Corp. | 4.10% | Biotechnology |
| BMRN | Biomarin Pharmaceutical Inc. | 4.07% | Biotechnology |
| MDVN | Medivation Inc. | 4% | Pharmaceuticals |
| AMLN | Amylin Pharmaceuticals Inc. | 3.99% | Biotechnology |
| VRTX | Vertex Pharmaceuticals Inc. | 3.97% | Biotechnology |
| CELG | Celgene Corp. | 3.97% | Biotechnology |
| SGEN | Seattle Genetics Inc. | 3.92% | Biotechnology |
| CBST | Cubist Pharmaceuticals Inc. | 3.89% | Biotechnology |

**TABLE 6.12    PowerShares Dynamic Biotechnology &
Genome Portfolio (PBE)
Expense Ratio (0.63%)    Top 10 Holdings (21 December 2009)**

| Ticker Symbol | Name | Weight | Sector |
|---|---|---|---|
| BIIB | Biogen Idec Inc. | 5.17% | Biotechnology |
| ALXN | Alexion Pharmaceuticals Inc. | 5.08% | Biotechnology |
| MIL | Millipore Corp. | 5.00% | Biotechnology |
| LIFE | Life Technologies Corp. | 4.91% | Biotechnology |
| WAT | Waters Corp. | 4.90% | Medical Equipment |
| AMGN | Amgen Inc. | 4.76% | Biotechnology |
| GILD | Gilead Sciences Inc. | 4.40% | Biotechnology |
| AFFX | Affymetrix Inc. | 3.15% | Biotechnology |
| REGN | Regeneron Pharmaceuticals Inc. | 3.14% | Biotechnology |
| AFFY | Affymax Inc. | 3.07% | Biotechnology |

The IBB, which has a 48 basis point expense load, owns about 125 positions, though the five largest positions represent more than 35% of the portfolio. The remaining 120 positions represent on average 0.5% of the total. Investing in biotech is all about investing in the future discoveries of the industry. It is likely that biotech companies will develop the drugs that will replace those that are coming off patent at the large pharmaceutical companies. They will also create the therapies that will transition medicine from its current state of treating symptoms to the point where it can treat and ultimately cure or prevent the underlying diseases. Even for the larger biotech companies, one successful drug can have a meaningful effect on its stock price. For the smaller companies, the ones that make up the remainder of the 120 stocks in the IBB, the effect on the stock price can be massive (up if the drug is successful and down if not). But because there are 120 such positions, any one stock's movement will not have much effect on the overall portfolio. If one company that represents a 0.5% position in the portfolio sees its stock price rise fivefold because of a successful trial, the ETF will see a benefit of only 2%. So owning the IBB gives exposure to potential blockbuster innovation but with substantial mitigation of both risk and reward.

An investor seeking more upside should consider the other two funds, PBE and XBI. PBE has 32 positions, the largest of which is 5% of the portfolio, and the smallest is 2.5%. Similarly XBI has about 27 positions. There is very little overlap in the portfolios, each of them owning a subset of the IBB portfolio. Over the past year PBE is up about 20% while XBI is up about 3%. That performance is not necessarily indicative of future results as both portfolios' companies have many drugs in trials. Because most of these companies are unfamiliar to most investors, the following description of a sample of companies from both funds should be instructive.

One of the positions that the two funds have in common is OSI Pharmaceuticals (OSIP). OSIP has a market cap of $2 billion. In 2009, the company had gross sales of $400 million, most of that coming from Tarceva, which is used to treat a type of lung cancer as well as pancreatic cancer. The drug is in trials for additional uses. The company is developing other cancer drugs as well. In addition, the company is developing products to address diabetes and obesity. The stock, which traded as high as $75 per share in 2004, recently was selling at $35 per share. The drugs that the company has in development give it a very large upside, although it will take years to commercialize the drugs in development. Because the company is working on drugs that address large unmet medical needs, it is perennially a takeover candidate for the big pharmaceutical companies looking to restock their pipelines. There is no question that this is a high risk/high reward stock that on its own would be too risky for most investors. But as 4% of XBI and 3% of PBE, it becomes an excellent addition to the portfolio.

One of the largest positions in XBI is Dendreon (DNDN), which has developed a therapy, called Provenge, for men with advanced prostate cancer. The company has completed one set of trials and is conducting others. In November 2009, the company applied for a license to manufacture and distribute the drug. The drug is an immunotherapy, designed to engage the patient's own immune system against the disease. The stock, which traded under $3 in March 2009, was priced at $25 at the end of December 2009. The reason for the rise was that in April, the company announced that a trial of the drug had been successful in extending the life of some men with advanced prostate cancer. The company has other products in development, but none that are close to fruition. This would have been a very risky stock to own individually but makes perfect sense as a 4% position in XBI. The market cap of DNDN is $3 billion. The potential sales of Provenge are in excess of $2 billion. If the drug is approved, the company will definitely be considered a takeover target.

Another portfolio company of XBI is Isis Pharmaceuticals (Isis). Isis is developing a number of drugs based upon antisense technology. The technology identifies the gene or genes responsible for causing a particular disease and allows for the creation of drugs that can regulate or even interfere with the activity of the gene. Isis has more than 1,500 patents for antisense applications. The company is developing a number of drugs for a variety of therapeutic areas including cardiovascular, metabolic, neurodegenerative, and inflammatory diseases. Since the company cannot develop more than a few drugs on its own, it is licensing patents to other drug developers. The upside potential for Isis is virtually limitless; if the technology achieves what is hoped, it has the potential to become one of the largest pharmaceutical companies in the world. The current market cap is about $1 billion. There is great risk associated with the technology in that it may ultimately be proven not to work. It is therefore an ideal portfolio company because, as one of three dozen components, it will not have a serious downside effect in case of failure, but can provide a substantial upside if successful.

A third company in the XBI portfolio is Myriad Genetics (MYGN). Myriad is one of the world leaders in molecular diagnostics, an important and rapidly expanding field of medicine. Historically, the word "diagnosis" creates a mental image of a doctor wearing a white coat armed with a stethoscope and tongue depressor, standing over a patient lying on an examination table. In that image, the doctor examines the patient, notes the symptoms being displayed, and pronounces the diagnosis of the underlying condition. It is, in essence, a look back at what the disease has already done to the patient. But companies like Myriad are changing the very meaning of diagnosis. It is becoming more of an assessment of what may happen to the patient in the future, a prognosis of disease that may occur years down the road. Take, for example, BRACAnalysis.

Myriad markets the BRACAnalysis, a diagnostic test for mutations in two genes (BRCA 1 and BRCA 2), which can indicate a woman's risk of developing breast cancer. Myriad markets similar tests for colorectal cancer, melanoma, and a test to determine a patient's chance of having a severe toxic reaction to chemotherapy. These tests allow the doctor and the patient to predict problems long before they occur. As medicine transitions from treating symptoms (after the fact) to intervening in or preventing the underlying disease, companies like Myriad will play a critical role in reducing the cost of care. A disease identified at the molecular level, before there are symptoms, can potentially be dealt with much more efficiently and with a far superior result for the patient. Myriad, and other companies, are developing dozens more gene-based diagnostics for early detection of disease. Myriad, which has a market capitalization of about $2.5 billion, has seen its stock price rise fivefold over the past five years. Most of the company's products are still in development. Because the technology of diagnosis is still evolving, Myriad must be considered a higher risk investment. It benefits the investor to own the XBI ETF where Myriad represents 3% of the portfolio because there is so much upside potential for the company.

Vertex Pharmaceuticals (VRTX), with a market capitalization of $7.5 billion, is one of the largest companies in the XBI portfolio. Vertex is working on several new therapies for major diseases including viruses, cystic fibrosis, autoimmune diseases, and cancer. Vertex currently markets one of the key medicines for the treatment of HIV. A success in any one of the ten drugs currently in trials would represent a major upside for the company's stock price. The company has two late stage trials for a drug to treat Hepatitis C, for which there currently is no medication. The drug to treat cystic fibrosis is also subject to two Phase III trials. The stock which was trading at a five-year high at the end of 2009 has doubled in price in the past 18 months. Again, this is a company with enormous upside potential that would carry too much risk as an individual position for the average investor. It represents 4% of XBI, meaning that the downside effect would be minimal, and the upside meaningful.

Onyx Pharmaceuticals (ONXX) specializes in treatments of various types of cancer. The company is typical of the high risk/high reward nature of biotech stocks. In the past ten years the stock has been as low as $3 per share and as high as $60. Recently it was trading around $30. The company has one approved product, Nexavar, which is used to treat both kidney and liver cancer. Nexavar is being tested for other indications, and the company has several other products in development. The drugs Onyx develops are designed to inhibit the development of tumors and cancer cells on a molecular basis. Nexavar sales in 2009 exceeded $1 billion, which demonstrates the potential value of this class of therapeutics. Again, the company has great potential but with a high degree of risk. Onyx has the added benefit of having commercialized a drug so the possibility that similar drugs will prove to be useful for other indications is somewhat higher.

In addition to the companies just discussed, there are 24 additional portfolio positions in XBI, each with a potentially exciting new therapy for an unmet need in medicine. While the positions individually are somewhat risky, the overall portfolio represents more than 100 drugs in trials. While most will not be commercially successful, the odds are that a number of them will succeed. Investing is not only about managing risk but also having the opportunity to earn an appropriate reward for the risk undertaken. XBI is certainly such an investment.

The largest portfolio position in the PowerShares Dynamic Biotechnology and Genome Portfolio (PBE) is Alexion Pharmaceuticals (ALXN). Alexion is devoted to developing revolutionary treatments for life-threatening and ultra-rare diseases. The company focuses on hematological and neurologic diseases, transplant rejection, cancer, and autoimmune disorders. Currently the company has one marketed drug, Soliris, which treats a rare blood disorder. The sales of Soliris in 2009 totaled $100 million. The drug is being tested on other conditions. The company has several other products in development including a new formulation for treating asthma and a promising treatment for leukemia. ALXN is about 5% of the PBE portfolio. The company's market cap is $4 billion, which provides plenty of room for appreciation if some of the drugs in development are ultimately successful.

Another 5% position in PBE is Life Technologies Corp. (LIFE). LIFE has a market cap of $9 billion and has seen its stock price rise from $20 to $50 in the past year. LIFE manufactures and sells the various tools that biotech companies need to develop their drugs including items such as gene sequencers and mass spectrometers and a variety of cell biology applications. These tools are unique since drug development for biotech companies (involving the manipulation of molecules and genes) is very different from the process to develop a classic pharmaceutical drug. LIFE has 3,600 patents and exclusive licensing arrangements, which give the company a strong proprietary position in the marketplace. The National Institutes of Health (NIH) handed out grants totaling nearly $30 billion to more than 200,000 recipients in 2009 and is expected to maintain that rate of funding for the next several years. Many of these research grant recipients will turn into commercial enterprises over the next few years, and these companies represent a growing and fertile market for companies like LIFE.

PDL BioPharma (PDLI) is a company whose market cap was over $4 billion in 2006 but which fell to under $1 billion in 2009. The stock represents about 3% of PBE. The company created an antibody humanization platform that it licenses to other biotech firms, which they use to create therapeutic drugs. The company receives a royalty stream from these licenses. It derives revenue from Genentech from two of that company's most successful cancer drugs, Herceptin and Avastin. PDLI also receives royalties from Elan/Biodec for Tysabri, a therapy for multiple sclerosis. Many analysts believe PDLI to be much undervalued. The stock was a high flier after the mapping of the human genome was complete in 2002, and the price got ahead of the company's development. The platform has been proven to work and now underpins some of the industry's most successful drugs. This is an ideal company for an aggressive biotech portfolio.

Exelixis (EXEL) develops small molecule drugs for the treatment of cancer, metabolic disorders, and cardiovascular diseases. It is a small-cap company with a market value of $800 million. The company has a variety of drugs at various stages of clinical development including a Phase III trial of a drug to treat thyroid cancer, which is being developed in partnership with Bristol-Myers Squibb (BMY). These partnerships benefit small biotech companies because the large pharmaceutical companies have the cash to pay for the trials and the distribution channels to market the drug. Many times these types of partnerships can lead to a sale of either the drug or the entire biotech company to the partner. Exelixis has several potentially exciting drugs but will likely need to raise more cash to commercialize them. This is one of the tricky aspects of valuing a biotech company. In general, the more successful a biotech company is, the more cash it requires. That is why having a deep-pocketed partner is a big advantage. But bringing in a partner too early (before there is any proof of concept) means that the valuation offered will take into account the associated risk and will therefore be very low. On the other hand, if a company waits too long to make a deal, it risks running out of cash and negotiating from desperation and having to give away most of the economics. Exelixis has great potential in its drugs, but it remains to be seen how successful the company will ultimately be. That is one of the primary reasons for its currently depressed stock price. But once again, the risk/reward ratio is attractive as a component in an ETF portfolio of biotech companies.

Alkermes (ALKS) is a company that focuses on chronic diseases such as nervous system disorders, addiction, rheumatoid arthritis, and diabetes. The company markets Risperdal, a long-acting treatment for schizophrenia and bipolar disorder. It sells Vivitrol, an injectable for the control of alcohol addiction. The company is testing similar drugs and a new injectable drug for the treatment of diabetes. The company's proprietary technology is used to enhance the therapeutic benefit of existing medications by making them last longer and engineering them for a slower release into the body. This is a platform that could potentially be applicable to dozens of medications. So once again, this is a company with fewer than one billion dollars of market capitalization that has great upside potential. It represents 3% of the PBE portfolio. It is possible that the technology becomes ubiquitous; it is just as likely that a superior technology comes along and proves to be a better product. But it is a worthy member of the ETF portfolio.

There has been a heated political debate in this country about healthcare. But nearly all of that debate has been about how to pay for it and how to include as many people as possible in the system (the question of access to the healthcare system is discussed earlier in the book). That is only a piece of the equation to making healthcare affordable. A more important piece is the evolution of the technologies and therapies of medicine so that we may produce better outcomes more efficiently—increasing healthcare quality. This process must be driven by innovation. Most Americans do not realize that the innovation we need is taking place. Healthcare will cost us $2.5 trillion in 2010, fully one-sixth of the GDP of the country. The emerging biotech companies are creating the products that will allow us to have better treatments with better outcomes at more affordable prices. Americans were happy to invest in a similar situation when Moore's Law was driving down the cost of semiconductors while they became faster and more powerful. Investors created real wealth in that process. And because there were no ETFs in the 1980s, investors had to pick just the right stocks or mutual fund manager to be successful. As the public becomes aware of the unmistakable trend in biotechnology, they will embrace these companies and the ETFs that own them in the same way.

# Medical Devices

The iShares U.S. Medical Devices Index Fund (IHI) owns approximately 38 of the major companies in this sector (see Table 6.13). An aging population is increasingly dependent on devices for the delivery of care from diabetes pumps to infusion therapy to prosthetic hips and knees to surgical tools. The device industry stands to be a primary beneficiary of both an aging population and longer lives. These companies have the added advantage of not being subject to the same rigorous and expensive trials that drug companies face.[2] These products can move from the inventor's bench to the market place quite speedily. IHI has about $300 million in assets under management, which is astonishingly low when one considers that the total market cap of the components is $180 billion. Many of these companies are quite profitable and on average are seeing their revenues grow at close to 20% per annum. The price/earnings ratio (PE) of the entire portfolio is 25 times trailing earnings. The expense load is 48 basis points. This is a portfolio that is destined to outperform the market over the next several years.

Medtronic (MDT) is the largest position in IHI representing 12% of the portfolio. It is the largest medical device company in the United States with a market cap of just under $50 billion. The product lines at Medtronic are both broad and deep. The company makes devices for neuromodulation, cardiovascular diseases, cardio rhythm modulation, spinal technologies, diabetes, and surgical devices. There are thousands of products in its catalog. Total revenues for 2009 were $15 billion. While this is a large and mature company, it still manages a healthy growth rate and is the market leader in every sector in which it competes.

**TABLE 6.13    iShares Dow Jones U.S. Medical Devices Index Fund (IHI) Total Expense Ratio (0.48%)    Top 10 Holdings (30 November 2009)**

| Ticker Symbol | Name | Weight | Sector |
|---|---|---|---|
| MDT | Medtronic Inc. | 12.1% | Medical Equipment |
| TMO | Thermo Fisher Scientific Inc. | 7.52% | Medical Equipment |
| SYK | Stryker Corp. | 6.83% | Medical Equipment |
| ZMH | Zimmer Holdings Inc. | 6.34% | Medical Equipment |
| STJ | St Jude Medical Inc. | 5.69% | Medical Equipment |
| ISRG | Intuitive Surgical Inc. | 5.62% | Medical Equipment |
| BSX | Boston Scientific Corp. | 5.09% | Medical Equipment |
| VAR | Varian Medical Systems Inc. | 3.97% | Medical Equipment |
| WAT | Waters Corp. | 3.92% | Medical Equipment |
| BEC | Beckman Coulter Inc. | 3.18% | Medical Equipment |

One of the newer and more exciting companies in the IHI portfolio is Intuitive Surgical, Inc. (ISRG) a company that was founded in 1995 and today has an $11 billion market cap. The stock recently touched $300 per share; it was less than $30 per share five years ago. ISRG is the manufacturer of the da Vinci robotic surgical system, which is used in a variety of surgeries routinely performed in hospitals; the surgeon sits at a computer console, and the system translates the surgeon's movements to instruments positioned inside the patient. In addition, the company sells a variety of surgical accessories and tools. The company has been able to sustain sales growth of at least 25% per year for the past five years. Robotic surgery is one of the breathtaking recent developments in medicine, yet most people know little about it. It is worth a trip to the company's website to see the system demonstrated (www.intuitivesurgical.com). The technologies are well protected by many patents and the company has an exceedingly bright future. ISRG is about 6% of the portfolio of IHI.

Knee and hip replacement are two of the fastest growing surgeries in healthcare. There are more than 500,000 knee replacements and 200,000 hip replacements in the United States every year. Many of those orthopedic replacement parts are provided by Stryker Corporation (SYK) whose stock makes up 7% of IHI. The company also sells the surgical tools and bonding agents needed for the surgeries as well as endoscopes and digital imaging systems. Seniors remain more active later in life than ever before, and it is common today for a healthy person to have a knee, hip, or joint wear out and become very painful. Joint replacement surgery is a growth industry and a completely appropriate investment focus for all who seek to participate in the economics of aging.

As this book goes to press, Congress is still debating healthcare legislation. It is impossible at this time to determine the impact on the industry. It appears, however, that the proposed increases in taxes and decreases in the Medicare budget could have a dampening effect on the performance of medical device companies in the short term. Such a dampening could reduce margins and retard innovation further impacting the outlook for these companies. This is only a possibility that must be noted. History shows that it is virtually impossible to stop innovation, and the overwhelming benefit of these devices should prevail giving these companies a bright future. Investors need to pay attention, however, as new legislation takes effect.

# Conclusion

The industry of healthcare is complex and in the throes of change. An investor wanting a comprehensive investment in the sector must be able to access the existing pharmaceutical companies, the emerging biotech companies, and the ever-expanding universe of medical device companies. It would be virtually impossible for individuals to build an adequate portfolio on their own. ETFs make the job simple and straightforward. A portfolio should include an allocation to one of the pharmaceutical ETFs, one of the broadly diversified healthcare ETFs, and one or more of the biotech and medical device ETFs. More conservative investors will want a larger allocation to pharmaceuticals and the broadly diversified healthcare funds, whereas more aggressive investors will want a larger allocation to biotech and medical devices. Typically, investors might make an equal allocation to all four categories, but each individual must measure her risk tolerance and adjust accordingly.

# Notes

[1] CROs may do drug research and development or run clinical trials.

[2] These companies are regulated but in a different manner than drugs.

# 7

# Climate Change and
# Understanding Green Investing

At the moment, our earth is undergoing unprecedented warming due to human activity, primarily from burning of fossil fuels to produce energy. The increasing concentration of greenhouse gases that raise terrestrial temperatures could dramatically alter our planet for the worse by leading to rising sea levels that flood coastal cities, increased desertification, death of coral reefs from ocean acidification, more wildfires, new disease pandemics, and creating more intense hurricanes that could threaten coastal areas. Climate change needs to be confronted before the damage is irreversible. In the short term, this can best be done by reducing greenhouse gas emissions, by developing and implementing cleaner forms of energy production, and by using energy more efficiently. This imperative to protect our planet presents a great opportunity for investors. Investing in technologies that will combat climate change, through Green ETFs, allows investors to profit from the move to a cleaner world.

## Understanding Climate Basics[1]

The atmosphere of earth is transparent to visible light, so when the skies are clear, the sun's energy passes through the atmosphere with ease. About 30% of light is reflected back into space, and the remaining 70% is absorbed by the ground and atmosphere and oceans. Some of that heat radiates back into space—otherwise, the earth would be cooked. However, the atmosphere contains water vapor and carbon dioxide ($CO_2$). While these gases allow the transmission of visible light, they absorb the infrared energy that the earth radiates. The atmosphere absorbs much of the energy before it goes into space. At a certain point, equilibrium is reached between incoming and outgoing energy, a process known as the *greenhouse effect*. This process keeps the earth's temperature relatively stable. Without its atmosphere, earth's temperature would fluctuate like the moon's, which goes from -230 degrees Fahrenheit (–110 degrees Celsius) at night to +230 degrees Fahrenheit (+110 degrees Celsius) during the day. The greenhouse effect keeps the earth habitable.

The largest amount of solar radiation hitting the earth strikes the equatorial region. The sun warms the air and water at the earth's surface. This heat causes water to evaporate from the earth's surface, which condenses to form clouds and rainfall, producing the tropical rains. Condensation releases heat, much of which is radiated into space. The remaining dryer, cooler air proceeds northward and settles down toward earth around 30 degrees from the equator, and it circulates back toward the equator in the trade winds. This pattern of air rising around the equator and settling down to earth around 30 degrees from the equator is known as the Hadley Cell. This pattern brings heat energy from the equator to the subtropics. Other circulation patterns bring the energy farther north. About half of the energy that comes from the equator moves through the atmosphere, and the other half through ocean currents. Ocean circulation is very important for Europe because it carries warm tropical surface water toward Europe, allowing it to be much warmer than it would be in the absence of these currents. If one of these circulation patterns, the Atlantic Meridional Overturning Circulations (AMOC) were to cease, as appears to have happened in the last glacial period, rapid climate change could occur in northern Europe and other regions.[2]

### Climate Is Constantly Changing

Climate always changes. Some changes are long term. Others are short term. Some are due to natural events, such as volcanic eruptions, and others are due to man. Since the industrial revolution, we have released increasing quantities of gases, such as carbon dioxide, methane, and others that trap infrared energy and warm the earth.

The Intergovernmental Panel on Climate Change (IPCC) of the United Nations Environmental Program and the World Meteorological Program has concluded that over the twentieth century, the earth's average surface temperature increased by about 0.6 degrees Celsius (1.1 degrees Fahrenheit) plus/minus 0.2 degrees Celsius (0.4 degrees Fahrenheit), and the earth's average surface temperature will go up between 1.4 degrees Celsius (2.5 degrees Fahrenheit) and 5.8 degrees Celsius (10.4 degrees Fahrenheit) from 1990 to 2100.[3]

### Greenhouse Gases Stick Around

Unlike many other pollutants, such as sulfur dioxide, that have short lives of hours or days in the atmosphere, greenhouse gases have long lives. Once emitted, carbon dioxide ($CO_2$) remains in the atmosphere for about 100 years. Others have even longer lives. This means that to stabilize atmospheric concentrations of $CO_2$ and temperatures requires reductions of global $CO_2$ emissions by 90%.[4]

As more greenhouse gases go into the atmosphere, the earth's temperature is expected to rise, assuming no other changes occur. Feedbacks in the system could affect the rate of change. For example, negative feedbacks can slow down, or reduce, the effects of global warming while positive feedbacks could speed up, or intensify, global warming. One example of a negative feedback is that since carbon dioxide is a plant fertilizer, increasing levels of carbon dioxide in the atmosphere could speed up the growth of plants, which will, in turn, take more carbon dioxide out of the atmosphere. This could slow the increase of carbon dioxide and slow the pace of warming.

On the other hand, as the earth warms, more snow and ice are expected to melt. Snow and ice reflect a good deal of sunlight. If they melt, the dark earth or ocean beneath them will not reflect as well, meaning the earth will absorb more energy which will increase earth's warming, an example of a positive feedback loop.

# Warming and Its Consequences

These feedbacks introduce some uncertainty into the climate change picture. However, it does appear that the earth's average temperature will increase over this century, although, all parts of the earth will not warm equally. The polar regions are expected to warm more than the tropics, and land regions are expected to warm more than oceanic regions.

The IPCC has made some general predictions about how the current pace of climate change could affect the earth. There are a number of events that the IPCC is 90% to 99% confident will occur in this century:

- Higher temperature maximums and an increased number of high temperature days over most land areas
- Higher temperature minimums along with fewer cold and frost days over most land areas
- Smaller difference between day and night time temperatures on land
- Increasing heat indexes (a combined measure of heat and humidity that measures human discomfort)
- More intense precipitation during storms

The IPCC also predicts other events with 66% to 90% confidence. These include

- Greater chance of dryer summers and risk of drought in certain areas
- Increase in windspeed in tropical cyclones in some areas
- Increase in rainfall during tropical cyclones

Some feel that changes in climate could shift ocean currents that currently warm Western Europe and could lead to dramatic climate change there, including rapid cooling when the warming waters no longer flow there.

# The Meaning of the Changes

It is anticipated that developed countries will undergo less impact from climate change than developing countries. There will be some likely impacts, though. Ski areas at lower altitudes may go out of business. More significantly, low lying cities and areas could be damaged badly by storm surges as oceans rise, which could be magnified by more intense storms. For example, airports and tunnels in New York

City could be flooded without protective structures. On the other hand, in the short term, warmer temperatures may mean more agricultural productivity in higher and middle latitudes.

Developing countries could face even greater threats—the impact on their economies will probably be larger than in the developed world. In addition, many poorer countries, such as Bangladesh, have large populations living near sea level, so sea level rise combined with storm surges could devastate these regions. Many low-lying countries do not have the resources of the Dutch, for example, to build protective levee systems.

Nature itself faces a tremendous challenge from climate change. It is hard for ecosystems, such as coral reefs, to adapt quickly enough to survive. New plant communities and species may emerge, and others may disappear forever. For example, New England could lose its current forest ecosystems. Decreasing biodiversity can make ecosystems more vulnerable to pests or diseases that live on a single species. Greater change is expected in the polar regions. The Arctic Ocean could be ice free in summer by the end of this century, opening up new shipping channels and exposing its ecosystems to new threats.

# Climate Change Could Happen Faster Than Expected

Climate change is expected to be gradual in the near term; however, certain events could speed it up, or increase its impact. These events include shifting of ocean currents, large scale melting of polar ice, changes in climate that could lead to destruction of ecosystems such as the Amazon rain forest, and the release of $CO_2$ stored in arctic permafrost. If one or more of these events take place, then climate change could have a greater and faster impact on the world, including on developed countries.

The increase of $CO_2$ in the atmosphere has already changed the oceans, making them more acidic. This could reduce the output of fisheries and lead to other environmental changes that affect sea life. Already coral reefs are dying due to higher temperatures, affecting fish stocks and tourism in certain areas.

Another pernicious effect on humanity could be that climate change may exacerbate the spread of infectious diseases. Climate change may make some regions more prone to various diseases, such as malaria. Unfortunately, many of these areas lack robust public health infrastructures, which could worsen the impact on people in those regions.

While the there may be uncertainty over the details about climate change, such as its pace and where changes will occur, there is agreement on two major points:

- Human activity is increasing the concentration of $CO_2$ and other long-lived greenhouse gases.
- The average temperature of the earth is increasing due to these gases and will continue to do so—altering the climate.

## What Needs to Be Done

To prevent greenhouse gases from permanently damaging the earth, emissions need to be reduced by about 90%, or existing greenhouse gases in the atmosphere have to be removed. The main source of $CO_2$ in the atmosphere comes from burning fossil fuels, with coal being the worst offender.

Moving to clean sources of energy, and/or reducing energy consumption, represent the fastest and most potent ways to reduce the emissions of $CO_2$ and stop climate change. Knowing how harmful climate change can be makes it imperative to stop it. One way to help stop it is by investing in technologies that will reduce greenhouse gas emissions. Investing in green technologies offers opportunity but also presents a risk/reward profile. If global warming accelerates, there will be more demand for these technologies and potentially higher returns for investors. If it doesn't happen—perhaps because of the widespread introduction of green technologies that reduce the chance of global warming—investors in those technologies still come out ahead in two ways—profiting from their investments and having and living in a climate that hasn't spun out of control. As with healthcare, many green technology companies are risky investments.

Buying in baskets is the way to go, because it allows investors to purchase across a sector—capturing many companies and often competing technologies, giving investors a better chance for success.

# Focus on Reducing Greenhouse Gas Emissions

Our focus in green technologies is on forms of energy production that reduce emissions of greenhouse gases, or technologies that increase energy efficiency and consequently reduce emissions. The following is a review of major developments designed to mitigate global warming. It focuses on the various technologies that can be easily accessed by investing in green ETFs and also helps investors understand the risks related to investing in these areas.

The goal of most green energy technologies is to create power, usually electricity, in ways that do not create emissions to exacerbate global warming. Most technologies revolve around cleaner methods of electricity generation. Others focus on reducing emissions through more efficient energy usage, cleaner transportation fuels, or less energy-intensive ways of moving goods.

Let's look at some of the alternative energy areas that investors can access through ETFs. Table 7.1 shows the amount of electric energy generated in the United States by source. Table 7.2 shows the breakdown of renewable electric production. Although renewable hydropower is the largest source of clean electric production in the United States, there is little opportunity for growth (and no hydropower ETFs), so we will not cover specific investments in that area.[5] Figure 7.1 and Figure 7.2, from Energy Information Administration data, provide an overview of U.S. greenhouse gas emissions. Figure 7.1 shows that the top fuel that contributes to carbon dioxide emissions is petroleum, and Figure 7.2 shows that the industry that produces the most carbon dioxide is the electric power industry, with coal being the major source of carbon dioxide in the electric power business. Following the figures and tables is an overview of major clean energy sources.

**TABLE 7.1    Total Electricity Generation by Fuel in 2008**

|                               | Billion KWh | Percent of Total Generation |
|-------------------------------|-------------|-----------------------------|
| Coal                          | 1995        | 48.47%                      |
| Petroleum                     | 45          | 1.11%                       |
| Natural Gas                   | 879         | 21.35%                      |
| Nuclear Power                 | 806         | 19.59%                      |
| Renewable Sources             | 373         | 9.07%                       |
| Other                         | 17          | 0.42%                       |
| Total Electricity Generation  | 4116        | 100.00%                     |

Source: Annual Energy Outlook

**TABLE 7.2    Total Renewable Generation in U.S. in 2008**

|                          | Generation (billion kilowatt hours) | Percentage |
|--------------------------|-------------------------------------|------------|
| Conventional Hydropower  | 248.79                              | 66.66%     |
| Geothermal               | 14.86                               | 3.98%      |
| Municipal Waste          | 16.51                               | 4.42%      |
| Wood and Other Biomass   | 38.79                               | 10.39%     |
| Solar                    | 2.10                                | 0.56%      |
| Wind                     | 52.15                               | 13.97%     |
| Total                    | 373.20                              | 100.00%    |

Source: Annual Energy Outlook

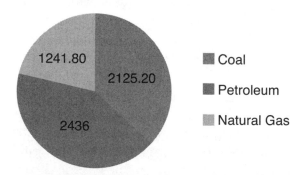

**Figure 7.1    U.S. energy-related carbon dioxide emissions by major fuel, 2008; million metric tons carbon dioxide equivalent.**

(Source: Energy Information Administration, Emissions of Greenhouse Gases in the United States, 2008, ftp://ftp.eia.doe.gov/pub/oiaf/1605/cdr)

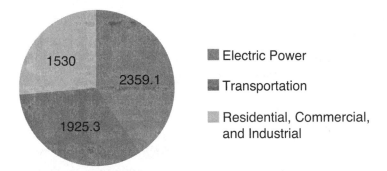

**Figure 7.2   U.S. energy-related carbon dioxide emissions by end-use sector, 2008; million metric tons carbon dioxide equivalent.**

(Source: Energy Information Administration, Emissions of Greenhouse Gases in the United States, 2008, ftp://ftp.eia.doe.gov/pub/oiaf/160)

# Wind

Man has used wind for years. Wind powered the growth of world trade through sailing ships. In the United States, prior to the Rural Electrification Act, it pumped water and generated electricity.[6] Falling fuel prices after World War II led to decreased interest in wind power. However, the push for green power has led to increased use of wind power around the world. Currently, wind power is one of the largest sources of clean energy in the United States.

## What Is It?

Wind is indirect solar energy. This is because winds arise due to uneven heating of the earth's surface by the sun. The winds that encircle the earth blow because the earth is heated more near the equator than at the poles. This causes air to rise up over the equator and descend near the poles, driving global air circulation (as discussed earlier in this chapter in the discussion about the Hadley Cell).

Wind turbines, modern windmills, use blades to capture the kinetic energy of wind and use it to rotate electric turbines that generate electric power. Wind power requires a large up-front investment, but has low maintenance costs and obviously no fuel costs.[7] The costs of wind power have fallen dramatically in recent years, thanks to new materials and new designs that have led to larger, more efficient turbines.

One obvious weakness of wind power is that the wind doesn't blow all the time. This means that wind power will not easily replace all other forms of energy. Alternate power sources are needed when the wind does not blow (or better energy storage devices). Wind needs backup power to fill in when it fails. The gap in power generation must be filled quickly or the network will go down. In addition, wind resources are often far from where electricity is consumed, requiring new long-distance transmission lines. Unfortunately, long-distance transmission lines take a while to build because of environmental disputes and arguments over who should pay for the lines. Also, much wind production takes place at night, when demand is low. Wind would be a more favorable energy source if its electric output could be stored to use when needed. One possibility is the electric car, which could charge at night, acting as a portable battery for wind power.

In the United States, in 2008, wind power generated 52 billion kilowatt hours of energy, about 1.3% of U.S. electric generation.[8] Still, that amount has been growing rapidly—production doubled between 2006 and 2008.[9]

It is hard to define what makes up the wind industry. Each fund manager—or index developer—has its own criteria of what makes up a wind company, such as the percent of revenues coming from wind-related operations. Wind funds tend to consist of companies that develop, or manage, wind farms, produce or distribute electricity from wind, and are involved in designing, manufacturing, or distributing materials and machinery designed for the wind energy industry.[10]

## Size of Market

It is hard to predict the precise size of the future wind power market. Although the United States has the most wind power production of any country in the world, it is not the leader by percentage of power generated. That title belongs to Denmark, where 20% of the power is generated by wind. It seems likely that the United States will increase its levels of electricity generated from wind. If the United States were to generate 20% of its power from wind, that would mean enormous growth in wind power—and good news for producers of wind turbines and related equipment, but that is unlikely at present, because the grid could not handle so much power from an intermittent source without reliability and stability.

## Risks

While wind power does have many environmental benefits, in terms of clean power, there are some environmental downsides. Windmills may prove hazardous to bird and bat populations. In addition, some criticize their aesthetics and find them noisy. But to be fair, a lot of people don't like transmission lines either.

One risk for investors in wind is that some competing alternate energy system may come along and undercut the price of wind. For example, if either solar or nuclear power becomes very cheap, they could undercut demand for wind power. In addition, most major wind turbine manufacturers are located outside the United States, so there is the risk of investing in foreign securities that was outlined in Chapter 1, "Understanding ETFs and Why They Beat Mutual Funds." Also, demand for electric power is affected by the overall economic situation. Setbacks in the economy could lead to decreasing demand for power and, consequently, decreasing demand for wind power as well. In addition, in hard economic times, regulators and politicians may cut funds for alternative energy programs, which could also decrease funding for wind power technologies. This may be one of the biggest risks for wind power investors. Wind power has flourished thanks to subsidies—direct or indirect—from governments. Many states have directed electric companies to purchase a set percentage of energy needs from renewable resources by a given date. Removal of that support, before wind power achieves grid parity, the point where it can economically compete with other fuels, could hurt wind power as an investment. In the United States a tax credit of 2.1 cents per kilowatt hour (KWh) applies to wind, solar, geothermal, and closed loop bioenergy (from crops grown for energy purposes). This credit is scheduled to expire in 2013. If it is not renewed, it could affect the competitiveness of wind (and other renewables).

Despite its risks, wind represents an area with growth potential in the coming years, provided continued measures are taken to reduce carbon emissions through regulation or taxation.

# Solar

The sun's rays power our human existence. They grow our crops and warm our lives. There is no reason they can't generate much of our electricity.

Slowly this is starting to happen as more and more solar energy is used to power our electric lifestyle. Solar energy can be used to provide heat directly, to heat water and spaces, and to generate electricity. The sun can generate electric power through photovoltaic devices and solar thermal power plants.

Solar funds typically consist of companies that produce solar power (with a large portion of their revenues coming from the sale of solar power), produce solar power equipment, install solar power equipment, and provide the raw materials used in manufacturing solar power equipment.[11]

## Photovoltaics

Photovoltaic devices, often known as solar cells, convert sunlight directly into electricity. Photovoltaic devices are made of semiconductors and generate electricity when photons, particles of solar energy, strike them. These cells can be combined in various sizes to power items as small as calculators or to generate enough power to feed into the electric grid.

## Solar Thermal Power Plants

Solar thermal power plants generate power by concentrating the sun's heat and using that heat to boil water to produce steam to drive a turbine that spins an electric generator.

These plants are usually relatively large to achieve economies of scale and tend to be located in hot, desert environments (at least in the United States).

## Size of Market

Solar energy has great potential. It is available everywhere—at some time during the year. According to one estimate, covering 4% of the earth's deserts—or the Gobi desert alone—with photovoltaics could meet all the world's electric needs.[12] At the moment, solar is still a small part of U.S. energy production—a fraction of wind power's contribution. Falling prices for panels, in conjunction with regulatory policies that favor solar power, help position this energy form for growth in the future.

Globally there is a large push toward solar. Many countries encourage the development of solar power through regulatory policies. For example, Germany encourages solar power through feed in tariffs. In the United States, California's regulatory policies have so encouraged solar power that it is now one of the largest solar markets worldwide. Spain also uses special electric tariffs to encourage use of solar energy.

Solar power in the United States is rapidly approaching grid parity—the point whereby solar power may be competitive with conventional power in many markets by 2012.[13] Photon Consulting, a firm that studies the solar market, predicts that the costs of solar power could fall below 10 cents/KWh by 2012 in the sunnier areas of the United States. Given that, today, the average retail customer in California pays over 15 cents/KWh—and 25 cents/KWh in Hawaii—that could prove beneficial to end users.[14]

### Risks

One of the most obvious drawbacks of solar energy is that it can only be generated when the sun shines. This means that, without development of adequate power storage, solar will not completely replace other sources of electric power. It may take longer for solar power to become competitive with fossil fuels, depending on prices of competing fuels and the state of regulation.

# Natural Gas

Natural gas, as a fossil fuel, is not a renewable form of energy, but it is one of the cleanest available power sources.[15] Natural gas's primary component is methane, made up of one carbon atom and four hydrogen atoms ($CH_4$). Natural gas is a fossil fuel resulting from great heat and pressure being applied to the remains of marine organisms from millions of years ago.[16] In 2008, natural gas provided about one-fourth of energy used in the United States.[17]

Natural gas has a major advantage over other fossil fuels, especially coal, the United States' number one source of electric power, in that it burns more cleanly than any of them. It emits less sulfur, carbon, or nitrogen than coal, or oil, and leaves almost no ash. Still, natural gas does produce carbon dioxide, but at a lower rate than other fuels. Typically, natural gas power plants emit over a third less carbon dioxide than those powered by oil or coal. Moving away from electric power produced from coal to natural gas could reduce U.S. carbon emissions significantly.

When it comes to investing in natural gas via ETFs, there is only one natural gas ETF—the First Trust ISE-Revere Natural Gas Index Fund. It includes companies involved in exploration for, and production of, natural gas.[18]

### Risks

Although it is cleaner than coal and oil, burning natural gas still emits greenhouse gases. Stricter greenhouse gas regulations in the future could lead to less demand for fossil fuels, including natural gas. Still, in the near term, natural gas represents a cleaner alternative to other fossil fuels that are burned to produce electricity.

Another major risk for natural gas as an investment is that demand for natural gas is also a function of the prices of competing fuels. When other fuels are less expensive, or if new renewable energy technologies produce electricity more cheaply than by burning gas, demand for gas may fall. Also natural gas demand is sensitive to weather. Warmer winters decrease demand for gas as a heating fuel. Cooler summers decrease demand for gas to produce electricity. In addition, because of its capital intensive nature, the gas industry is sensitive to increased interest rates.[19]

# Nuclear

Nuclear energy comes from releasing the energy that is tied up in the bonds that hold atoms together. These bonds hold a tremendous amount of energy that can be used to make electricity.

The most commonly used fuel for nuclear fission is uranium, a nonrenewable fuel source. It needs to be processed to become nuclear fuel. In nuclear fission, a small particle called a neutron is used to bombard a uranium atom, which splits it, releasing energy as heat and radiation. This process releases more neutrons, which bombard other uranium atoms, and the process repeats again and again, known as a chain reaction. Fission in nuclear reactors creates heat that is used to boil water and produce steam that is used to spin a turbine and generate electricity.

Nuclear power plants do not produce air pollution or carbon dioxide. Some emissions may result from processing the uranium used in nuclear reactors. On the downside, nuclear power plants generate highly radioactive waste that needs to be stored in special pools or storage containers. No long-term storage facility for nuclear waste exists in the United States.

The dangerous nature of nuclear power has long generated opposition to it. Also, because of its dangerous nature, it is a heavily regulated industry.

For years some environmentalists opposed development of nuclear power. However, concern over climate change and a search for fuels that don't emit greenhouse gases has brought new attention to nuclear power, which may lead to increasing development of nuclear plants and their related industries.

For investors in nuclear funds, the industry consists of[20]

- Uranium mining
- Uranium enrichment
- Uranium storage
- Equipment for the nuclear industry
- Nuclear fuel transportation
- Nuclear plant infrastructure
- Nuclear power generation

### Regulatory Risk

Regulatory risk is no small matter for nuclear power. Some countries have called for closing working nuclear facilities for ideological reasons. In some countries, political forces have slowed development of waste storage facilities. International nuclear proliferation issues have stalled processing of fuels and construction of reactors. Prospects for a nuclear revival in the United States rely heavily on subsidies.

# Clean Energy and Clean Technologies

The clean energy and clean technologies categories are a bit of a catchall for funds that are made up of a number of industries and do not represent a pure industry-based approach to clean power.

The clean energy funds tend to have a number of companies in various areas. Their mandates are broad. In addition to wind and solar, they may have geothermal energy, hydropower, and biomass energy. Here is an overview of the subsectors.

### Geothermal

Geothermal energy is heat that comes from within the earth. This heat can be used to create steam to run electric generators or to heat buildings. Geothermal plants are typically located in areas near the boundaries of the earth's plates, areas characterized by volcanoes and earthquakes. Geothermal plants emit less than 1% of the carbon dioxide of a conventional fossil fuel plant.[21]

### Biofuels

Biofuels are produced from plants and animal waste. These forms of energy are renewable because plants are constantly growing, and man and animals are constantly producing waste.

Some examples of biofuels include wood, crops, manure, and some forms of garbage.

These fuels can be burned to produce electricity or heat buildings. Some forms of biomass can be converted into methane (a component of natural gas) or fuels for transportation such as ethanol and biodiesel.

Burning these fuels is not the greenest choice, however, due to pollution and emission of greenhouse gases. Some point out that when wood is burned, for example, it simply releases the carbon it had previously absorbed from the atmosphere, so there may be no net addition of carbon. In contrast, when coal is burned, it releases new carbon into the atmosphere. One potential problem with biofuels is if more food products, such as corn, are diverted to biofuel production, it may raise food prices around the world, impacting poor people most. If food prices rise, people may cultivate forested areas to grow their own food, creating other environmental problems, such as removing trees that absorb carbon dioxide. However, in the future, biofuels may be developed from nonfood crops, or plant wastes, which may alleviate some problems with these fuels.

### Hydropower

Hydropower is generated by using the kinetic energy of falling water to spin turbines that generate electricity. This type of power has high capital costs to build but low operating costs. In the United States, most good hydropower sites have already been developed, so there is not much potential for growth. In addition, hydropower is not environmentally benign, since the dams required to trap the water often alter aquatic ecosystems. The building of large dams in the Pacific Northwest devastated salmon populations. Hydropower is still a major, and growing, source of power in Brazil and parts of Asia. It is a major source of power in Canada. Still, new sources of water-based power, such as tidal power, could be new sources of clean power.

### What Is a Clean Energy Fund?

Clean energy funds can consist of companies that are in the business of developing alternative energy resources, developing new, cleaner environmental technologies, and improving energy efficiency. Since their mandates are broad, the only way to really see what these funds are about is to dissect the portfolio.

For example, PowerShares describes the following sectors as part of the clean energy universe:[22]

- **Cleaner utilities**—Use cleaner methods to generate electricity—wind, solar, biofuel, geothermal, and hydroelectric.
- **Energy conversion**—Devices that convert fuel into electric power.

- **Generation efficiency and smart distribution**—Companies that work to improve the efficiency of existing electric generation and distribution systems, including software that helps companies better manage demand and reduce losses from the grid.

- **Power storage**—Energy storage technologies, such as batteries and flywheels that provide storage for alternative power sources, and make it easier to implement technologies that generate power from intermittent sources such as wind and sun.

- **Hydrogen and fuel cells**—Hydrogen extracted from water could represent a clean fuel. Fuel cells are a highly efficient way of generating electricity from hydrogen and other fuels. These technologies are still far from widespread adoption.

- **Demand-side energy saving**—Technologies to reduce energy demand.

- **Services and suppliers**—Companies providing services to the alternative energy industry, such as consultants, research and development, and forecasting, among others.

## What is Cleantech?

Cleantech as a concept is even more nebulous than clean energy. It is hard to sum up what cleantech encompasses. Here is how PowerShares describes cleantech in its prospectus for the PowerShares Cleantech Portfolio:

> "Cleantech Indices LLC ("Cleantech" or the "Index Provider") considers a company to be a cleantech company if it derives at least 50% of its revenues or operating profits from cleantech businesses. Cleantech businesses are defined as those that provide knowledge-based products (or services) that add economic value by reducing costs and raising productivity and/or product performance, while reducing the consumption of resources and the negative impact on the environment and public health. The Underlying Index focuses on companies which are leaders in the innovation and commercial deployment of cleantech products across a broad range of industries including, but not limited to, alternative energy, energy efficiency and transmission, air and water

purification, advanced materials, eco-friendly agriculture, transportation, manufacturing efficiency, recycling and pollution prevention."[23]

Cleantech is a catchall for all sorts of companies with a lot of leeway for the index provider to use in choosing the index members. Investors who want to invest in this area should look at these funds to get an idea of what is in them and to see if they fit with the investor's view of what a green investment is and if the fund makes sense for her. This does not mean they are bad investments, just that it can be hard to pin them down to see how they fit into green trends.

The risks of cleantech funds relate to the demand for the products of the companies in the fund and potential regulatory changes that could affect particular industries.

# Risks That Span the Green Spectrum

While there are many opportunities to profit from investing in ETFs based on companies that develop technologies for reducing greenhouse gas emissions and creating new sources of clean energy, that doesn't mean there aren't risks as well. Investors need to understand factors that could jeopardize their portfolios.

## *Demand Comes from Mandates—Not from Energy Customers*

At the moment, the demand for these technologies is not a function of consumer demand, but of governmental regulatory policies. (This is less true for energy efficiency, because it often saves energy users money.) In the industrial revolution, innovation arose from consumer demand—people wanted railways, for example, because they were faster and more powerful than horse transportation, or electric lights because they were better than candles. However, the same demand does not exist for green power, like wind power for example, because clean wind power runs people's TVs as effectively as dirty power from coal.[24] In addition, clean energy may not be attractive in the short term because it is more expensive than other forms of electric generation.

At the moment, a lot of the funding for green power depends on governments and related agencies. Starting up a business in a risky area can require a large amount of capital. This could put green power developers at the mercy of government funding or policies, such as alternative energy subsidies. For example, in some states, green power is subsidized by utility consumers who often have to pay higher electric rates that are used to invest in green projects. These regulatory schemes represent transfers from ratepayers to green power developers—and in many cases the ratepayers may not have a choice as to whether to pay. As long as green technology depends only on government policies or regulations to drive its future—regulations and policies that can change at the whim of politicians or regulators—green technology faces a difficult future. Cleantech may increase the production costs of existing energy sources. For example, carbon capture and sequestration would add to the production cost of electricity and would face opposition, as a result, from large power users. Clean power doesn't necessarily mean cheaper power.

Still, as green power develops—and the technology improves—we may get past the point where this market is simply driven by regulation and subsidies. New technologies may bring the price of electricity production down to compete with current energy sources.

### Overseas Investment Risk

Many green companies are based and trade on stock markets outside the United States. This brings foreign securities risk to many of these ETFs. As mentioned in Chapter 1, there are a number of risks from investing overseas, although there may be benefits from currency fluctuations in buying foreign shares if the dollar depreciates. Some risks include more volatile markets, less reliable financial information, higher transaction and custody costs, which can make for a more expensive ETF, foreign taxes, and less liquid markets.[25] Instability in certain foreign countries may make it difficult for a fund to invest there or repatriate the proceeds of its investments back to the United States.

The main risk of overseas funds to investors is foreign currency risk. The stocks in an ETF may be priced in a different currency, or have earnings in a foreign currency, which exposes the investor to the risk that changes in exchange rates could affect the investor's holdings—advantageously or harmfully.

### Small Company Risk

Many alternative energy companies are small. Smaller companies are often more vulnerable to general market moves or adverse economic developments.[26] In addition, their securities may be less liquid than those of larger companies and have greater price volatility than larger, more established companies. This volatility could stem from limited trading volumes in shares or the state of the company's finances, depth of corporate management, and the fact there is often little publicly available information on less prominent companies. These companies are often subject to greater market risk than larger, more established companies.[27]

### Competing Fuels

One of the major risk factors for investing in green energy is the price of competing fuels. Green fuels and green technologies do not exist in a vacuum. They compete against other green fuels and conventional fuels. If one green fuel, say solar, becomes a cheaper way of providing energy than wind, then the solar industry may outperform the wind industry. In the short term, however, the fate of many green fuels is affected by conventional electric-generating competitors—notably coal and natural gas. Some analysts mistakenly believe that the price of oil determines the success of green power. However, that comparison misses the mark, because, in the United States, oil is primarily used as a transportation fuel, whereas most green technologies are used to generate electricity. When a utility has the capabilities to switch between different fuels, they are able to choose the lowest cost fuels. A slow economy could induce pressure to relax regulations on using green power to allow utilities to once again buy cheaper, dirtier fuels to power their plants.

## Technological Change

It is hard to predict which particular green technology will win out in the long run. It could be some of them, it could be all that are currently available, or some new technology could come along that makes all current methods of green energy production obsolete.

It is hard to predict how technological change will affect the various green technologies. Within the various subsectors, there may be competing technologies. For example, one type of solar cell may turn out to be better than another, and the companies with the superior technology will outperform the ones with inferior technology. It can be hard to predict these eventualities, so by buying an ETF that encompasses the whole solar sector, an investor doesn't have to choose the right technology, thereby minimizing some of the risk. The key factor is to be aware that technology is fluid and investments in these areas may be ones to buy and hold, but not ones to buy and forget.

# The Three Wild Cards

Before concluding, it is necessary to consider the three wild cards of green power that could change the economics of the game for all involved.

## Inexpensive Carbon Capture and Sequestration

The first wild card is inexpensive carbon capture and sequestration (CCS).[28] If means can be found to bring down the costs of CCS, that would change the picture for electric generation and make possible the continued, or increased, use of cheaper coal. CCS represents an opportunity for those involved in the business, mainly chemical engineering and pipeline companies, and would provide added competition for renewable and nuclear energy providers.

## The Electric Car

The second wild card is the electric car. The electric car might produce fewer greenhouse gases, even now, than the internal combustion engine. It will charge up at night when generators aren't running fully. If renewable power charged electric cars, then the environment would really come out ahead. In addition, the cars could be considered as storage batteries for renewable power. The main roadblock is that much of the distribution grid needs time at night to cool down. Widespread use of electric cars might require improved infrastructure to handle the demand.

### Biotech Fuels

The third wild card is biotech fuels. It might be possible to have genetically engineered organisms to eat $CO_2$ and then produce new fuels that are close to petroleum in composition. Craig Venter, the scientist who sequenced the human genome, has engaged in a joint venture with Exxon to create oil from algae (which consumes $CO_2$). Other scientists have considered developing organisms to absorb nuclear waste, coal ash, and $CO_2$ at power plants.

Obviously it's too early to tell how any of these wild cards will play out, but it is good to keep them in mind as you make your green investment decisions. There may be new funds that will capitalize on one, or more, of these wild card technologies.

# Conclusion

Investing in green ETFs represents a way to profit from the move to a cleaner, more sustainable world, without the difficulties that come from investing in individual companies in what can be risky areas. It is hard to predict which specific technologies, let alone companies, will succeed as the best way to battle climate change. However, by investing in baskets of companies in particular sectors, investors have a better chance of getting some winners along with the inevitable losers—and the winners will drive the performance of these sector ETFs. In addition, investing in these areas can serve as a global climate change insurance policy for investors. If the crisis accelerates, then many of these companies may have the technologies to help alleviate the problems. Or, if these companies provide the technologies that keep the problems from worsening, then society comes out ahead and we all benefit. The need to combat climate change is clear to the majority of scientists who specialize in the area. The companies that get in on this wave have great potential for growth. Climate change is real. Steps will be taken to combat it. Investors can profit by investing in green technologies that will improve the environment.

# Notes

[1] This material is summarized and adapted from Granger Morgan's and Jay Apt's "Basic Tutorial on Climate Change" background paper for "The Insurance Industry and Climate Change," a workshop held in Washington D.C. on May 8-9, 2006. Convened by the NSF-supported Center for Climate Decision Making to identify needs in analysis and decision research. Morgan and Apt teach in the Department of Engineering and Public Policy at Carnegie Mellon University.

[2] Matthias Hofmann and Stefan Rahmstorf. "On the Stability of the Atlantic Meridional Overturning Circulation," *PNAS Early Edition*. http://www.pnas.org/content/early/2009/11/05/0909146106.full.pdf.

[3] Morgan and Apt, "Basic Tutorial on Climate Change," 7.

[4] Ibid.

[5] In fact, some small dams are being removed in the United States because of the harm they do to fish populations and aquatic habitats. In addition, most good hydropower sites in the United States have been developed. In other countries, notably Brazil and China, significant hydropower development is still underway.

[6] Homer Rustebakke, ed., *Electric Utility Systems and Practices*, fourth edition (New York: John Wiley & Sons, 1983), 30.

[7] Richard Asplund, *Profiting from Clean Energy: A Complete Guide to Trading Green in the Solar, Wind, Ethanol, Fuel Cell, Carbon Credit Industries, and More* (Hoboken, N.J.: John Wiley & Sons, 2008), 133.

[8] Energy Kids, U.S. Energy Information Administration, "Wind Basics," http://tonto.eia.doe.gov/kids/energy.cfm?page=wind_home-basics.

[9] Ibid.

[10] First Trust Portfolios, First Trust Exchange-Traded Fund II, *Prospectus*, 28.

[11] Van Eck Global, Market Vectors, *Prospectus*, May 1, 2009, 54.

[12] Energy Kids, U.S. Energy Information Administration, "Solar Basics," http://tonto.eia.doe.gov/kids/energy.cfm?page=solar_home-basics.

[13] Photon Consulting, "Solar Power in Focus," http://www.photonconsulting.com/files/true_cost_exec_sum.pdf.

[14] U.S. Energy Information Administration, http://www.eia.doe.gov/cneaf/electricity/epm/epmxlfile5_6_a.xls.

[15] Methane, however, can be harvested from decaying matter, such as that found in landfills. However, most natural gas used in the United States comes from fossil sources from millions of years ago.

[16] Using devices called digesters, natural gas can also be produced from organic material, such as plant and animal waste. This process does not take millions of years, but the amount of gas is small relative to that brought up from beneath the earth's surface through drilling.

[17] Energy Kids, U.S. Energy Information Administration, "Natural Gas Basics," http://tonto.eia.doe.gov/kids/energy.cfm?page=natural_gas_home-basics.

[18] First Trust Exchange-Traded Fund, *Prospectus*, May 1, 2009, 40.

[19] Ibid., 11.

[20] Van Eck Global, Market Vectors, *Prospectus*, May 1, 2009, 37.

[21] Energy Kids, U.S. Energy Information Administration, "Geothermal Basics," http://tonto.eia.doe.gov/kids/energy.cfm?page=geothermal_home-basics.

[22] PowerShares "Green ETFs: Now, some of the most innovative ETFs on the planet are all about saving it," 5.

[23] PowerShares Exchange-Traded Fund Trust, *Prospectus*, August 31, 2009, 14.

[24] Jonathan Guthrie, "Green start-ups in need of a Charge," *Financial Times*, December 30, 2009, 10.

[25] U.S. investors may qualify for a foreign tax credit when investing in global funds, provided that more than 50% of the index is made up of non-U.S. companies. Otherwise, investors only qualify for a tax deduction, which in all likelihood means they pay more taxes on their overseas investments.

[26] First Trust Exchange-Traded Fund, *Prospectus*, May 1, 2009, 7.

[27] Ibid.

[28] This is whereby carbon, instead of going into the atmosphere, is trapped and buried underground.

# 8

# Green ETFs: Overview and Analysis

There is an unmistakable new wave rolling across the business and investment landscapes of the United States. Its shape and substance are still somewhat difficult to define, *but the color is certainly green.* Businesses are seeking practices that are environmentally friendly, energy neutral (or sustainable), and socially beneficial. Investors are looking at not only sales and revenues but also whether a company behaves responsibly toward the planet. The wave is small but growing. The global warming debate rages on, but there are some irrefutable facts. The nation is highly dependent on fossil fuels—we import more than half of the petroleum we consume. We continue to flood the atmosphere with greenhouse gas (GHG) emissions, which scientists have shown trap heat in the atmosphere. The damage being done is difficult to measure, but everyone can agree there is some effect. At the same time, the country seriously needs job growth. We have lost five million jobs over the past three years and must create at least one million jobs per year to sustain economic growth in the future. Existing industries will be hard pressed to provide even half of that total. Green industries including alternative fuels (like ethanol), sustainable energy sources (wind and solar), and clean technologies have the potential to create millions of jobs, many of which will be semiskilled or unskilled. But many green tech companies are relatively young and small, so it is difficult to predict which will prevail. Fortunately, there are ETFs in this area that can help investors participate in innovation without incurring single-stock risk. Currently seven ETFs are worthy of consideration for green investors in that they invest in the major subsectors and have at least $100 million in invested assets. These are listed in Table 8.1.

**TABLE 8.1    Green ETFs with Market Cap Greater than $100 Million**

| Industry Category | Fund Company | Fund Name | Ticker | Expense Ratio |
|---|---|---|---|---|
| *Clean Energy* | | | | |
| | Invesco PowerShares Capital Mgmt LLC | PowerShares WilderHill Clean Energy Portfolio | PBW | 0.69% |
| | Van Eck Associates Corporation | Market Vectors Global Alternative Energy ETF | GEX | 0.62% |
| *Gas* | | | | |
| | First Trust Advisors LP | First Trust ISE-Revere Natural Gas Index Fund | FCG | 0.60% |
| *Wind Power* | | | | |
| | First Trust Advisors LP | FirstTrust Global Wind Energy ETF | FAN | 0.60% |
| *Solar Energy* | | | | |
| | Claymore Advisors LLC | Claymore/MAC Global Solar Index ETF | TAN | 0.70% |
| *Nuclear Energy* | | | | |
| | Van Eck Associates Corporation | Market Vectors Nuclear Energy ETF | NLR | 0.61% |
| *Clean Technology* | | | | |
| | Invesco PowerShares Capital Mgmt LLC | PowerShares Cleantech Portfolio | PZD | 0.67% |

The complete contents of each ETF are in Appendix B, "Green ETFs."

# Clean Energy

The largest green ETF is the PowerShares WilderHill Clean Energy Portfolio (PBW) shown in Table 8.2. The total assets of the fund are about $700 million, which is invested in 52 companies. These are, in general, smaller companies. The total market cap of all the components of PBW is just over $100 billion. Fuel cells, solar, semiconductors, basic materials, and utilities are represented in the portfolio. The largest position is in Trina Solar, Ltd. (TSL). Trina is a

Chinese company that manufactures and sells solar modules to residential, commercial, and industrial customers. The company has a market cap of $1.3 billion and is listed on the New York Stock Exchange. Sales for the company were $100 million in 2007 and then skyrocketed to more than $1 billion in 2009. The stock rose from $5 at the beginning of 2009 to $50 at the end of the year.

**TABLE 8.2    PowerShares WilderHill Clean Energy Portfolio (PBW) Expense Ratio (0.69%)    Top Ten Holdings (24 December 2009)**

| Ticker Symbol | Name | Weight | Sector |
| --- | --- | --- | --- |
| TSL | Trina Solar Ltd. (ADS) | 4.41% | Energy—Alternate Sources |
| CREE | Cree Inc. | 3.95% | Information Technology |
| JASO | JA Solar Holdings Co. Ltd. (ADS) | 3.78% | Industrials |
| RBCN | Rubicon Technology Inc. | 3.66% | Information Technology |
| AMSC | American Superconductor Corp. | 3.51% | Industrials |
| YGE | Yingli Green Energy Holding Co. Ltd. (ADS) | 3.25% | Industrials |
| BWEN | Broadwind Energy Inc. | 2.93% | Industrials |
| IRF | International Rectifier Corp. | 2.89% | Information Technology |
| PANL | Universal Display Corp. | 2.84% | Information Technology |
| ITRI | Itron Inc. | 2.74% | Information Technology |

Because innovation in the United States has lagged in the last several years, many of the new green technologies have been developed overseas. A significant percentage of the "green" ETFs have portfolio companies headquartered in Europe and Asia. The stocks of these companies are traded publicly in the United States. JA Solar (JASO), headquartered in Shanghai, has a market cap of about a billion dollars and manufactures solar cells, which are used to convert sunlight into electric power. This rapidly growing company has seen its sales grow from $90 million in 2006 to close to $900 million in 2009.

American Superconductor Corp. (AMSC), 3.5% of PBW with a market cap of $1.8 billion, is typical of the kind of company one finds in this portfolio. This company, which manufactures large wind turbine systems, turbine components, and the technology to connect turbines to the grid, has seen its sales quadruple in the past two years. In 2009 alone, the stock price rose from $11 per share to more than $40 per share. And yet, this is a company that most equity investors know nothing about. In fact, most of us have never heard of the company. The same is true for most of the component companies. It would be very difficult for the average investor, even those with a background in technology, to adequately research and assess a company like JASO. Even after doing the research in an absolute sense (just looking at this one company), relative analysis is an order of magnitude harder. When two new technologies are competing in a marketplace, even if they are both qualified to succeed, one may ultimately prevail at the expense of the other. (Think VHS versus Beta when videocassette recorders were introduced.) *Purchasing an ETF allows an investor to own all the competing technologies.* When one reviews the growth that has already taken place in this space and then considers the potential going forward, the ultimate winners of the competition are likely to be very large companies, and a portfolio that owns all the competitors will reap enough benefit from the successful firms to more than compensate for the failures.

### Battery Companies

Advanced Battery Technologies (ABAT) manufactures rechargeable lithium batteries for cell phones, personal computers, and other electronic devices. It is one of several small battery manufacturers in the PBW portfolio. The market cap is $250 million, and the company represents 1% of the portfolio. The company is headquartered in the United States and manufactures its products in China. Similarly, Ener1, Inc. (HEV) is a U.S. company that manufactures lithium batteries in Korea. Portable power is an important part of the clean technology revolution, and anyone who owns an electronic device is aware that battery life and recharging capabilities are evolving. There is likely to be a breakthrough in this technology, but most investors would not have a chance of handicapping the competition. The ETF allows for ownership of all of the key players.

There are several industrial technology companies in the PBW ETF. Included are Quanta Services (PWR) and Valence Technology

(VLNC). Quanta provides services for designing, installing, and maintaining all sorts of network infrastructure, including power grids. Its market cap is $4 billion, and its sales have doubled to nearly $5 billion in the past two years. Valence develops electric power systems for hybrid vehicles. This is a microcap stock trading at $1 per share but presumably is included in the portfolio because the growth of hybrid cars is expected to be explosive in the next decade, perhaps reaching two million units per year by 2015 (up from about 500,000 in 2009). The PBW portfolio combines some more mature companies with some that are virtually startups with high risk/reward ratios. VLNC is certainly in that category. In addition to these three companies, there are 20 small industrial companies in the PBW portfolio, each participating in a narrow sector of green technology.

### Efficiency Companies

Another significant group of companies in the portfolio is involved with electronic innovations that reduce energy usage (some of these companies are considered as part of the information technology sector). This group represents about 30% of the portfolio. The largest of these positions is Cree (CREE), about 4% of the total portfolio. CREE, a $5 billion company, manufactures light emitting diode products which are energy-saving devices. The company operates in Asia and the United States. Rubicon Technology (RBCN) also makes light emitting diodes, as well as several other green products for industrial applications and processes, including semiconductors. This company, with a $400 million market cap, has seen its sales double in the past two years. Maxwell Technologies (MXWL) manufactures a variety of energy storage and power delivery products. The products are used in a wide variety of applications such as consumer electronics, aerospace, automotive, and renewable energy. The company's stock rose from $4 per share to more than $20 per share during 2009, and the market cap is approaching $500 million. Sales have grown by 40% per year for the past two years, and though the company is not yet profitable, it is nearing the break-even point. Itron (ITRI) manufactures meters to measure the use of gas, water, electricity, and heat. The company's sales grew substantially from $600 million in 2006 to

nearly $2 billion in 2009. It represents about 3% of the PBW port-
folio. Comverge (COMV) makes the tools that allow electric utilities
and grid operators to monitor and control peak and base load capacity issues while delivering power to customers. These tools increase
the ability to more efficiently use energy to create electricity. The
company has seen its stock price triple, and sales double, in the past
two years.

Beyond the companies just described, there are 40 more positions in the portfolio, and many of these firms have exciting cutting
edge technologies. Of course, many of them will ultimately be unsuccessful, or will move into different business lines. At the same time,
new companies will be added to the index on which the ETF is based.
If functioning properly, the ETF keeps its positions in the successful
companies and replaces those that are not viable. The total market
cap of the ETF components will increase as the business grows. PBW
is the right core holding for an ETF investor seeking to participate in
green investing. Green investing has great promise for investors. As
this portfolio has 52 components, it is likely to have a significant number of successes and failures. Since no one position is more than 4%
of the portfolio, and most are at 2%, this ETF has the potential to
outperform the overall market. There are other green ETFs that are
more concentrated and therefore have the potential for greater outperformance in the event this sector takes off in a major way.

One such fund is the Van Eck Market Vectors Global Alternative
Energy ETF, which currently has $200 million invested in it (see
Table 8.3). This fund has only 30 components. The largest position is
in Vestas Wind Systems, headquartered in Denmark, which is the
largest wind energy company in the world. The next four largest positions are in First Solar (solar panels), Cree (light emitting devices),
Iberdrola Renovables (a Spanish wind company), and Kurita Water
Industries, a Japanese manufacturer of water treatment facilities.
While this fund is diversified across different alternative energies, it
has one or two major positions in each different alternative. As it is
still early in the evolution of these various technologies, it is entirely
possible that this focus will miss the ultimate winners in the competition. For most investors who lack the specific knowledge to compare
the technologies of competitors, this fund is likely too concentrated.

**TABLE 8.3   Van Eck Market Vectors Global Alternative Energy ETF (GEX) Expense Ratio (0.62%)   Top Ten Holdings (24 December 2009)**

| Ticker Symbol | Name | Weight | Sector |
|---|---|---|---|
| VWS DC | Vestas Wind Systems A/S | 9.11% | Industrials |
| FSLR | First Solar Inc. | 6.62% | Industrials |
| CREE | Cree Inc. | 5.99% | Information Technology |
| IBR SM | Iberdrola Renovables S.A. | 4.93% | Utilities |
| 6370 JP | Kurita Water Industries Ltd. | 4.70% | Industrials |
| WFR | MEMC Electronic Materials Inc. | 4.28% | Information Technology |
| GAM SM | Gamesa Corp. Tecnologica SA | 4.26% | Industrials |
| VER AV | Verbund - Oesterreichische Elektrizitaetswirtschafts AG | 4.05% | Energy—Alternate Sources |
| ITRI | Itron Inc. | 4.01% | Information Technology |
| REC NO | Renewable Energy Corp. AS | 3.64% | Industrials |

# Natural Gas

Natural gas is a far cleaner fuel than oil—and much cleaner than coal, the dirtiest of fossil fuels. In addition, natural gas is extremely plentiful in the United States, and the United States produces nearly all the natural gas it consumes. While oil and gasoline are the primary fossil fuels we consume, a retrofit to natural gas is technologically feasible. The oil companies, a firmly entrenched oligopoly if there ever was one, have resisted this change vigorously. But, at the end of 2009, Exxon announced it was acquiring XTO Energy, a major natural gas producer. It is logical to assume other major oil companies will inevitably move in the same direction, making natural gas–producing companies appealing for investors. One fund that captures many of these companies is First Trust ISE-Revere Natural Gas Fund (FCG), shown in Table 8.4. The following companies represent the portfolio of FCG.

**TABLE 8.4    First Trust ISE-Revere Natural Gas Index Fund (FCG)
Expense Ratio (0.60%)    Top Ten Holdings (24 December 2009)**

| Ticker Symbol | Name | Weight | Sector |
|---|---|---|---|
| DPTR | Delta Petroleum Corporation | 4.44% | Oil Companies—Exploration and Production |
| BEXP | Brigham Exploration Company | 3.82% | Oil Companies—Exploration and Production |
| NFX | Newfield Exploration Company | 3.55% | Oil Companies—Exploration and Production |
| RRC | Range Resources Corporation | 3.54% | Oil Companies—Exploration and Production |
| SWN | Southwestern Energy Company | 3.54% | Oil Companies—Exploration and Production |
| PQ | PetroQuest Energy, Inc. | 3.52% | Oil Companies—Exploration and Production |
| PXD | Pioneer Natural Resources Company | 3.52% | Oil Companies—Exploration and Production |
| KWK | Quicksilver Resources Inc. | 3.52% | Oil Companies—Exploration and Production |
| CHK | Chesapeake Energy Corporation | 3.50% | Oil Companies—Exploration and Production |
| COG | Cabot Oil & Gas Corporation | 3.46% | Oil Companies—Exploration and Production |

As of December, 2009, FCG had $400 million in assets under management. This is a very small amount, as the 31 positions in this fund have a total market cap of more than $500 billion. Royal Dutch Shell, with a market cap of $180 billion, is a 3% position in the fund. It would not be surprising at all to see the assets in this fund grow to several billion dollars over the next three years. XTO Energy, which will exit the index when the merger with Exxon concludes, represented about 3.4% of the portfolio when the deal was announced. Exxon's purchase price represented a 25% premium over XTO's stock price at the time. It is reasonable to expect similar transactions with comparable premiums in the future. On that basis alone, this is an attractive ETF to own. In addition, the component companies have bright futures if they remain independent. A few examples are discussed in the following paragraphs.

Southwestern Energy (SWN) represents about 3.5% of the portfolio. SWN produces gas in Texas, Oklahoma, Arkansas, and Pennsylvania. The company has a $16 billion market cap and has seen its stock price rise from $6 per share to more than $50 in the past five years (which has not been a particularly favorable period for natural gas). The company has publicly announced it expects production of natural gas to rise by 35% in 2010 over the previous year.

Chesapeake Energy Corp. (CHK) explores for, and produces, natural gas all across the United States. It has proven reserves of more than 12 trillion cubic feet of natural gas and more than 40,000 wells. The company has a $16 billion market cap and more than $11 billion in revenues. EnCana Corp. (ECA), market cap $24 billion, is a Canadian company based in Calgary with substantial natural gas reserves in both Canada and the United States. Its total natural gas reserves measure 14 trillion cubic feet. Apache Corp. (APA), a $35 billion market cap company, has natural gas reserves in the United States as well as South America, Europe, the Middle East, and Australia. These are just a sample.

Natural gas is poised to see a surge in demand over the next several years as illustrated in Figure 8.1. Investors must be cautious though as the price of oil could significantly influence its usage. The price of oil, as of this writing, is about $75 per barrel and most analysts predict the price will be at that level, or higher, in the coming

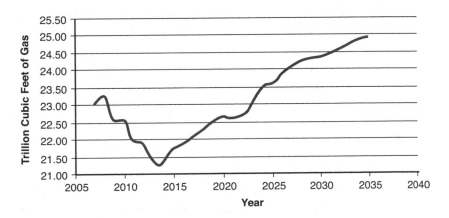

**Figure 8.1   Natural gas usage and projections**

(Source: http://www.eia.doe.gov/oiaf/aeo/excel/aeotab_13.xls)

years. At that level, natural gas is a viable alternative to oil. If oil were to drop to $50 per barrel or less, then the interest in natural gas might wane, despite its superior cleanliness and small environmental impact. However, new drilling technologies that lower production costs, such as new methods for extracting gas from shale, could open up large new reserves and put downward pressure on prices, keeping gas competitive with oil.

Moreover, if the world economy recovers and demand for fossil fuels increases, the demand for natural gas is limitless.

Today only a few cars in the United States can run on natural gas. (They were sold by Honda in California when petroleum prices reached $4 per gallon in 2008.) In fact, Italy, with one-fifth the population of the United States, has about five times the number of natural gas vehicles. Increasing the number of natural gas vehicles could provide a great benefit to the natural gas industry, with the companies in the FCG portfolio as the prime beneficiaries.

# Wind, Solar, and Nuclear Power

If the fossil fuel prices continue to rise, alternative energy sources will grow more attractive. Wind energy, solar power, and nuclear energy are the three most commercially viable alternatives at this time. There is an ETF for each of these subsectors: the First Trust Global Wind Energy ETF (FAN), the Claymore/MAC Global Solar Index ETF (TAN), and Van Eck Nuclear Energy ETF (NLR). These ETFs are currently rather small ($200 million in TAN and $100 million in FAN). The companies in the portfolios are mostly small, and largely unknown, but the technologies are exciting and could prove very profitable. Aggressive investors will want to own at least a small position in each of these funds.

## Wind Power

First Trust's Global Wind Energy ETF (FAN) (see Table 8.5), owns 52 positions. The way the index is constructed, about 66% of the portfolio (35 companies) is invested in firms primarily involved in wind energy. The rest of the positions are in companies that have only some commitment to the industry. Two companies in the portfolio are General Electric and Royal Dutch Shell, between them representing more than $350 billion of market cap, but, obviously, only a tiny fraction of their revenues come from wind. Both companies represent small (little more than 1%) positions in the fund. On the other hand, the ten largest positions represent 50% of the portfolio, and it is the performance of these positions that will largely drive the returns derived from owning this ETF. Most of these companies are headquartered outside the United States, but most are investing substantial funds in the U.S. market. Here is a look at some of these companies:

**TABLE 8.5   First Trust Global Wind Energy ETF (FAN)**
**Expense Ratio (0.60%)   Top Ten Holdings (24 December 2009)**

| Ticker Symbol | Name | Weight | Sector |
|---|---|---|---|
| EDPR.PL | EDP Renovaveis SA | 7.79% | Energy—Alternate Sources |
| IBR.SM | Iberdrola Renovables | 7.30% | Utilities |
| VWS.DC | Vestas Wind Systems | 6.75% | Industrials |
| RPW.GY | REpower Systems AG | 5.92% | Power Conversion/Supply Equipment |
| GAM.SM | Gamesa Corporacion Tecnologica, SA (Gamesa) | 5.58% | Industrials |
| HSN.LN | Hansen Transmissions | 5.53% | Industrials |
| BWEN | Broadwind Energy, Inc. | 5.16% | Industrials |
| IFN.AU | Infigen Energy | 4.61% | Energy—Alternate Sources |
| NDX1.GY | Nordex AG | 4.39% | Energy—Alternate Sources |
| FRS.SM | Fersa Energias Renovables SA | 3.08% | Energy—Alternate Sources |

EDP Renewables (EDPR listed in London) is the wind energy unit of Energias de Portugal. It recently announced a $3 billion investment in wind energy in the United States. It currently ranks as the third largest wind producer in the United States. The company has a market cap of $8 billion. Wind power is more widespread in Europe than in the United States. The company's future success is tied to commercial viability of the wind industry in the United States. It is building out its infrastructure to deliver power and should see revenues increase over the next few years.

Broadwind Energy (BWEN) sells both wind turbines and their components. The company was founded in 2003 in Illinois, had $6 million in sales in 2006, and reached $250 million in sales in 2009, achieving a market cap of $900 million. The company provides components and services to other companies in the wind industry and so is well-positioned should wind become a key source of energy.

REpower Systems (RPW), a billion dollar market capitalization company, based in Germany with subsidiaries in the United States and 11 other countries, is another wind turbine manufacturer. It represents 6% of the FAN portfolio. Vestas Wind Systems has installed 40,000 wind turbines in 63 countries, making it the largest wind turbine company in the world.

Hansen Transmissions N.V., based in Belgium, is building wind turbines in Europe and China. It also represents 6% of the portfolio and recently had a $700 million market cap.

Wind has become a $90 billion business worldwide. It has moved from startup to upstart in the energy world. While the future of this business is difficult to predict, no one doubts it has a future. The mostly small, but growing companies that dominate this portfolio currently have bright prospects. An investor who believes in green technologies should have an allocation to this fund. For some investors, it may be only 5% of their allocation to green. For true believers, and those seeking substantial upside, that could be increased to 20%.

### Solar Power

The Claymore/MAC Global Solar Index ETF (TAN) is a broadly diversified portfolio of companies that participate in the solar industry (see Table 8.6). This includes producers of solar power equipment, fabrication companies that make solar panels, solar cell manufacturers, and companies that distribute, install, and integrate solar solutions into energy systems. There are 30 holdings in the portfolio, and those companies have a total market cap of $90 billion. At the end of 2009, the fund held $182 million of assets under management. Many of these companies have seen great volatility in their stock prices as the outlook for solar rises and falls based on the prices of competing sources of electricity, and more importantly at the moment, regulatory mandates.

**TABLE 8.6 Claymore/MAC Global Solar Index ETF (TAN)
Expense Ratio (0.70%)    Top Ten Holdings (24 December 2009)**

| Ticker Symbol | Name | Weight | Sector |
|---|---|---|---|
| FSLR | First Solar Inc. | 8.17% | Industrials |
| REC | Renewable Energy Corp. AS | 6.08% | Industrials |
| STP | Suntech Power Holdings ADR | 5.46% | Industrials |
| TSL | Trina Solar Ltd-Spon Adr | 5.42% | Energy—Alternate Sources |
| SWV | Solarworld AG | 4.98% | Electronic Components— Semiconductors |
| WFR | Memc Electronic Materials Inc. | 4.91% | Information Technology |
| YGE | Yingli Green Energy - ADR | 4.82% | Industrials |
| SPWRA | Sunpower Corp-A | 4.62% | Information Technology |
| CSIQ | Canadian Solar Inc. | 4.08% | Power Conversion/ Supply Equipment |
| JASO | Ja Solar Holdings Co Ltd. | 4.07% | Industrials |

The largest holding in TAN is First Solar (FSLR), which manufactures solar electric power modules to convert sunlight into electricity. The company has seen its sales quadruple in just three years from $400 million in 2006 to $1.6 billion in 2009. First Solar went public at the end of 2006. The stock closed at $24 on the first day of trading (the market cap was under $1 billion). A little more than a year later the stock traded at more than $300 per share and ended 2009 at $135 with an $11 billion market cap. The $300 price was reached as oil soared to $140 per barrel. This rapidly growing company has enormous potential if competing energy sources move higher in price, and should do well even if prices stabilize. Suntech Power Holdings (STP), headquartered in China, manufactures photovoltaic cells and systems that create electricity from sunlight for a variety of customers including commercial buildings, farms, and public utilities. This is another rapidly growing company whose revenues have tripled to $2 billion per year in the past three years. It is the second largest solar company in the world. The stock is listed on the

NYSE, and it makes up about 6% of the TAN portfolio. Trina Solar (TSL) is a similar company to Suntech, also headquartered in China, which represents another 6% of the portfolio.

Evergreen Solar (ESLR) is a Massachusetts-based company that manufactures the silicon wafers that are the primary components of the photovoltaic cells that make up solar panels. Evergreen is a $300 million market cap company whose stock was at $1.50 at the end of 2009.

Solarfun Power Holdings (SOLF) also has a market cap of around $300 million, is headquartered in China, and also makes components for photovoltaic cells. Each company represents nearly 2% of the portfolio. There are about a dozen other investments of the same size in the portfolio. It is unlikely that all of these companies will survive; more likely one or two of them will emerge as the leaders in their business. The beauty of an ETF is that the investor gets to own 15 companies, each with a market cap of $200 to $300 million, without having to pick the ultimate survivors. If the solar business matures, there could be two companies that dominate, and each easily could have a market cap of $10 billion or more. The market cap of all 15 today is about $3 billion, so the upside potential is great without the investor having to incur single stock risk. For this reason, owning TAN makes perfect sense for the long-term investor.

### Nuclear Power

The third leg of the alternative investment portfolio is nuclear energy. Van Eck Associates offers the Market Vectors Nuclear Energy ETF (NLR) (see Table 8.7). This ETF, with $150 million in assets, tracks the Deutsche Bank Nuclear Energy Index. While no nuclear power plants in the United States have been hooked into the grid since 1996 (most construction activity is outside the United States), rising fossil fuel prices, energy security concerns, and fear of global warming have stimulated interest in nuclear power. Nuclear energy currently accounts for 16% of the world's electricity. World demand for electricity is expected to double by 2030. If nuclear energy maintains its current share of the market, it will grow nicely. There is reason to believe that nuclear will grow even faster, and the alternative energy investor needs to have some exposure to these companies.

**TABLE 8.7  Market Vectors Nuclear Energy ETF (NLR)**
**Expense Ratio (0.61%)   Top Ten Holdings (24 December 2009)**

| Ticker Symbol | Name | Weight | Sector |
|---|---|---|---|
| CEG | Constellation Energy Group Inc. | 8.47% | Electric Utilities |
| CCJ | Cameco Corp. | 8.44% | Non-Ferrous Metals |
| 7011 JP | Mitsubishi Heavy Industries Ltd. | 7.98% | Machinery—General Industry |
| EDF FP | EDF | 7.90% | Electric Utilities |
| EXC | Exelon Corp. | 7.60% | Electric Utilities |
| PDN AU | Paladin Energy Ltd. | 4.52% | Non-Ferrous Metals |
| ERA AU | Energy Resources of Australia Ltd. | 4.48% | Non-Ferrous Metals |
| 1963 JP | JGC Corp. | 4.44% | Engineering/R&D Services |
| UUU CN | Uranium One Inc. | 4.40% | Non-Ferrous Metals |
| CEI FP | Areva SA | 4.36% | Energy—Alternate Sources |

There are 25 component companies in the ETF with a total market cap of about $100 billion. These include uranium miners, power plant operators, and manufacturers of key components. The largest position in the fund is Cameco Corp. (CCJ), a Canadian company that is a fully integrated nuclear company. It has a mining division that produces uranium in both Canada and the United States, a fuel services division that refines and converts the uranium, and an electricity division that generates and sells the power. The company's market cap is $12 billion, and total revenues exceeded $2.5 billion in 2009. Cameco is the second largest uranium miner in the world. The seventh largest uranium miner is Uranium One (UUU on the Toronto Stock Exchange). UUU represents 4.4% of the NLR portfolio. Paladin Energy, about 4.5% of the portfolio, has operating uranium mines in Australia and Africa.

Exelon Corp. (EXC) operates utilities in northern Illinois and Southeastern Pennsylvania. It generates most of its electricity from nuclear energy. It has a market cap of $33 billion, pays a 5% dividend and represents about 7.6% of the portfolio. Because it is a well established utility with predictable earnings, it represents a good core holding for the NLR ETF.

# Clean Technology

The PowerShares Cleantech Portfolio (PZD) in Table 8.8 is similar in theme to the Van Eck Market Vectors Global Alternative Energy ETF. In fact, it owns nearly all the same positions as the GEX but also has 50 additional component companies. It is truly an international fund that includes companies on five continents operating in all forms of alternative energy.

**TABLE 8.8  PowerShares Cleantech Portfolio (PZD)**
**Expense Ratio (0.67%)   Top Ten Holdings (24 December 2009)**

| Ticker Symbol | Name | Weight | Sector |
| --- | --- | --- | --- |
| GLW | Corning Inc. | 3.47% | Information Technology |
| CREE | Cree Inc. | 3.16% | Information Technology |
| 483410 | Schneider Electric S.A. | 2.93% | Industrials |
| 572797 | Siemens AG | 2.86% | Industrials |
| 710889 | ABB Ltd. | 2.74% | Industrials |
| B29NWR | Iberdrola Renovables S.A. | 2.54% | Utilities |
| 465853 | Novozymes A/S | 2.50% | Materials |
| ADSK | Autodesk Inc. | 2.44% | Information Technology |
| ANSS | Ansys Inc. | 2.39% | Information Technology |
| NLC | Nalco Holding Co. | 2.37% | Materials |

# Conclusion

While it is difficult to predict how long it will take for the United States to convert to cleaner, cheaper fuels, we are undoubtedly moving in that direction. The price of oil has held up well during a severe recession and was still trading at $73 per barrel at the end of 2009. If the world economy recovers, that price could very well rise thereby accelerating the growth of solar, wind, and nuclear. Take a look at the projections in Figure 8.2. Clearly, an investor with a diversified portfolio must have a significant allocation to energy. Some may prefer to simply own the PBW while continuing to invest in traditional oil and gas firms. Others may want to shun fossil fuels and build a diversified portfolio in green energy. A prudent investor would do well to invest 25% of her energy allocation in each of the four ETFs described earlier (PBW, FAN, TAN, and NLR). Those investors more inclined, for whatever reason, toward one specific modality (solar, for example) should simply reduce the allocation to PBW and increase the investment in the particular ETF they favor by that same amount.

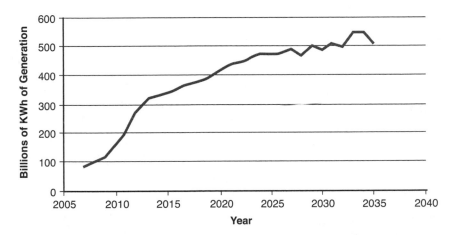

**Figure 8.2    Projected growth in non-hydropower renewable generation in the United States**

(Source: http://www.eia.doe.gov/oiaf/aeo/excel/aeotab_16.xls.)

# 9

## Why We Need to Invest in Infrastructure and How to Do It

On August 1, 2007, a bridge over the Mississippi River in Minnesota collapsed in the middle of rush hour, killing 13 people and injuring 145 more. A bridge that supported a part of the interstate highway system fell into a river without any warning. This shocked many Americans. They read about these sorts of disasters happening in various developing countries around the world, but those things happened over there. Didn't they? Then, here was a bridge—built in the 1960s—collapsing in a major American city. Something seemed wrong.

In August 2003, the Great Northeast Blackout plunged the northeastern United States into darkness in the largest power loss in history. This blackout started when an overheated, sagging power line in Ohio contacted a tree, which led to a disruption that tripped off more than 400 transmission lines and generating units at 261 power plants.[1] Most of New York, parts of Pennsylvania, Ohio, Michigan, and two Canadian provinces lost power. All this happened because of a system that was not robust, and the fact that a utility failed to prune trees to keep them away from transmission wires. Eleven people died as a result of the blackout.[2] Is this the kind of obsolete power system we want?

In 2005, Hurricane Katrina swept through the Gulf Coast of the United States. The levees that were supposed to protect the city of New Orleans failed. This infrastructure, built by the U.S. Army Corps of Engineers, the nation's most venerable engineering organization, failed to protect New Orleans. Chaos reigned. People who could not make it out of town on their own huddled in the city's convention center and football stadium. The population of New Orleans subsequently shrank substantially. New Orleans's protective infrastructure failed. All these events, in addition to countless studies, point out the need to invest anew in our infrastructure—the structural foundations of a society.[3] Infrastructure includes the "roads, bridges, sewers, etc., regarded as a country's economic foundation."[4] Without good infrastructure, it is hard to develop—and maintain—a smoothly operating and successful economy.

Working infrastructure permits people to go about their business and enables businesses to function efficiently. For example, the server farms that provide data storage need to be kept properly cooled. Without reliable electric delivery, server farms' operations could be compromised, crippling computers across the country.

Without good working infrastructure, our economy will suffer. To maintain its prosperity, the United States has no choice but to invest in its aging infrastructure now.

# What Is Infrastructure?

Our infrastructure is the systems that allow us to function in our lives. When you get up in the morning, you rely on water utilities to provide you with your morning shower. Electric and gas utilities provide the power you need to make breakfast. Your region's transportation infrastructure enables your children to go to school and you to go to work or run errands. When it works well, people don't pay much attention to infrastructure. When it doesn't work, they notice. If you can't drink the water, or the power is out, or traffic is jammed due to road repairs, or your train is late because of track problems, then your infrastructure is not functioning well and is impacting business efficiency and adding a cost to your lives.

## What Is the Problem?

We don't expect our infrastructure to make headlines, such as when bridges fall or levees give way. But when these things happen, we are reminded of our serious problems. Because we don't always notice the condition of our infrastructure because we are conditioned to take it for granted, or have familiarity with its workings, we don't necessarily know if it is safe and properly cared for—as evidenced by the cases of the bridge in Minnesota, the Great Northeast Blackout, and the flooding of New Orleans after Hurricane Katrina. The problem has several aspects: We have aging structures that are very difficult to replace, we cannot adequately inspect all projects, and rebuilding is extremely costly and provides substantial inconvenience to people and business.

### What Are Infrastructure Issues?

One problem with much of our infrastructure is that it is old. In many cities, for example, water pipes are often more than 100 years old. In addition, much of this infrastructure has not been adequately maintained. When systems are not maintained well, they tend to be inefficient.

Let's review the status of U.S. infrastructure based on an analysis made by the American Society of Civil Engineers (ASCE) in its "2009 Report Card for America's Infrastructure."[5] The ASCE's analysis gives letter grades to various parts of American infrastructure based on an analysis by leading civil engineers. The average grade for the United States in 2009 was a D.

The grading scale is as follows (grades can be modified by + or -):

- A = Exceptional
- B = Good
- C = Mediocre
- D = Poor
- F = Failing

Following is an overview of many major infrastructure needs taken from the ASCE report. We have focused on those needs that are open to investment through ETFs.

# Drinking Water

Drinking water earned a grade of D- in the society's report card. U.S. drinking water systems face an annual shortfall of some $11 billion per year to replace aging water facilities that are nearing the ends of their useful lives and need upgrades to comply with current and future federal water regulations. However, this shortfall does not take into account increased demand over the next 20 years. Federal assistance has been reduced to local water systems, leading to forecasted gaps between projected revenues and investments that water systems will need to spend on infrastructure improvements. Clean drinking water is essential to life and public health, and properly run systems also help foster economic development. Disruptions to water services can adversely affect health and can damage property (think bursting water mains) and hamper fire services. One example of the shortfall in water infrastructure is that leaking pipes waste about 7 billion gallons per day of clean drinking water. This means that 15% of the water supplied to the public is wasted.

Because most water operations in the United States are run by government agencies, the major opportunities will probably lie in providing services to these water agencies, rather than owning and operating water facilities, because privatization, at least until now, has not taken off in the United States.

# Wastewater

Wastewater earned a D- in the ASCE survey. Every year aging wastewater systems discharge billions of gallons of untreated wastewater into surface waters. These discharges can be environmentally harmful and close beaches to swimming. The U.S. Environmental Protection Agency (EPA) estimates that the United States needs to invest close to $400 billion in the next 20 years to update or replace existing wastewater systems and build new plants to meet rising demand for treatment services. The current condition of plants is poor due to lack of investment in the plants, equipment, and failure to make necessary capital improvements. Many plants are at the ends of their useful lives. Older systems exceed their capacity during heavy precipitation events and discharge raw sewage into surface waters. Federal assistance has not kept pace with needs. Wastewater infrastructure cannot continue to be neglected, because it is vital to our public health.

# Aviation

Aviation infrastructure received a D in the ASCE report. This is probably no surprise to anyone who has flown recently. The future doesn't look much better. The Federal Aviation Administration (FAA) predicts 3% annual growth in air travel. As if current delays aren't bad enough, they are expected to increase because the air traffic control system is outdated. The largest source of delays is the operation of the whole National Aviation System (NAS).[6] Better management of airports and airways could reduce these numbers and make the system more efficient. In addition, delays are very costly. In 2008, the Joint Economic Committee of Congress released a report entitled, "Your Flight Has Been Delayed Again," which estimated the annual cost of delays to the economy at $41 billion.

The failure to modernize the air traffic control system means that the delay situation will not improve dramatically, unless new systems are put into place.

# Bridges

Bridges received a C in the ASCE report. About one in four of the nation's bridges is considered structurally deficient, or functionally obsolete.[7] These bridges often have weight and speed limits that restrict traffic volumes and may create delays or congestion. While the number of deficient and obsolete rural bridges has been falling, the number of deficient and obsolete bridges is increasing in urban areas. Bridges are typically built to last about 50 years, and the average bridge age in this country is 43 years. The coming years could see great needs in bridge maintenance and repairs from this aging infrastructure.

The ASCE estimates that $17 billion needs to be spent annually to improve bridges, but only $10.5 billion is spent on construction and maintenance. The cost of replacing just one large bridge, New York's Tappan Zee Bridge across the Hudson River, could total some $15 billion.

# Rail

Rail received a C- in the ASCE report. Rail transportation is one of the most efficient ways to transport goods. For example, freight trains are three times as fuel-efficient as trucks. Traveling by passenger rail uses 20% less energy per mile than car travel. However, one of the factors that could hamper growth of both forms of transport is that passenger railroads and freight railroads usually share the same tracks. Freight railroads own most of the rail lines that passenger lines use, and they often take priority over passenger rail, which can make passenger rail slow and unreliable.

The rail system offers great economic and environmental potential for the United States, but few improvements have been made in recent years. Demand for freight transportation is expected to double by 2035. The ASCE estimates that $148 billion in improvements will be needed to accommodate this demand—and the large, Class I railroads, will probably pay some 90% of those costs.

Intercity passenger rail in the United States, in the Amtrak system, saw ridership climb from 2007 to 2008. Because of increasing ridership and an aging infrastructure, Amtrak has significant capital needs for upgrades, especially in the highly traveled Northeast corridor where some of the electrical system was installed in the 1930s. Amtrak is approaching capacity in some regions and will need to upgrade its fleet in the coming years. The Obama administration has launched a push for high-speed rail, and California is developing its own high-speed rail program. High-speed rail has proven very popular in Europe and in Asia. It could compete with short haul airline flights in certain markets. Getting to a high quality intercity rail system will take significant investment. The Passenger Rail Working Group has estimated that spending about $8 billion per year through 2050 could produce a modern rail network. While the costs are substantial, there could be significant benefits, about $4 billion in energy savings alone, not counting the benefits from reducing the need to expand capacity in other transportation modes.

# Roads

Roads received a D- in the ASCE report. It noted that road congestion is increasing, and the cost to improve roads is rising. Americans spend 4.2 billion hours a year stuck in traffic, which costs the economy $78.2 billion—$710 per motorist. Poor road conditions present physical dangers to drivers and their passengers and also lead to $67 billion a year in auto repairs. According to the report card, about one-third of major U.S. roads rank in poor, or mediocre, condition, and some 45% of urban highways are congested. The current spending of $70.3 billion for highway capital improvements falls short of the $186 billion per year needed to improve conditions.

The report also notes that change is needed in the way the highway infrastructure is managed including the use of new technologies and innovative ways to operate road systems. New forms of intelligent roadway systems could be safer and more efficient for travelers. However, without funding or new ways of managing roads, this won't happen. It is likely that private road operators could play a part in upgrading these systems.

New ways of financing roads are also needed. The Highway Trust Fund, the primary funding source for federal highways, built on gasoline excise taxes, is moving toward negative balances if current trends continue. The ASCE recommends shifting away from revenues collected from gasoline taxes to fees users pay that are aligned more directly with the benefits they derive. For example, tolls could be increased during peak travel hours. This might discourage some users and help reduce highway congestion, thus reducing the need to expand road systems. There is no question that innovation is needed—and it could come from private companies that are found in the infrastructure ETFs.

# Transit

Transit received a D in the ASCE report. Anyone who has ridden one of the newer transit systems found in Europe, and then one of the older ones found in the United States, can easily see why. Still, transit use grew 25% between 1995 and 2005—faster than any other transport mode. Nonetheless, about half of U.S. households do not have access to bus or rail transit. The Federal Transit Administration estimates that $15.8 billion annually is needed to maintain conditions, and $21.6 billion is needed to bring transit up to good condition. In 2008, the federal outlays for transit totaled $9.8 billion—far short of what was needed. Transit needs a lot of work. Many of the major systems were built more than a century ago. The condition of rail transit stations is poor. According to the Federal Transit Administration, only 49% of U.S. rail transit stations are considered in adequate or good condition, and 51% are substandard, or worse.

Transit systems make major contributions to a region's economic health and have environmental benefits as well, especially important as we confront climate change.

# Energy

Energy received a D+ in the ASCE report. It notes that the U.S. system requires heavy duty investment in new power generation, needs to improve efficiency in its existing generation plants, and needs to invest in transmission and distribution systems. The system for transmitting and distributing electric power is overloaded because demand has grown; however, new transmission lines have not been added to match that increase. Since 1990, electric demand has increased 25%, while construction of transmission facilities fell 30%. This congestion often prevents operators from removing the lines for necessary maintenance, which can lead to systemwide failures due to unexpected outages.

Slowly more money is being invested in transmission, but a lot needs to be done across the entire electric infrastructure. The ASCE estimates that the utility industry as a whole needs to invest some $1.5 trillion to $2 trillion by 2030. The industry is spending about that amount now and faces financing problems. However, the smart grid could cost $100 to $900 billion more over the next 20 years. Then add in the costs of carbon dioxide ($CO_2$) removal and climate change prevention, and you have a big potential funding shortfall. Still, keeping the status quo has significant costs. It has been estimated that power outages and poor power quality cost the country between $25 billion and $180 billion per year. Those costs could increase if power quality worsened or outages became more frequent or increased in duration.

The local distribution system that brings electricity to the customer is inadequate also, because it is not always designed for reliability. Squirrels crawl into transformers and get electrocuted, and a whole city blacks out. Having distribution systems above ground makes them vulnerable to falling trees and high winds. Yes, it may cost more to bury lines underground, but there could also be an increase in reliability for those who want to pay for it.

Our information economy needs a reliable electric system. Unless investment is made in the coming years in generation, transmission, and distribution facilities, electric service quality will fall, and costs will rise. New technologies have the potential to improve our current electric system and change the way the grid works for the better. However, the utility system is not set up for large inputs of alternative energy, and the grid is unreliable. In addition, aboveground transmission and distribution makes the system vulnerable to weather and other dangers.

# Investing in Infrastructure Could Have Major Payoffs for Society

To sustain our society, we need to invest in infrastructure. Without working infrastructure, it is difficult for a society to function effectively and to prosper.

U.S. infrastructure has been decaying for years. We are at a critical juncture. If we continue to let it collapse, we threaten our economic and social well-being. Without clean water, good transportation, and reliable energy systems, it will be hard for the United States to compete globally and grow our economy, let alone sustain our quality of life. Falling bridges, large-scale blackouts, and flooded metropolises are not the future we want. Investments in our infrastructure will be costly but will probably save us money in the long term, and the benefits are enormous. Each dollar we spend now reduces costs by 25 cents per year into the future. After four years, we will have earned back our investment. Spending that money now would provide benefits that last for a long time to come. This could mean a big payoff for investors who choose to put their money into companies focused on improving infrastructure.

# Understanding Infrastructure Investing with ETFs

Our economy requires a robust, resilient infrastructure. Rebuilding infrastructure can help provide a stronger foundation that will help the United States grow its way out of the Great Recession. ETFs allow investors to buy into various infrastructure sectors without exposure to single stock risk. In addition, because many of the big infrastructure companies do not trade on U.S. markets, ETFs make it easier for individual investors to access these companies. For investors who want to participate in what promises to be an important growth sector, an understanding of the industries, and their risks, will better prepare investors to succeed.

# General Infrastructure Investing

Infrastructure is made up of a broad range of industries, including water, transportation, and energy. This variety gives fund managers a lot of leeway in deciding what goes into an infrastructure ETF. With a fund that invests across the infrastructure spectrum, its nature can only be determined by looking at what goes into the index, and consequently the fund. Looking at the weightings for the various industries in the fund is important, because, given the broad nature of these funds, it is hard to tell by the fund's category (general infrastructure) what is in the portfolio. This is also important to see how the fund fits into your current portfolio—notably how the fund's industry weightings overlap with your current allocations.

Still, the ultimate choice of what goes into an index fund comes down to what the index provider chooses to place into that infrastructure basket. There don't seem to be clear cut lines as to what belongs in an infrastructure fund—as opposed to lines that delineate an electric utility fund, for example. Examining the fund and its contents can help you determine whether a particular infrastructure fund fits in your portfolio. It may help to see how iShares defines infrastructure for its iShares S&P Global Infrastructure Fund (IGF) compared to how PowerShares defines its Emerging Markets Infrastructure Portfolio (PXR).

iShares S&P Global Infrastructure Fund (IGF) includes the following:

- Energy storage and transportation infrastructure (e.g., management or ownership of oil and gas storage and transportation)
- Airport services
- Highways
- Rail tracks
- Marine ports and services
- Electric, gas, and water utilities

PowerShares Emerging Markets Infrastructure Portfolio (PXR) builds its fund around infrastructure construction and development in emerging market countries. It includes the following industries in its fund:

- Construction and engineering
- Construction machinery
- Construction materials
- Diversified metals and mining
- Heavy electrical equipment
- Industrial machinery
- Steel

The two funds define infrastructure in two very different ways. The iShares fund is more about infrastructure ownership and operations, whereas the PowerShares fund focuses more on construction and building. Their risks differ, because their component areas differ.

### Risks

The iShares fund, in addition to transportation- and utilities-specific risk, also has these risks:

- The energy sector is cyclical, and its fortunes are related to commodity prices.
- Government regulation.
- Energy companies often operate in countries where their assets may be subject to expropriation.

The risks of an infrastructure fund depend on what is in it. For funds with utilities, water, and transportation components, consult the risk sections for each of those industries later in this chapter.

The risks of the iShares fund are tied to the energy and utilities sectors, transportation, and industrial sectors.[8] The fortunes of companies in the energy sector depend on commodity prices.

Transportation and utility risks are covered in their respective sections later in the chapter.

The PowerShares fund has these risks relating to infrastructure:

- A poor economy may hamper infrastructure spending.
- High interest costs could prevent projects from being built.
- Environmental regulations can stop or slow down projects.
- Government rate regulation could affect profitability.
- Rising energy prices or decreasing demand for gas or electricity could reduce profitability.

# Materials

The expansion of infrastructure—or the rebuilding of current infrastructure—will require large amounts of materials and other resources. Investing in the materials sector, and possibly metals and mining, offers another way to potentially profit from the movement to improve infrastructure.

## What Are Materials Funds?

To the layperson, the concept of materials can sound a bit confusing. After all, isn't everything made of materials? MSCI Barra through its Global Industry Classification System (GICS) makes up the industry from the following subsectors:

- Chemicals
- Construction materials
- Metals and mining
- Paper and forest products

*Risks*[9]

Companies in the materials sector deal primarily in commodities—an ounce of gold is an ounce of gold, no matter who mines it. This commodity orientation means that the companies are affected significantly by levels and volatility of commodity prices. In addition, given that many of these products are imported, the value of the dollar can affect the price of the products imported into the United States. Also, periodically worldwide production of materials exceeds the demand due to slow economic activity, which hurts profits across the industry. These industries are often subject to extensive environmental regulation. Interest rates and cross border competition affect the ability of companies in the industry to raise capital. Economic cycles have a strong effect on this sector, also.

## Metals and Mining

Metals and mining is an industry that falls within the materials sector. Investors in both materials and metals and mining ETFs may want to see the extent of the overlap in the funds, before they buy, to avoid overweighting the metals and mining sector. Steel stands out as a sector that might benefit from increasing infrastructure spending, given its importance in reinforcing concrete. MSCI Barra considers the following industries as part of metals and mining:[10]

- **Aluminum**—Aluminum producers, bauxite miners, and aluminum recyclers. Excludes companies that produce aluminum building materials.
- **Diversified metals and mining**—Companies that produce or extract metals or minerals that are not covered by the other classifications here.
- **Gold**—Producers of gold and related products. Includes companies that mine or process gold and South African finance houses that mainly invest in, but do not operate gold mines.
- **Precious metals and minerals**—Companies that mine precious metals and minerals that don't fall under the gold classification. Includes platinum miners.
- **Steel**—Producers of iron, steel, and related products.

Some funds not based on the MSCI Barra criteria also include coal miners.

### Risks

State Street lists the following risks for its SPDR S&P Metals & Mining ETF (XME):[11]

- International political and economic developments
- Energy conservation (mainly for mining ETFs with coal companies)
- Success of exploration projects
- Commodity prices
- Tax and other government regulations

# Utilities

Utilities provide energy (gas and electric) and water to customers. They are industries with large capital infrastructure. Here is an overview of what the utility industry includes, according to MSCI's Global Industry Classification Standard, which is used to divide up industries into different sectors and subindustries for investment analysis. The utility industry includes:[12]

- **Electric utilities**—Companies that produce or distribute electricity.
- **Gas utilities**—Companies that are mainly in the business of distributing and transmitting natural gas. Excludes companies that are mainly involved in gas exploration and production. Also excludes gas pipeline companies that operate in competitive markets.
- **Multi-utilities**—Utilities that are diversified into more than one utility sector in addition to their core operations, be they in electric, gas, or water.
- **Water utilities**—Companies that purchase and redistribute water to consumers (includes large-scale water treatment systems).

- **Independent power producers and energy traders—** Independent power producers, gas and power marketers, and/or integrated energy merchants. Excludes electric transmission and distribution companies that fall under the electric utilities subindustry. These companies are more volatile than traditional utilities.

### Risks

The utility sector, due to its highly regulated nature, faces numerous risks peculiar to that industry.[13] The rates utilities charge their customers are often subject to review, and oversight, by government regulators. Although rates are adjusted to reflect rising prices, and other costs, there may be lag between the increase in costs and the time that the utility is granted the rate relief that allows it to raise rates to cover those costs. During this period, a company's earnings could be hurt. In addition, utilities, which are very capital-intensive companies, can be affected by interest rate jumps that can affect the long-term borrowing used to finance new plants and infrastructure.

# Water

Although it is considered a utility subindustry, according to Morgan Stanley's Global Industry Classification Standard, given the great interest in water ETFs, not only for their infrastructure component, but also for their environmental and public health importance, water deserves its own space for investors. The water industry is about more than just the water utilities that provide drinking water. Fund companies tend to consider a company as part of the water industry if it receives more than 50% of its revenues from the water business. These are the major categories of companies in the water industry:[14]

- **Water utilities**—Regulated companies that deliver water to residential, commercial, and industrial users. They are usually subject to environmental and economic regulations.
- **Treatment**—Water treatment makes water suitable for end users—whether for drinking or other uses. For humans, water needs to be safe to drink. For industrial users, water may be

treated to remove or add certain chemicals that affect its properties. Wastewater treatment cleans up water after it has been used and returns it to the environment in an environmentally friendly form. Treatment companies are involved with maintaining the physical, chemical, and biological integrity of water and wastewater.

- **Analytical/monitoring**—Companies that analyze, test, and monitor water and wastewater quality. They can provide the services or the technology needed to assess compliance with water and wastewater quality regulations.

- **Infrastructure/distribution**—Companies that supply the products used to construct water infrastructure. This includes the manufacturers of pipes, pumps, valves, and other water distribution equipment. These companies also service and supply the water distribution network and provide technologies that are used to maintain, upgrade, and restore distribution networks, which may be more cost-effective than new construction.

- **Water resources management**—Consulting, engineering, and technical services firms that develop irrigation and other water management systems.

- **Conglomerates**—Companies that are major players in the water business, but are so large or diversified that water contributes a small part of their revenues.

### Risks

Given the importance of water to public health and safety, water companies are subject to high levels of environmental regulation. Water utilities may also be subject to economic regulation that governs the prices they can charge customers. In addition, the water industry, which is very capital intensive, can be affected by rises in interest rates, which can affect the long-term borrowing used to finance new plants and infrastructure that is often needed to comply with environmental regulations.

# REITS

The American economic recovery will require the return of a vibrant real estate industry. All previous economic rebounds have included a substantial amount of new construction to house the expanding economy. While the buying and selling of individual properties is not practical for everyone, investors can access the real estate markets through real estate investment trusts (REITs). A REIT is a corporation or trust that pools capital to invest in real estate, either directly (an equity REIT) or by loaning money for mortgages or buying existing mortgages or mortgage-backed securities (a mortgage REIT). Equity REITs earn their money from income from leasing or selling property, and mortgage REITs earn their money from interest on the money they lend. REITs are required to distribute 95% of all income they earn, which in good economic times can represent a substantial return for investors.

## *Diversification*

REITs can serve to diversify an investor's overall portfolio because, historically, they have low correlation with the U.S. stock market.[15] Larry Swedroe and Jared Kizer sum up the benefit of this sort of diversification as "ideally, when one investment 'zigs,' another 'zags.'"[16] This diversification can counter the effects of volatile equities in an investor's portfolio.

Swedroe and Kizer explain why the performance of REITs differs from other equities:

- The long-term nature of leases means that rents are more stable than corporate earnings.
- Real estate returns are driven primarily by the relatively stable rents, not the capital gains that dominate equity returns.
- Landlords are not trying to create new technologies, new businesses, or new services to a market, so their business may be less risky than others.
- Dividends account for about 60% of REIT returns, which helps stabilize returns.[17]

When buying REITs, investors are urged to diversify. REIT ETFs make this relatively simple in that the investor can buy a package of REITs.

### Risks

One thing that investors need to know is that dividends from REITs are not considered qualified dividends and are taxed at ordinary income tax rates. (As of this writing, qualified dividends are taxed at the lower, long-term capital gains tax rate.) Investors may want to place their REIT investments in a tax-deferred or tax exempt account.[18] However, investors in international REITs may face a quandary. If they own international REITs, they may wind up paying foreign taxes. If those REITs are held in a tax free account, they cannot credit those taxes against their U.S. taxes, which effectively increases the expense ratio for that particular fund.

REITs are subject to the risks that come with direct ownership of real estate. These risks include the following:[19]

- Decreases in real estate values
- Overbuilding
- Increased competition and other risks arising from economic conditions
- Increases in operating costs and property taxes
- Changes in zoning laws
- Casualty or condemnation losses
- Environmental liabilities
- Rent controls

A well-diversified REIT will have funds from different geographical markets to hopefully reduce the effects of some of the risks previously mentioned. However, other factors, notably changes in interest rates can affect the valuation of the whole real estate securities market, which could have a significant effect on the fund. Or, as we saw in 2008, a credit crunch that reduces the real estate industry's access to debt can hurt the whole market at once.

# Transport

When the global economy recovers, trade probably will rebound as well. Transport ties economies together. In certain cases, investing in transportation can be an infrastructure investment, especially in the case of railroads, where they often own their own track as well as rolling stock. In Chapter 10, "Infrastructure ETFs: Overview and Analysis," we take a look at ocean shipping and other transportation ETFs. Here is an overview of those areas.

## Ocean Shipping

MSCI Barra defines the marine subindustry as companies that provide maritime transportation of passengers or goods. It excludes cruise ships, which fall under the hotels, resorts and cruise lines subindustry. Claymore, in its Claymore/Delta Global Shipping ETF, is made up of companies that derive over 80% of their revenues from:

- Seaborne transport of dry bulk goods
- Leasing and /or operating of tanker ships, container ships, specialty chemical ships, and ships that transport LNG or dry bulk goods[20]

## Risks

Shipping activity is a function of global trade. Decreased trade means decreased shipping. Shipping companies' fortunes are also tied to the goods they can carry. According to Claymore:

> "Companies in the global shipping industry are subject to volatile fluctuations in the price and supply of energy fuels, steel, raw materials and other products transported by containerships. In addition, changes in seaborne transportation patterns, weather patterns and events including hurricane activity, commodities prices, international politics and conflicts, port congestion, canal closures, embargoes and labor strikes can significantly affect companies involved in the maritime shipping of crude oil, dry bulk and container cargo."[21]

### Transportation

Transportation relies on economic activity. As the economy improves, it is likely that more goods will be transported and more people will travel. In addition, the government may invest in infrastructure projects, which could benefit companies that are involved in transportation. One proxy for the transportation sector can be found in the industries that make up iShares Dow Jones Transportation ETF (IYT). The sector consists of the following:

- Airlines
- Trucking
- Railroads
- Air freight
- Transportation services
- Industrial services
- Marine transportation

### Risks

Since transportation is a service industry, its fortunes are tied to the health of the economy. Economic factors, fuel prices, labor relations (railroads are unionized), and insurance costs have significant effects on transportation providers. Some transportation companies may also have substantial government regulation or oversight, which can affect their businesses.[22]

# Conclusion

Understanding the infrastructure sector, and its many subindustries, will enable investors to better understand how to put their money to work there. ETFs make it easy for investors to access the various areas of infrastructure without having to pick individual companies. They can select particular themes that appeal to them, or invest in extremely broad funds. This can allow investors to capitalize on the rebuilding of aging infrastructure in the United States.

# Notes

[1] Robert Galvin and Kurt Yeager with Jay Stuller, *Perfect Power: How the Micro Grid Revolution Will Unleash Cleaner, Greener, and More Abundant Energy* (New York: McGraw Hill, 2009), 18.

[2] Scientific American, "The Northeast Blackout—Five Years Later," http://www.scientificamerican.com/article.cfm?id=2003-blackout-five-years-later.

[3] Definition for "Infrastructure," *The Oxford Dictionary and Thesaurus*, American Edition (New York: Oxford University Press, 1996), 765.

[4] Ibid.

[5] Report Card for America's Infrastructure, http://www.infrastructurereportcard.org/.

[6] Although weather is often considered a major source of delays, it is important to distinguish between extreme weather, which prevents flying and the other category of weather that causes what are called NAS (National Aviation System) delays. This weather slows operations, but does not prevent flying. According to the Bureau of Transportation Statistics, "Delays or cancellations coded 'NAS' are the type of weather delays that could be reduced with corrective action by the airports or the Federal Aviation Administration." In 2008, NAS delays accounted for about 33% of all delays. Extreme weather accounted for about 3% of delays.

[7] A structurally deficient bridge is not unsafe, but has limits on speed and weight. Structural deficiency represents deterioration over time. A functionally obsolete bridge is not unsafe, but has older design features and geometry and cannot easily handle current vehicles, vehicle weights, and traffic volumes. A bridge designed in the 1930s, for car widths of the 1930s, with 1930s shoulder widths, that has not been updated could be considered functionally obsolete.

[8] iShares, *2009 Prospectus to Shareholders: iShares S&P Global Infrastructure Fund,* August 1, 2009.

[9] Adapted from *Select Sector SPDRs Prospectus*, January 31, 2009, 9.

[10] MSCI, "GICS (Global Industry Classification Standard), Effective after close of business (US, EST), Friday, August 29, 2008," http://www.mscibarra.com/resources/xls/GICS_map2008.xls.

[11] SPDR Series Trust, *Prospectus*, October 31, 2008, 38.

[12] MSCI "GICS (Global Industry Classification Standard)," Effective after close of business (US, EST), Friday, August 29, 2008, http://www.mscibarra.com/resources/xls/GICS_map2008.xls.

[13] Adapted from *Select Sector SPDRs Prospectus*, 9-10.

[14] PowerShares, *PowerShares Exchange-Traded Fund Trust*, 83-84.

[15] Larry E. Swedroe and Jared Kizer, *The Only Guide to Alternative Investments You'll Ever Need* (New York: Bloomberg Press, 2008), 6.

[16] Ibid.

[17] Ibid., 8.

[18] Ibid., 9.

[19] These risks are from the SPDR DJ Wilshire REIT ETF Prospectus from October 31, 2008. The ETF is now called the SPDR Dow Jones REIT.

[20] Claymore, "Investment Options," http://www.claymore.com/etf/fund/SEA.

[21] Claymore Securities, Claymore Exchange-Traded Fund Trust 2, *Prospectus*, 28.

[22] iShares, 2009 Prospectus to Shareholders: iShares S&P Global Infrastructure Fund, August 1, 2009, 5.

# 10

## Infrastructure ETFs: Overview and Analysis

To rationalize an investment in equities, an investor must believe that the country will ultimately prosper. If one does not believe that, then it is necessary to look to hard assets or precious metals or some other store of value. Some believe that the cleverer among us can accumulate wealth by investing in gold, silver, or emerging markets while we neglect our own economy, continuing to lose jobs, piling up deficits, and failing to create new technologies that will increase our standard of living. There is no scenario where the few can profit while most of their fellow citizens suffer. In the last decade, financial firms have moved away from investing in sustainable businesses that create real economic utility and toward casino capitalism, whereby they make large bets on short-term macroeconomic outcomes (oil prices, gold prices, mortgage rates, derivatives, etc.). The economic crisis of 2008 and the resulting recession demonstrated clearly that this type of activity is an anathema to the financial well-being of the United States.

Much has been made of the conflict of interest between Main Street and Wall Street, but there is a critically important aspect that has not been discussed. Casino capitalism, the placing of large bets on macroeconomic outcomes involving commodities, precious metals, interest rates, and currencies were once the exclusive purview of investment banks and hedge funds. Today, largely through the development of ETFs, this type of trade is available to all. Making bets on volatile sectors produces results quickly, far more quickly than a longer term investment in healthcare, alternative energy, or infrastructure. Investors are drawn to these momentum plays for their instant gratification. Investment advisors and brokers are equally attracted to these trades because it gives them the opportunity to create an instant track record. But such a trading strategy is unsustainable, except for the most talented and well-equipped participants. Recently we have seen large firms spend billions of dollars on technology that lets them engage in high frequency trading at lightning speed. There will be a few winners in this arms race, but most will not be able to keep up. Worse, though, is the fact that this is no way to build an economy. It does not fund businesses, create jobs, or advance the innovation we need to drive productivity, which ultimately drives our standard of living. Casino capitalism is simply a competition where there are a few winners and many losers from an investment perspective, but whereby all members of society lose out from an economic perspective. Investing for the long term, building sustainable businesses that advance technology, and creating commerce and jobs (and exportable products) is the only way to build a successful economy and real permanent wealth.

Critical to our success as a nation is our infrastructure, which is in severe disrepair. For most of the twentieth century, Americans could travel anywhere in the world and from the moment they arrived at the airport would recognize that their infrastructure—from roads and bridges, to buildings, telecommunications, transportation systems, and educational institutions—was far superior to anything they would see in a foreign country. Today, the opposite is true. We have neglected infrastructure while other countries have built anew based on modern technology. There can be no prosperity without a substantial investment in the basic workings of our country.

Now, we are just coming out of the deepest recession since the Great Depression of the 1930s. The federal deficit has grown by more than $1 trillion due to the cost of bailing out the banks from the subprime mortgage fiasco. The federal government must lead the way in rebuilding our infrastructure, and that will mean more deficit spending. The political resistance to such efforts could retard such progress. On the other hand, even as the economy recovers, there has been no sign of job growth, without which a recovery is unsustainable. It is likely, through a combination of spending, tax cuts, and other incentives, that the government will encourage infrastructure

investment over the next several years. Investors looking to participate in the rebuilding of prosperity will do well to allocate a portion of
their investment dollars to infrastructure. There are several ETFs
that target infrastructure in different ways, depicted in Table 10.1.
The complete listing of each ETF, with all their components, is in
Appendix C, "Infrastructure ETFs."

**TABLE 10.1   Infrastructure ETFs with Market Capitalization Over $100 Million**

| Fund Area | Fund Company | Fund Name | Ticker | Expense Ratio |
|---|---|---|---|---|
| *Infrastructure* | | | | |
| | BlackRock | iShares S&P Global Infrastructure Index Fund | IGF | 0.48% |
| | Invesco PowerShares Capital Mgmt LLC | PowerShares Emerging Infrastructure Portfolio | PXR | 0.75% |
| *Materials* | | | | |
| | BlackRock | iShares Dow Jones U.S. Basic Materials | IYM | 0.47% |
| | BlackRock | iShares S&P Global Materials | MXI | 0.48% |
| | State Street Bank & Trust Co. | Materials Select SPDR | XLB | 0.22% |
| | State Street Bank & Trust Co. | SPDR S&P Metals & Mining | XME | 0.35% |
| | Vanguard | Vanguard Materials ETF | VAW | 0.25% |
| *Utilities* | | | | |
| | BlackRock | iShares S&P Global Utilities Sector Index Fund | JXI | 0.48% |
| | BlackRock | iShares DJ U.S. Utility Sector Index Fund | IDU | 0.48% |
| | State Street Bank & Trust Co. | Utilities Sel Sect SPDR Fund | XLU | 0.22% |
| | Vanguard Group Inc. | Vanguard Utilities ETF | VPU | 0.25% |

**TABLE 10.1   Infrastructure ETFs with Market Capitalization Over $100 Million  (cont.)**

| Fund Area | Fund Company | Fund Name | Ticker | Expense Ratio |
|---|---|---|---|---|
| *Water* | | | | |
| | Claymore Advisors LLC | Claymore S&P Global Water Index ETF | CGW | 0.70% |
| | Invesco PowerShares Capital Mgmt LLC | PowerShares Global Water Portfolio | PIO | 0.75% |
| | Invesco PowerShares Capital Mgmt LLC | PowerShares Water Resource Portfolio | PHO | 0.64% |
| *Transportation* | | | | |
| | BlackRock | iShares Dow Jones Transportation Average | IYT | 0.47% |
| | Claymore Advisors LLC | Claymore/Delta Global Shipping | SEA | 0.95% |
| *REITS* | | | | |
| | BlackRock | iShares Cohen & Steers Realty Majors | ICF | 0.35% |
| | State Street Bank & Trust Co. | SPDR Dow Jones REIT | RWR | 0.25% |
| | | Vanguard REIT Index ETF | | |
| | Vanguard | | VNQ | 0.11% |

Infrastructure investing per se has not, to date, attracted significant investor assets. Although there are more than two dozen ETFs devoted to the sector, only 14 of them have received at least $100 million in assets, and all the funds together have about $3.5 billion. In addition to these ETFs, an investor will want to own at least one of the three major real estate ETFs that own a portfolio of real estate investment trusts (REITs).

# Utilities

Four infrastructure ETFs are devoted to investing in utilities; the largest is Utilities Select SPDR Fund (XLU) (see Table 10.2) with $2.5 billion of investment, the iShares DJ US Utility Sector ETF (IDU) (see Table 10.3) has $430 million, the Vanguard Utilities ETF (VPU) (see Table 10.4) has about $400 million, and the iShares S&P Global Utility Funds (JXI) (see Table 10.5) has about $200 million.

**TABLE 10.2   Utilities Select SPDR Fund (XLU)**
**Expense Ratio (0.22%)   Top Ten Holdings (23 December 2009)**

| Ticker Symbol | Name | Weight | Sector |
|---|---|---|---|
| EXC | Exelon Corp. | 8.8% | Electric Utilities |
| SO | Southern Co. | 7.2% | Electric Utilities |
| D | Dominion Resources Inc. | 6.32% | Electric Utilities |
| FPL | FPL Group Inc. | 5.91% | Electric Utilities |
| DUK | Duke Energy Corp. | 5.61% | Gas, Water, & Multiutilities |
| PEG | Public Service Enterprise Group | 4.54% | Electric Utilities |
| PCG | PG&E Corp. | 4.51% | Electric Utilities |
| AEP | American Electric Power Inc. | 4.5% | Electric Utilities |
| ETR | Entergy Corp | 4.23% | Electric Utilities |
| FE | FirstEnergy Corp. | 3.9% | Electric Utilities |

**TABLE 10.3   iShares DJ US Utility Sector Index Fund  (IDU)**
**Expense Ratio (0.48%)   Top Ten Holdings (30 November 2009)**

| Ticker Symbol | Name | Weight | Sector |
|---|---|---|---|
| EXC | Exelon Corp. | 7.26% | Electric Utilities |
| SO | Southern Co. | 5.83% | Electric Utilities |
| DUK | Duke Energy Corp. | 4.9% | Gas, Water, & Multiutilities |
| D | Dominion Resources Inc. | 4.9% | Electric Utilities |

**TABLE 10.3   iShares DJ US Utility Sector Index Fund  (IDU)**
**Expense Ratio (0.48%)   Top Ten Holdings (30 November 2009) (cont.)**

| Ticker Symbol | Name | Weight | Sector |
|---|---|---|---|
| FPL | FPL Group Inc. | 4.46% | Electric Utilities |
| PEG | Public Service Enterprise Group | 3.64% | Electric Utilities |
| PCG | PG&E Corp. | 3.58% | Electric Utilities |
| ETR | Entergy Corp. | 3.52% | Electric Utilities |
| AEP | American Electric Power | 3.5% | Electric Utilities |
| FE | FirstEnergy Corp. | 3% | Electric Utilities |

**TABLE 10.4   Vanguard Utilities ETF (VPU)**
**Expense Ratio (0.25%)   Top Ten Holdings (30 September 2009)**

| Ticker Symbol | Name | Weight | Sector |
|---|---|---|---|
| EXC | Exelon Corp. | 7.50% | Electric Utilities |
| SO | Southern Co. | 5.70% | Electric Utilities |
| FPL | FPL Group Inc. | 4.90% | Electric Utilities |
| D | Dominion Resources Inc. | 4.60% | Electric Utilities |
| DUK | Duke Energy Corp. | 4.60% | Gas, Water, & Multiutilities |
| PEG | Public Service Enterprise Group Inc. | 3.60% | Electric Utilities |
| ETR | Entergy Corp. | 3.60% | Electric Utilities |
| PCG | PG&E Corp. | 3.40% | Electric Utilities |
| AEP | American Electric Power Co. Inc. | 3.40% | Electric Utilities |
| FE | FirstEnergy Corp. | 3.20% | Electric Utilities |

**TABLE 10.5   iShares S&P Global Utilities Sector Index Fund (JXI)
Expense Ratio (0.48%)   Top Ten Holdings (30 November 2009)**

| Ticker Symbol | Name | Weight | Sector |
|---|---|---|---|
| EOAN | EON AG | 7.97% | Electric Utilities |
| GSZ | GDF SUEZ | 6.42% | Gas, Water & Multiutilities |
| ENEL | Enel SPA | 4.03% | Electric Utilities |
| IBE | Iberdrola SA | 4.01% | Gas, Water & Multiutilities |
| RWE | RWE AG | 3.98% | Gas, Water & Multiutilities |
| EXC | Exelon Corp. | 3.36% | Electric Utilities |
| 9501 | Tokyo Electric Power Co. Inc. | 3.23% | Electric Utilities |
| NG/ | National Grid PLC | 2.83% | Electric Utilities |
| SO | Southern Co. | 2.71% | Electric Utilities |
| DUK | Duke Energy Corp. | 2.29% | Gas, Water & Multiutilities |

The three U.S. utility ETFs—XLU, IDU, and VPU—have nearly identical holdings, and therefore the same performance and similar expense loads. Each of the funds owns the major utility companies across the United States. The five largest positions in each fund are Exelon (EXC), Southern Co. (SO), Dominion Resources (D), FPL Group (FPL), and Duke Energy (DUK).

Exelon has about 5 million electricity customers in Illinois and Pennsylvania. Southern Co. has about 4.5 million customers in Alabama, Florida, Georgia, and Mississippi. Dominion has 2.5 million customers in Virginia and North Carolina, Ohio, Pennsylvania, and West Virginia. FPL has 4.5 million customers in Florida, and Duke has 4 million customers primarily in the Carolinas, Indiana, Kentucky, and Ohio. As utilities are good dividend payers, each ETF yielded about 4% at the end of 2009. In an economic recovery, the demand for power should rise as GDP increases, so this group of utilities is an excellent core portfolio. Since these ETFs all own the same portfolio and are otherwise almost identical, anyone of them can be used in an investment strategy.

The fourth utility fund is JXI, a global fund that has about 90 components including utilities in Europe, Asia, and South America. It has a somewhat higher yield than its U.S.-based counterparts at 5.38% as of November 30, 2009. Because it has more positions, the exposure to the main U.S. utilities is somewhat diluted. The tradeoff is that the investor gets international exposure. This may be attractive to some investors, but there is no real risk reduction in diversifying away from U.S. utilities. Since most investors are not familiar with foreign markets, this fund is only for those who insist upon the international exposure.

# Water

One of the unmistakable economic trends taking place throughout the world is the emergence of a large new middle class, particularly in developing nations. Some estimate that more than 800 million people will become middle class in the next decade in Brazil, Russia, India, and China (the so-called BRIC countries). These people will want and need western quality food, shelter, and clothing. Demand is emerging for clean and plentiful water, which, of course, is a given in the west. The infrastructure of water systems is therefore going to be a high growth business for years to come. There is an ETF that owns the companies involved in this industry, the Power-Shares Water Resources Portfolio (PHO) (see Table 10.6), which has $1.3 billion in assets. The portfolio owns companies that treat and deliver potable water as well as companies that provide services and technologies to this industry. This international portfolio has 30 component companies.

There are very few pure plays in the water business. That is, companies that are involved in water infrastructure and delivery are generally creating products that can be used in other areas of the energy equation. For example, the largest position in PHO is URS Corp., which is involved in engineering, architecture, construction, and maintenance of a wide range of infrastructure facilities, including electricity transmission, installation of clean air technologies, transportation networks, port and harbor maintenance as well as water supply and water treatment and conveyance systems. This San Francisco–based company has a $4 billion market cap and represents about 5.2% of the PHO portfolio. Investors should understand that many portfolio companies included in specialized ETFs are there only because a significant percentage of their business is derived from that specialty. More often than not, a company in a specialized portfolio derives much (even a majority) of its revenues from other businesses. This may mean that some companies will fall out of the index that underlies the portfolio. The PHO tracks the Palisades Water Index, which has as its criteria that the companies chosen be small- or mid-cap companies and that they "participate" in the water business. It happens that, for nearly all the component companies, their business outside of water is related to infrastructure so an investment in this fund, while not exclusively about water, is appropriate for these purposes.

**TABLE 10.6   PowerShares Water Resources Portfolio (PHO)
Expense Ratio (0.64%)   Top Ten Holdings (23 December 2009)**

| Ticker Symbol | Name | Weight | Sector |
|---|---|---|---|
| URS | URS Corp. | 5.15% | Industrials |
| ACM | AECOM Technology Corp. | 5.11% | Industrials |
| TTEK | Tetra Tech Inc. | 5.08% | Industrials |
| DHR | Danaher Corp. | 4.92% | Industrials |
| VMI | Valmont Industries Inc. | 4.71% | Industrials |
| ITRI | Itron Inc. | 4.71% | Information Technology |
| ROP | Roper Industries Inc. | 4.15% | Industrials |
| VE | Veolia Environnement (ADS) | 4.15% | Gas, Water, & Multiutilities |
| BMI | Badger Meter Inc. | 3.96% | Industrials |
| FLS | Flowserve Corp. | 3.87% | Industrials |

Four other companies are each about 5% of PHO: AECOM Technology, Tetra Tech, Itron, and Danaher. AECOM provides engineering, technical support, and logistics management for water and wastewater facilities as well as for transportation systems, bridge and tunnel construction, highways, airports, power transmission, and mass transit systems. Tetra Tech is an engineering, design, and consulting firm specializing in environmental projects. Itron, a $3 billion market cap company, manufactures water meters for commercial and residential use, data collection systems to manage and analyze information coming from those meters, as well as payment systems and other market-based solutions applicable to both the water and electricity industries. Danaher is a broadly diversified company that manufactures products for the commercial, industrial, consumer, and medical markets. It is the largest company in the portfolio with a market cap of $25 billion. The Professional Instrumentation Division of Danaher manufactures water monitoring systems, leak detection systems, submersible turbine pumps, and wastewater solutions.

Also included in the portfolio are several smaller companies that are more specialized in the business of water. Mueller Water Products (not listed here but in Appendix C, Table C.5) manufactures and markets a range of water infrastructure, flow control, and piping component system products for use in water distribution networks and water treatment facilities in the United States and Canada. It has a $900 million market cap. Layne Christiansen provides water and wastewater related services and products, including hydrological studies, site selection, well design, drilling and well development, pump installation, and well rehabilitation. American Water Works provides water and wastewater services to about 15 million customers in 32 states and Canada. A similar company, Aqua America serves about 3 million customers. Finally Calgon Carbon Corp. provides water treatment and purification systems and services for a variety of water consumers including potable water and industrial users. PHO is a comprehensive portfolio that will track the increased demand for clean water in the years to come.

PowerShares also offers a Global Water Portfolio (PIO) (see Table 10.7), which currently has $300 million in assets. There is very little overlap with PHO as the emphasis is on building a truly international portfolio. The largest position in the fund is Nalco, a Tennessee-based company that provides water treatment services to customers all over the world. Arcadis N.V. is a generalized infrastructure company, headquartered in the Netherlands. It is 6% of the portfolio. Stantec, a Canadian company develops environmental solutions for water treatment, distribution, and storage. The portfolio also includes companies from China, the Middle East, South America, and Europe. Virtually all of these companies are unknown to most investors. The portfolio does have more direct exposure to emerging markets where water infrastructure is in heavy demand.

**TABLE 10.7    PowerShares Global Water Portfolio (PIO)**
**Expense Ratio (0.75%)    Top Ten Holdings (23 December 2009)**

| Ticker Symbol | Name | Weight | Sector |
|---|---|---|---|
| NLC | Nalco Holding Co. | 6.18% | Water Treatment Systems |
| ARCAD | ARCADIS N.V. | 5.99% | Industrials |
| HYF | Hyflux Ltd. | 5.73% | Gas, Water, & Multiutilities |
| STN | Stantec Inc. | 5.68% | Industrials |
| TTEK | Tetra Tech Inc. | 5.14% | Industrials |
| SEV | Suez Environnement S.A. | 4.87% | Gas, Water, & Multiutilities |
| VMI | Valmont Industries Inc. | 4.67% | Industrials |
| KRA1 | Kemira Oyj | 4.49% | Materials |
| 6370 | Kurita Water Industries Ltd. | 4.40% | Industrials |
| VIE | Veolia Environnement S.A. | 4.07% | Gas, Water, & Multiutilities |

PIO outperformed PHO in recent years by about 10% per year. Investors who are comfortable owning companies that are not listed in the United States and therefore about which it is more difficult to get current information, may want to allocate a portion of their water funds to PIO. For most investors, PHO is sufficient. Claymore offers a Global Water Portfolio (CGW) (see Table 10.8) that has many of the same positions at PIO (albeit with a different allocation). The expense load of CGW is 70 basis points compared to 75 basis points for the CIO. Over the past three years, PIO has consistently outperformed CGW by a significant margin. While there is no guaranty this outperformance will continue, at this point in time PIO has produced superior returns. An investor wanting to invest in the international component of the water business would do well to split that investment between these two funds.

**TABLE 10.8    Claymore S&P Global Water Index  (CGW)**
**Expense Ratio (0.70%)    Top Ten Holdings (24 December 2009)**

| Ticker Symbol | Name | Weight | Sector |
|---|---|---|---|
| GEBN | Geberit AG | 10.05% | Industrials |
| VIE | Veolia Environnement | 7.62% | Gas, Water, & Multiutilities |
| UU/ | United Utilities GRP Plc. | 6.45% | Gas, Water, & Multiutilities |
| 6370 | Kurita Water Industries Ltd. | 5.21% | Industrials |
| DHR | Danaher Corp. | 5.09% | Industrials |
| SVT | Severn Trent Plc. | 4.99% | Gas, Water, & Multiutilities |
| NLC | Nalco Holding Co. | 4.81% | Water Treatment Systems |
| ITT | ITT Industries Inc. | 4.41% | Industrials |
| WOR | Worleyparsons Ltd. | 3.56% | Engineering/R&D Services |
| PNN | Pennon Group PLC | 3.48% | Gas, Water, & Multiutilities |

# General Infrastructure Funds

Two ETFs seek to make investments across the entire spectrum of infrastructure. They are the iShares S&P Global Infrastructure Index Fund (IGF) (see Table 10.9) and the PowerShares Emerging Infrastructure Portfolio (PXR) (see Table 10.10).

**TABLE 10.9    iShares S&P Global Infrastructure Index Fund (IGF)**
**Expense Ratio (0.48%)    Top Ten Holdings (30 November 2009)**

| Ticker Symbol | Name | Weight | Sector |
|---|---|---|---|
| TRP | TransCanada Corp. | 4.84% | Energy |
| ENB | Enbridge Inc. | 4.48% | Energy |
| ABE | Abertis Infraestructuras SA | 4.39% | Industrials |
| EOAN | E.ON AG | 3.93% | Utilities |
| TCL | Transurban Group | 3.77% | Industrials |
| GSZ | GDF Suez | 3.69% | Utilities |
| ATL | Atlantia SPA | 3.69% | Industrials |

**TABLE 10.9   iShares S&P Global Infrastructure Index Fund (IGF)
Expense Ratio (0.48%)   Top Ten Holdings (30 November 2009) (cont.)**

| Ticker Symbol | Name | Weight | Sector |
|---|---|---|---|
| SE | Spectra Energy Corp | 3.55% | Energy |
| WMB | Williams Cos Inc. | 2.99% | Energy |
| IBE | Iberdrola SA | 2.85% | Utilities |

**TABLE 10.10   PowerShares Emerging Infrastructure Portfolio (PXR)
Expense Ratio (0.75%)   Top Ten Holdings (23 December 2009)**

| Ticker Symbol | Name | Weight | Sector |
|---|---|---|---|
| ABB | ABB Ltd. | 3.75% | Industrials |
| CAT | Caterpillar Inc. | 3.63% | Industrials |
| VALE | Vale S.A. (ADS) | 3.58% | Materials |
| DG.PA | Vinci S.A. | 3.51% | Industrials |
| FWLT | Foster Wheeler AG | 3.06% | Industrials |
| REU1.BE | Reunert Ltd. | 2.86% | Industrials |
| USR.MU | Shanghai Electric Group Co. Ltd. | 2.61% | Industrials |
| LT.NS | Larsen and Toubro Ltd. Gdr Reg S | 2.56% | Industrials |
| JIX.DE | Jiangxi Copper Co. Ltd. | 2.52% | Materials |
| KBR | KBR Inc. | 2.49% | Industrials |

IGF owns the largest infrastructure companies around the world. The portfolio includes companies involved in energy and transportation infrastructure, airports, highways and rail services, marine ports, and electric, gas, and water utilities. There are 78 component companies located in 21 countries with 20% of those companies located in the United States.

The largest position (5%) is in TransCanada Corp., a $25 billion company that operates natural gas pipelines across Canada, Mexico, and South America and also owns several electricity generation facilities. Also representing 5% of the portfolio is Enbridge, another Canadian pipeline company that transports oil and natural gas. Abertis, 4%

of the portfolio, is a Spanish company with a variety of activities managing toll roads, telecommunications systems, airports, car parks, and logistics terminals. It operates throughout Europe and in Asia. Spectra Energy, a $13 billion company, is involved in gas transmission and distribution in the United States and Canada. GDF Suez is a French natural gas and electricity supplier. The other 70 plus companies in the portfolio are located all over the globe and are positioned at various stages of the supply chain of energy, power, and construction. An investment in this portfolio gives the investor a world view of infrastructure with a slight bias toward the United States.

PXR, PowerShares Emerging Market Infrastructure Portfolio, takes a different approach. PXR is designed to mirror the overall performance of the stocks of companies involved in the development of new infrastructure in emerging market economies. A variety of industries is included in this definition, and PXR includes construction and engineering, construction machinery, construction materials, diversified metals and mining, heavy electrical equipment, industrial machinery, and steel. Structures to be built include roadways, railroads, pipelines, power grids, seaports, and communication systems vital for day-to-day life. The PXR ETF performed extremely well in 2009 rising from $17 per share to more than $44. During the same time period, IGF performed well but not at the same rate, rising from $20 to $35 per share. Emerging markets have greater upside because they are growing from a lower base, but the risks are commensurately larger as well. Most of the companies in the PXR portfolio are unknown to most investors as many of them are located in Asia (35% of the portfolio), South Africa (12%), and Brazil (9%). Only 8% of the portfolio is based in the United States. Half of that position is represented by Caterpillar, the large manufacturer of construction and mining equipment. This portfolio should be seen as highly speculative and is likely to be very volatile as the emergence of developing countries' economies generally travels a very rocky road.

# Basic Materials

A component of infrastructure investing that should be included in the portfolio is basic materials. The basic materials components are chemicals, forestry and paper, industrial metals, and mining. These are the building blocks of construction and power. There are currently five ETFs that own the basic materials companies. The iShares Dow Jones Basic Materials ETF (IYM) (see Table 10.11) has 75 component companies covering all basic materials but is heavily weighted toward chemical companies, which make up 50% of the portfolio (with Dow, DuPont, Praxair, and Air Products & Chemicals alone making up more than one quarter of the fund). IYM has $800 million of investor assets. The other iShares ETF for basic materials investing is the iShares S&P Global Materials Sector Index Fund (MXI) (see Table 10.12). This fund, with $900 million in investor assets, is weighted far more heavily toward metals and mining, which represents nearly 60% of the portfolio while chemicals make up 30%. The two largest mining companies in the world—BHP Billiton and Rio Tinto—together make up 16% of the portfolio. There are more than 125 positions in the portfolio, and about 80% of those companies reside outside the United States.

**TABLE 10.11   iShares Dow Jones U.S. Basic Materials Sector Index Fund (IYM)**
**Expense Ratio (0.47%)   Top Ten Holdings (30 November 2009)**

| Ticker Symbol | Name | Weight | Sector |
|---|---|---|---|
| FCX | Freeport-McMoRan | 8.94% | Industrial Metals & Mining |
| DOW | Dow Chemical | 8.33% | Chemicals |
| DD | DuPont (E.I.) De Nemours | 7.68% | Chemicals |
| NEM | Newmont Mining Corp. | 6.72% | Mining |
| PX | Praxair Inc. | 6.63% | Chemicals |
| APD | Air Products & Chemicals Inc. | 4.29% | Chemicals |
| AA | Alcoa Inc. | 3.19% | Industrial Metals & Mining |
| NUE | Nucor Corp. | 3.17% | Industrial Metals & Mining |
| BTU | Peabody Energy Corp. | 3.11% | Mining |
| ECL | Ecolab Inc. | 2.78% | Chemicals |

**TABLE 10.12    iShares S&P Global Materials Sector Index Fund (MXI)
Expense Ratio (0.48%)    Top Ten Holdings (30 November 2009)**

| Ticker Symbol | Name | Weight | Sector |
| --- | --- | --- | --- |
| BHP | BHP Billiton Ltd. | 7.91% | Metals & Mining |
| BLT:LN | BHP Billiton Plc. | 4.24% | Metals & Mining |
| RIO:LN | Rio Tinto Plc. | 4.04% | Metals & Mining |
| BAS | Basf SE | 3.67% | Chemicals |
| AAL | Anglo American Plc. | 3.45% | Metals & Mining |
| VALE/P | Vale SA Adr. | 3.21% | Metals & Mining |
| MON | Monsanto Co. | 2.83% | Chemicals |
| ABX | Barrick Gold Corp. | 2.40% | Metals & Mining |
| XTA | Xstrata Plc. | 2.15% | Metals & Mining |
| PKX | POSCO-ADR | 2.15% | Metals & Mining |

State Street has two SPDRs for infrastructure investing: XLB (see Table 10.13; $1.8 billion in assets) is the Material Sector Portfolio, and XME (see Table 10.14; $800 million) focuses on metals and mining. The XLB, like its counterpart from iShares, IYM, is weighted toward the chemical companies. XLB is a more focused fund with 31 component companies as compared to 75 in IYM. The largest positions are Monsanto 12%, Dow 9%, Freeport McMoRan 9%, and DuPont 8%. It is notable that the expense load of XLB at 22 basis points is less than half of that of IYM (47 basis points). XME owns only metals and mining companies and has only 30 components. Most of those components are contained in the broader XLB. Only an investor seeking additional exposure to metals and mining would be interested in such a fund, and those investors would likely do better by taking a position in the ETFs that own metals directly like the SPDR Gold Shares (GLD), which gives investors direct ownership of the metal.

**TABLE 10.13   Materials Select SPDR (XLB)**
**Expense Ratio (0.22%)   Top Ten Holdings (23 December 2009)**

| Ticker Symbol | Name | Weight | Sector |
|---|---|---|---|
| MON | Monsanto Co. | 12.46% | Agricultural Chemicals |
| FCX | Freeport-McMoRan | 9.71% | Metal—Copper |
| DOW | Dow Chem Co. | 8.89% | Chemicals—Diversified |
| DD | Du Pont E I De Nemours & Co. | 8.34% | Chemicals—Diversified |
| PX | Praxair Inc. | 6.82% | Industrial Gases |
| NEM | Newmont Mining Corp. | 4.75% | Gold Mining |
| AA | Alcoa Inc. | 4.45% | Metal—Aluminum |
| APD | Air Prods & Chems Inc. | 4.4% | Industrial Gases |
| NUE | Nucor Corp. | 4.13% | Steel—Producers |
| IP | Intl Paper Co. | 3.45% | Paper & Related Products |

**TABLE 10.14   SPDR S&P Metals & Mining ETF (XME)**
**Expense Ratio (0.35%)   Top Ten Holdings (23 December 2009)**

| Ticker Symbol | Name | Weight | Sector |
|---|---|---|---|
| PCX | Patriot Coal Corp. | 4.62% | Energy |
| ATI | Allegheny Technologies Inc. | 4.48% | Materials |
| TIE | Titanium Metals Corp. | 4.44% | Materials |
| CNX | Consol Energy Inc. | 4.42% | Energy |
| X | United States Steel Corp. | 4.31% | Materials |
| MEE | Massey Energy Corp. | 4.27% | Energy |
| ANR | Alpha Natural Resources Inc. | 4.27% | Energy |
| ACI | Arch Coal Inc. | 4.18% | Energy |
| BTU | Peabody Energy Corp. | 4.14% | Energy |
| WLT | Walter Energy Inc. | 4.05% | Materials |

Vanguard offers a Materials ETF (VAW) (see Table 10.15) as well. This is a broad index with 125 stocks and a low expense load. It has the same major positions as the IYM and the XLB, a similar overall portfolio, and a highly correlated performance.

**TABLE 10.15   Vanguard Materials ETF (VAW)**
**Expense Ratio (0.25%)   Top Ten Holdings (30 September 2009)**

| Ticker Symbol | Name | Weight | Sector |
|---|---|---|---|
| MON | Monsanto Co. | 9.60% | Agricultural Chemicals |
| DD | EI Du Pont de Nemours & Co. | 6.60% | Chemicals—Diversified |
| FCX | Freeport-McMoRan | 6.40% | Metal—Copper |
| DOW | Dow Chemical Co. | 6.40% | Chemicals—Diversified |
| PX | Praxair Inc. | 5.70% | Industrial Gases |
| NEM | Newmont Mining Corp. | 4.80% | Gold Mining |
| APD | Air Products & Chemicals Inc. | 3.70% | Industrial Gases |
| NUE | Nucor Corp. | 3.40% | Steel—Producers |
| AA | Alcoa Inc. | 2.90% | Metal—Aluminum |
| ECL | Ecolab Inc. | 2.50% | Chemicals—Specialty |

# Shipping and Logistics

As the U.S. economy recovers, China continues to grow, and the rest of the world develops, demand for new and improved infrastructure will be limitless. One of the bottlenecks economies will face will be in shipping and logistics with regard to the basic materials. There are two transportation sector ETFs that investors need to know about. One is iShares Dow Jones Transportation Fund (IYT) (see Table 10.16), which currently has about $450 million of investor assets. It owns the major shipping and rail companies including FedEx, United Parcel, Union Pacific, and CSX Corp. Recently, Warren Buffet announced that his Berkshire Hathaway Company would acquire Burlington Northern Railway. His reasoning was that the demand for basic materials was to going to increase and stay elevated for decades. The IYT owns several railroad positions along with trucking and air freight companies. The ETF, with $440 million in assets, has seen its price double between March 2009 and the end of 2009. Continued economic recovery should bode very well for these companies.

**TABLE 10.16   iShares Dow Jones Transportation Average Index Fund (IYT)**
**Expense Ratio (0.48%)   Top Ten Holdings (30 November 2009)**

| Ticker Symbol | Name | Weight | Sector |
|---|---|---|---|
| BNI | Burlington Northern Santa Fe | 13.36% | Railroads |
| FDX | FedEx Corp. | 11.29% | Delivery Services |
| UNP | Union Pacific Corp. | 8.48% | Railroads |
| UPS | United Parcel Service-Cl B | 8.09% | Delivery Services |
| CHRW | C.H. Robinson Worldwide Inc. | 6.43% | Trucking |
| CSX | CSX Corp. | 4.96% | Railroads |
| NSC | Norfolk Southern Corp. | 4.88% | Railroads |
| GMT | Gatx Corp. | 4.68% | Commercial Vehicles & Trucks |
| JBHT | Hunt (JB) Transport Services Inc. | 4.55% | Trucking |
| LSTR | Landstar System Inc. | 4.53% | Trucking |

Marine shipping is likely to increase dramatically over the next several years as it becomes necessary to move raw materials and finished goods, not only within countries, but between them as well. Recognizing this trend, Claymore has created an ETF (SEA) (see Table 10.17) that focuses exclusively on global maritime shipping firms. The portfolio companies are involved in the seaborne transport of dry goods, specialty chemicals, and liquid natural gas. The fund only invests in companies headquartered in developed markets. There are 42 portfolio companies; about one-third of them are in Asia. Six of the companies are headquartered in the United States, and six are in Greece. The remainders are European. Teekay Corporation and two of its publicly traded subsidiaries, Teekay LNG Partners and Teekay Shipping, together make up about 13% of the portfolio. Teekay, which is based in Canada, provides a variety of tanker ships to carry oil and chemicals as well as liquid natural gas worldwide. It also provides fixed rate tankers for lease and operates a fleet of spot market ships. Frontline (shown in Appendix C, Table C.16) is a Bermuda based company that operates coal carriers as well as oil tankers and oil/bulk/ore (OBO) ships. Frontline is about 4% of the portfolio. Seaspan, located in the Marshall Islands, operates container ships in the Pacific, primarily out of Hong Kong. The SEA ETF has accumulated only $120 million of investor assets, but that should grow substantially over the next few years. Any infrastructure investor needs to have a position in this ETF.

**TABLE 10.17  Claymore/Delta Global Shipping Index ETF (SEA) Expense Ratio (0.65%)   Top Ten Holdings (24 December 2009)**

| Ticker Symbol | Name | Weight | Sector |
| --- | --- | --- | --- |
| TNK | Teekay Tank-CL A | 4.35% | Marine Transportation |
| OSG | Overseas Shipholding Group | 4.22% | Marine Transportation |
| EURN | Euronav NV | 4.22% | Marine Transportation |
| SFL | Ship Finance International Ltd. | 4.17% | Marine Transportation |
| TGP | Teekay LNG Partners | 4.13% | Marine Transportation |
| GMR | General Maritime Corp. | 4.02% | Marine Transportation |
| TK | Teekay Shipping Corp. | 3.95% | Marine Transportation |
| NMM | Navios Maritime Partners | 3.94% | Marine Transportation |
| SSW | Seaspan Corp. | 3.93% | Marine Transportation |
| 9101 | Nippon Yusen KK | 3.80% | Marine Transportation |

# Real Estate

There are three major real estate ETFs: the iShares Cohen and Steers Realty Majors (ICF) (see Table 10.18), the SPDR Dow Jones REIT ETF (RWR) (see Table 10.19), and the Vanguard REIT ETF (VNQ) (see Table 10.20). A Real Estate Investment Trust (REIT) is a corporation that invests in real estate but does not pay taxes. At least

90% of the income earned must be distributed to the shareholders (the income may be taxable). A REIT is to real estate investing what a mutual fund is to stocks. There are REITs that specialize in residential properties, others buy commercial properties, others own retail malls, and still others specialize in warehouses or healthcare facilities or hotel properties. The three major REIT ETFs own a portfolio of all the major REITs. While there is some slight variation in the specific apportionment of the funds between the various ETFs, the overall portfolios are very similar, and the performance of the three ETFs has been identical over the past several years. In fact, the ten largest positions in each ETF are the same ten REITs. They are as follows:

> AvalonBay Communities (Multifamily residential) AVB
>
> Boston Properties Inc. (Office parks) BXP
>
> Equity Residential (Multifamily residential) EQR
>
> HCP Inc. (Healthcare properties) HCP
>
> Health Care REIT (Healthcare properties) HCN
>
> Host Hotels & Resorts Inc. (Hotels) HST
>
> Public Storage (Self-storage warehouses) PSA
>
> Simon Property Grp. Inc. (Regional shopping malls) SPG
>
> Ventas Inc. (Healthcare properties) VTR
>
> Vornado Realty Trust (Regional shopping malls) VNO

**TABLE 10.18   iShares Cohen & Steers Realty Majors Index Fund (ICF) Expense Ratio (0.35%)   Top Ten Holdings (30 November 2009)**

| Ticker Symbol | Name | Weight | Sector |
| --- | --- | --- | --- |
| SPG | Simon Property Group Inc. | 7.91% | Regional Malls |
| PSA | Public Storage | 7.65% | Public Storage |
| VNO | Vornado Realty Trust | 7.24% | Diversified |
| BXP | Boston Properties Inc. | 6.58% | Office |
| HCP | HCP Inc. | 6.50% | Healthcare |
| EQR | Equity Residential | 6.26% | Apartments |
| VTR | Ventas Inc. | 4.77% | Healthcare |

**TABLE 10.18    iShares Cohen & Steers Realty Majors Index Fund (ICF)**
**Expense Ratio (0.35%)    Top Ten Holdings (30 November 2009) (cont.)**

| Ticker Symbol | Name | Weight | Sector |
|---|---|---|---|
| HST | Host Hotels & Resorts Inc. | 4.50% | Hotels |
| PLD | ProLogis | 4.11% | Industrial |
| AVB | AvalonBay Communities | 4.09% | Apartments |

**TABLE 10.19    SPDR Dow Jones REIT ETF (RWR)**
**Expense Ratio (0.25%)    Top Ten Holdings (24 December 2009)**

| Ticker | Name | Weight | Sector |
|---|---|---|---|
| SPG | Simon Property Group Inc. | 10.76% | Regional Malls |
| VNO | Vornado Realty Trust | 5.92% | Diversified |
| PSA | Public Storage | 4.93% | Self-Storage |
| BXP | Boston Properties Inc. | 4.48% | Office |
| EQR | Equity Residential | 4.41% | Apartments |
| HCP | HCP Inc. | 4.22% | Healthcare |
| HST | Host Hotels & Resorts Inc. | 3.46% | Hotels |
| AVB | AvalonBay Communities Inc. | 3.22% | Apartments |
| PLD | ProLogis | 3.17% | Industrial |
| VTR | Ventas Inc. | 3.15% | Healthcare |

**TABLE 10.20    Vanguard REIT ETF (VNQ)**
**Expense Ratio (0.11%)    Top Ten Holdings (30 September 2009)**

| Ticker Symbol | Name | Weight | Sector |
|---|---|---|---|
| SPG | Simon Property Group Inc. | 9.60% | Regional Malls |
| VNO | Vornado Realty Trust | 5.00% | Diversified |
| PSA | Public Storage | 4.60% | Self-Storage |
| BXP | Boston Properties Inc. | 4.30% | Office |
| EQR | Equity Residential | 4.10% | Apartments |
| HCP | HCP Inc. | 4.10% | Healthcare |
| HST | Host Hotels & Resorts Inc. | 3.40% | Hotels |

**TABLE 10.20   Vanguard REIT ETF (VNQ)**
**Expense Ratio (0.11%)   Top Ten Holdings (30 September 2009) (cont.)**

| Ticker Symbol | Name | Weight | Sector |
|---|---|---|---|
| VTR | Ventas Inc. | 2.90% | Healthcare |
| AVB | AvalonBay Communities Inc. | 2.80% | Apartments |
| PLD | ProLogis | 2.60% | Industrial |

This portfolio represents comprehensive ownership of all forms of real estate in the United States. As the country enters the second decade of the twenty-first century, unemployment is in excess of 10%, historically a very high figure. Venture investment, the source of capital for new companies, is at a 20-year low. Historically, 80% of new job growth has come from startup companies. If the country is to experience a return to prosperity, millions of jobs must be created. When that happens, commercial real estate will have to house all those workers. The dearth of financing for new construction means that capacity is not being increased. While vacancies are high as 2010 begins, economic recovery and job creation will fill that space. The disposable income available to the newly employed will eventually lift both the multifamily and retail markets. Current valuations represent an excellent entry point for investors to establish a position in real estate. Anyone of the three ETFs described here will give investors the comprehensive portfolio they need.

## Conclusion

Biotechnology and green technologies are exciting new fields of endeavor. Infrastructure is, in a word, boring. But we will not be able to build exciting new industries if there is not an adequate physical plant in which they can prosper. There are about 6.3 billion human beings on the planet, and that number is expected to grow to 9 billion by 2050. At the same time, as other countries around the world see their economies develop, their middle classes are expanding rapidly. It is expected that 800 million will join the middle class in this decade alone, many of them in China and India. This creates a talent pool that will be very attractive to new industries and the new companies that are formed within them. The United States must rebuild its infrastructure to remain competitive in this new paradigm. At the same time, in our new globalized economy, investors have the opportunity to participate in the growth that will occur in the world markets.

ETFs afford us the opportunity to invest in our own future while at the same time benefiting from the expanding economies around the world. The ETFs described here allow investors to avoid single country risk and single industry risk. In this rapidly changing world, it is difficult to forecast which new industries will mature first. We do not have to try to guess, but rather can build a comprehensive portfolio that allows us to participate in what promises to be a very bright future.

# 11

## Putting It All Together: Building a Three Paths ETF Portfolio

Building a portfolio is a personal matter. Investors have different objectives and different tolerances for risk. Investors need to know themselves in terms of their own risk profile. The suggested portfolios in this chapter are just that—suggestions. Three categories of portfolios are described here: conservative (lower risk), balanced (moderate risk), and aggressive (higher risk). All of these portfolios involve some risk of loss of principal, as does any investment in the stock market. Because all of the described portfolios are made up of ETFs, investors do get the benefit of diversification. Remember, diversification is a two-edged sword. Diversification is a tool of capital preservation. But precisely because the well-diversified portfolio owns a broad range of stocks, there will be both winners and losers among the components. This is particularly true in an emerging industry such as biotech or green technologies. The success of one company may cause the failure of another with a competing, but ultimately inferior, technology. The rationale for owning all the competitors is that the resulting value created by the surviving companies is large enough to make the overall portfolio profitable. Imagine if there had been Internet ETFs available during the tech boom of the 1990s. There likely would have been one that owned portals, one for search engines, and an ETF of major retail sites. There may have been five or six search engine companies in the portfolio with only one survivor—Google. At the end of 2009, Google's market capitalization hit $200 billion, up from its IPO value of just less than $30 billion. The sixfold increase in the price of Google would have more than paid for the failed investments in the other search engine companies. Owning the retail sites would have meant owning Amazon and Pets.com. The post-IPO value of Amazon was $450 million while at the end of 2009 it was $60 billion. Pets.com had a post-IPO value of $300 million in 2000 and went bankrupt several months later. The beauty of the ETF that owns all the competitors in a growing industry is that the winners more than pay for the losers.

The attributes of investing in healthcare, particularly biotech, green technologies, and infrastructure are obvious. Yet, these sectors attracted little investor capital in 2009. Rather, the money has flowed to macroeconomic bets on precious metals, commodities, energy, foreign currencies, and emerging market equities. All of these bets paid off handsomely in 2009, and the results were realized in a matter of months. This, of course, plays into the instant gratification desires of today's investors. But, as we saw in the bursting of the dot-com bubble in 2000, the housing bubble in 2006, and the credit crisis of 2008, eventually the macroeconomic trades gets too crowded. When investors pour capital into relatively illiquid assets, naturally those assets rise in price. As other investors become aware of the price rise, they jump on the bandwagon. But eventually, there are no more buyers, and inevitably the price collapses. The reason is simple: there is an equilibrium price for any of these assets based upon the fundamentals of supply and demand, but the forces of speculation drive the price higher. The momentum of the price increase accelerates as demand increases. Financial advisors, seeking to create a track record, pile into such a momentum trade. But ultimately, the fundamentals will prevail. In the past decade, each of the bubbles created in this way burst, with the result being that most investors wound up losing money.

The process of building real sustainable wealth is slow and methodical. The personal computer was introduced in the United States in 1981. This event launched the information age in which we currently live. In 1981, nobody had a PC at home. Today, virtually every investor does. Similarly, there were almost no cell phone users in 1981, and today they are ubiquitous. The companies that have successfully participated in these industries have become part of the fabric of American industry. Macroeconomic bets on commodities, precious metals, and energy do not afford the investor such an opportunity. After the crises of the last decade, it is critically important that the American financial markets get back to the basics of investing. It is a cliché to say that we all want to own "the next Microsoft" or "the next Amazon," but we must realize that the patience required to do so is mutually exclusive with instant gratification. We are now presented with the opportunity to own the next great industries of the U.S. economy: healthcare, green technologies, and infrastructure. The next generation of great American companies is certainly included in these portfolios, and by purchasing the ETFs the investor does not have to figure out which company will grow into Amazon or fall like Pets.com.

In 2009, U.S. investors poured $35 billion into emerging market ETFs as compared to a net outflow of $2 billion in 2008. Much of this money flowed into ETFs related to China. Investors see China, with its annual GDP growth rate of 9%, as having limitless upside potential. But in 2009, we saw the recall of toys laden with lead, defective pharmaceuticals, tainted pet foods, and a variety of food related issues involving imports from China. An earthquake in January 2009 devastated two Chinese schools demonstrating that there are serious building code issues. While China's gross domestic product is growing, the pains associated with growth are being felt. At an analogous time in U.S. history, the period of the Industrial Revolution in the latter half of the nineteenth century and early in the twentieth century, the nation endured several recessions and bank panics and twice barely avoided bankruptcy. The U.S. economy was growing then just as the Chinese economy is growing now. In addition, the Chinese population is nearly 20 times larger than was the U.S. population in 1900. Further, the average investor has no insight into what is happening in China, and most investors are simply attracted by the fact that the prices of Chinese stocks are rising. We have no idea whether such price rises are justified. But logic tells us that when prices rise unabated, they inevitably get ahead of the fundamentals. When that happens, the corrections are sudden—and devastating.

In 2009, at the same time investors sent $35 billion to emerging markets, the capital outflows from U.S. stocks totaled $85 billion. We are investing heavily in countries we do not understand and forsaking the companies that can, and will, create a new prosperity in the United States. We are not doing this because, as investors, we believe emerging market companies are superior. In fact, most of us

have no idea what they do. We are buying these securities because
we see them rising in value and because a parade of pundits showing
up on our TV screens tell us that the U.S. economy can no longer
compete. We are told that we must invest globally in a globalized
economy. While that statement has some truth to it, there is more
than one way to achieve that exposure. For example, the pharmaceutical industry gets more than half its sales from (and will derive much
of its growth from) international markets. New technologies for
alternative energy and infrastructure construction, primarily being
created in the United States and developed markets, will find eager
buyers in the developing world.

The downside of investing in the industries that are the subject of
this book is that there will be no instant gratification. There, in fact,
will be failures, delays, and disappointments. This is no different than
the experience of the companies that built our Internet and wireless
telecommunications networks. The indexes that underlie the ETFs
will adjust, removing the failed companies and replacing them with
those that have new promise. (Just as a hypothetical ETF owning
Internet search engines would have owned some losers it would have
eventually discarded in favor of Google.) The process will take an
indeterminate amount of time, measured in years and ultimately (like
the Internet and telecom companies) in decades. At the end of that
process, however, real sustainable wealth will have been created.

Each individual investor must decide how much of his or her
investable assets should be allocated to these industries. For some, it
may be as little as 10% or 20%. Investors seeking to maximize income
from their investments will not find suitable yields in these portfolios.
Investors whose time horizon for holding investments is at least five
years and preferably ten, may want to make a significant allocation to
the ETFs described here. There is no question that prosperity cannot
return to the United States unless major strides are made in these
areas. The technologies are about at the same point in their evolution
as Internet companies were in 1980—or about five to ten years from
real commercial success. For investors with a long-term outlook who
share that perspective, it is appropriate to allocate 50% of investable
assets to these portfolios.

It is important that investors understand both their objectives and their risk tolerance. These portfolios are not for investors seeking capital preservation. Rather these funds seek appreciation. The saying goes, you diversify to stay rich (preserve capital); you concentrate to get rich (seek appreciation). ETFs offer a blend—diversified concentration. It is possible to buy a fund that concentrates on owning solar companies but is adequately diversified in that it owns all the major competitors. The failure or demise of one company will not have a significant impact on the overall portfolio. If solar energy becomes a viable alternative to fossil fuels, several of these now small-cap companies could become large caps and, as happened with companies such as Amazon and Google, be worth hundreds of times their current value, providing a handsome return on investment even if all the other portfolio companies end up being worthless.

Table 11.1 lists our recommendation for building a portfolio using ETFs discussed in this book. It shows the name, symbol, assets as of December 31, 2009, and a suggested allocation from the perspective of three different types of portfolios: conservative, balanced, and aggressive.

**TABLE 11.1   Model Portfolios Based on Risk Tolerance**

| ETF | Symbol | Assets (mm) | Conservative | Balanced | Aggressive |
|---|---|---|---|---|---|
| Global Health | IXJ | $510 | 10% | 5% | 0% |
| SPDR Biotech | XBI | $310 | 5% | 5% | 5% |
| Bio & Genome | PBE | $200 | 0% | 5% | 15% |
| Clean Energy | PBW | $200 | 10% | 10% | 5% |
| Natural Gas | FCG | $400 | 5% | 5% | 10% |
| Wind | FAN | $100 | 0% | 5% | 5% |
| Solar | TAN | $180 | 0% | 5% | 10% |
| Nuclear | NLR | $150 | 0% | 5% | 5% |
| Utilities | XLU | $2,500 | 15% | 5% | 0% |
| Water | PHO | $1,300 | 5% | 5% | 5% |
| Materials | XLB | $1,300 | 10% | 5% | 5% |

**TABLE 11.1    Model Portfolios Based on Risk Tolerance (cont.)**

| ETF | Symbol | Assets (mm) | Conservative | Balanced | Aggressive |
|---|---|---|---|---|---|
| Metals | XME | $800 | 5% | 10% | 10% |
| Transport | IYT | $400 | 10% | 5% | 0% |
| Shipping | SEA | $120 | 5% | 5% | 10% |
| REIT | VNQ | $4,000 | 15% | 10% | 5% |

Table 11.1 shows strictly hypothetical portfolios, and the percentages are meant to be a guide to investors. Some of the ETFs described in this book are not included in our model portfolio, but that does not at all mean they are not worthy investments. Rather, we have chosen a sample that we believe provides the combination of broad diversification with upside potential that most investors are seeking.

Note that the total assets in the ETFs in the Table 11.1 model portfolio are around $15 billion. Contrast that with the $100 billion that is invested in emerging market ETFs or the $43 billion invested in GLD, the ETF that owns gold bullion. Consider that the market cap of Amazon is now $60 billion (in essence four times greater than these 16 ETFs combined). Remember that Amazon's market cap at its IPO was about $450 million. There are more than 2,000 companies in the aggregate in these ETFs, and if only a few of them are successful on the same scale as Amazon; these portfolios will be profitable.

## Conclusion

The model portfolios in Table 11.1 are meant only to be a guide. Some investors will decide they want to put more of their assets into certain sectors based on knowledge of, or belief in, those areas. There is no one correct portfolio. ETFs are transparent; investors always know the component companies and the investment allocation to those companies. An investor who wishes to put in the time to build a portfolio based on a more intricate analysis is able to do so. This would not be possible with a mutual fund because the portfolio alterations by a manager are not immediately known to the investing public.

We can all look back to the early 1980s and wish we had invested in a portfolio of telecom, computer hardware, and software companies. In the 1990s, we would have invested in baskets of companies that built and populated the Internet. We are at a similar inflection point in the investment cycle now. The sectors described here will be the best performing if we are to have a prosperous economy. This time we are fortunate to have ETFs that give us exposure in a broadly diversified way to the innovation that is coming.

# 12

## Conclusion

"Investing is an act of faith." So wrote John Bogle, the founder of the Vanguard Group, in his book *Common Sense on Mutual Funds* published in 1999. And it was true. Investors turned their money over to professional money managers and trusted them to invest prudently, certainly with the investors' best interests at heart. But over the past ten years, money managers have not lived up to that faith. Today institutional investors (mutual funds and pension plans) account for more than 70% of equity ownership in the United States, up from about 50% ten years ago. Our "faith" has allowed these managers and advisors to build a system that rewards the professionals regardless of how poorly they perform. They have created compensation structures that reward short-term speculation. Thus the turnover of the average investor's account has tripled, from 75% to 250%, in the past decade. The combination of turnover and fees has exploded the revenue streams of financial advisors and brokerage firms.

While all this was going on, the past ten years have become a hotbed of innovation of new financial products. Credit default swaps, which are essentially bets on the default of a particular corporation or state or even a country, and collateralized debt obligations, the driving force behind the subprime mortgage fiasco, have become all the rage and have attracted trillions of dollars. Exchange traded funds have given investors access to asset classes they could never own before, including direct ownership of precious metals and agricultural commodities, emerging markets, currencies, and hedge fund replication strategies. All these new investments appeared in the past ten years, and investors quickly embraced them, particularly professional investors. Remember, professional investors want to attract us as clients; to do so, they want to create a successful track record as soon as possible. In addition, professional investors need to justify their existence. They are attracted to new products, because the average investor knows nothing about them. They have poured hundreds of billions of dollars into emerging markets, precious metals, energy, and foreign currencies. These are all bets on a weak dollar, inflation, and the success of foreign economies at the expense of the United States. Ultimately, such a strategy makes no sense. If we divert the capital that would otherwise fund the future of the United States, essentially betting against it, we will create a self-fulfilling prophecy. More importantly, let's assume, for a moment, that these investments succeed. What would that mean for the economy of the United States? The dollar will have collapsed, gas will be $10/gallon, and other economies will be effective competitors for the world's resources. The United States will be in a severe economic tailspin. So the investors who succeed with this strategy may have more money, but they will live in a poorer economy. There are many who are predicting exactly that fate for the country and are therefore recommending these doomsday portfolios. But it is the doomsday portfolios that will cause the decline, as much as any other factor. Remember, the U.S. economy has been here before. Economic conditions 30 years ago were arguably worse than they are today.

## We've Seen This All Before— Travel in Time Back to 1980

1980 was a particularly bad year for the U.S. economy. We were experiencing a severe recession. We just emerged from the 1979 energy crisis, which had driven the price of oil to $50 a barrel from $10 just a few years earlier and had created long lines at the gas pumps. Inflation was running at 13%, the highest rate in U.S. history, and the unemployment rate was 10% (exactly where it stood at the beginning of 2010). The press, at the time, carried stories about the complete inability of the economy to generate new jobs and the likelihood that unemployment would remain high for years to come. The United States was dealing with terrorism as well—53 Americans were being held hostage in its embassy in Iran. But, in fact, the energy crisis abated as new supplies came to the market, and the price of a barrel of oil dropped to $10 by 1985. The unemployment rate dropped to 7% in 1985 and to 5% in 1990. By 2000, it was well under 4%. Inflation was less than 3% by 1985. But in 1980, things looked dreadful. So what happened?

Two companies went public in the fall of 1980. One was Apple Computer, then a three-year-old company that raised $60 million in its IPO. The other was Genentech, the then four-year-old biotech company. Genentech's IPO was priced at $35 per share, which represented a multiple of 1.750 times its current earnings. The stock closed at $71 per share on its first day of trading. Both companies had a first day market capitalization of well under $1 billion. Roche bought Genentech in 2009 for $45 billion, and Apple's market cap at the beginning of 2010 was $200 billion.

The businesses of these companies, genetic engineering and personal computing, represented a stark departure from the manufacturing-based economy of the 1970s. We, as a nation, while unaware of what was happening, were beginning the transition away from manufacturing and into the information age and were witnessing the birth of the biotechnology industry. It is at these inflection points in the economy that the opportunity for great wealth creation is presented to investors.

Twenty-five years earlier, the IPOs of IBM and Xerox represented a similar watershed event. Inevitably, these events occur when the economy is in crisis, when the "old economy" (at that time) is tired. Economists refer to this process as "creative destruction," whereby innovative companies provide technology that is more valuable to society than that of their predecessors, increasing productivity and raising our standard of living. Inevitably, these companies arise at times of economic distress when investors are fearful and risk capital is hard to find.

In 1980, much like today, many experts were negative about the prospects for the U.S. economy. Interest rates were at an all-time high, and some were predicting the prime rate could reach an astonishing 30%. Thirty-year treasury bonds were being sold with a yield of 20%—with few takers. Both inflation and unemployment were at double digit levels, and there was talk that both were becoming endemic to society. There was a sense that there was no innovation on the horizon, nothing to carry us out of our doldrums, and certainly nothing that could create millions of jobs. The fact is that the world was about to change, and the Apple and Genentech IPOs were just a hint of what was to come. But because investors analyze the economy on a legacy basis, by looking back at the market, most could not see what was coming, even though it was right around the proverbial corner.

## How Did We Get out of the Mess?

In the next few years, Microsoft, Cisco, Dell, eBay, Juniper Networks, WorldCom, Sprint, and dozens more would appear on the scene and revolutionize our economy. Yet, investors were slow to catch on. Investors who embraced these companies in a diversified manner made a great deal of money. But this required hard work. There were no ETFs that grouped the companies by sector enabling an investor to buy a basket of software companies or wireless telecom companies. No mutual funds focused on the new technologies. So the smart money, venture capitalists and private equity, which had the time and resources necessary to do the research, had a tremendous advantage over the average investor. With hindsight, we all wish we had owned a basket of these companies. But at the time, most of us would have convinced ourselves that these companies could not succeed, either because of economic conditions or because their business was too different from the traditional businesses to which we had become accustomed. Therefore, most investors missed this opportunity.

In 1985, five years after Apple went public, when millions of personal computers were being purchased annually, we were still investing in the "old economy." The ten most actively traded stocks in the United States in 1985 were AT&T, MCI, IBM, Phillips Petroleum, Unocal, Exxon, Beatrice, Apple Computer, American Express, and Middle South Utilities. With the exception of IBM, none of these companies were new economy participants. By 1990, the list had some more technology companies, but there was still a heavy weighting toward more venerable companies: MCI, Phillip Morris, Telematics International, Intel, AT&T, Citicorp, Oracle Systems, IBM, General Electric, and Apple Computer. Today the list would include Microsoft, Intel, Cisco, Apple, Google, Amazon, and Yahoo.

# 2010 Looks a Lot Like 1980

In 2010, we are at a point in our economic evolution that is very similar to 1980. Our existing economy is struggling. We are experiencing double digit unemployment. Our plants and factories are running well below capacity. Our economy is stagnating before our eyes. We are in desperate need of creative destruction. That process starts with capital formation. Capital is the life blood of new businesses without which they cannot exist. But capital formation is completely stalled in the United States, just as it was in 1980. In part that is attributable to the recent credit crisis and the resulting unwillingness of the banks to lend to anyone but the most credit worthy borrowers. But, in addition, investors are reluctant to take on any risk in these uncertain times.

Ultimately, there are only two motivators for investors—fear and greed. The pendulum of sentiment swings back and forth between the two but does so unpredictably, as can be seen in the level of initial public offerings (IPOs). We have been in a fearful pattern for several years now. There were only 63 IPOs in the United States in 2009, creating $22 billion in new capital for corporations. Contrast that with 2000 (which turned out to be the end of the bull market that began in 1982), which was the peak of the Internet bubble (and the height of the greed cycle for investors), when there were 406 IPOs that raised approximately $100 billion for the issuers.

# IPOs Signal Renewal of Faith in Markets

At the beginning of 2010, there were already 60 IPOs in registration, setting the stage for what could become a very big year for new issues. If the IPOs issued early in the year succeed, momentum could be created to bring additional products to market and a bandwagon effect could develop.

When the bull market began in 1982, there was approximately two trillion dollars invested in money market funds. Unlike today, when a money market account earns a fraction of one percent, in 1980 the average earnings of these accounts exceeded 12%. Despite that unprecedented return, when the bull market took hold, more than half of the two trillion dollars in money market funds found its way to the stock market in less than three years. At the beginning of 2010, there was nearly four trillion dollars in money market funds earning an average of 20 basis points (1/5 of one percent). This pitiful return will be a lot easier to part with than the 12% available 30 years ago. When that money gets over its fear and rushes to the market, the result can be far more dramatic than what occurred in the 1980s.

There are some obstacles to a new prosperity. The biggest one is that investors have far more choices today than they did 30 years ago. And many investors are convinced that holding stocks for the long run is not as lucrative as short-term trading and speculation. While that may have been true over the past ten years, it was not the case for 20 years before that. The Dow Jones Industrial Average was at 1,000 at the beginning of 1982 and rose to over 10,700 in March 2000. In January 2010, the Dow Jones was at about that same level, 10,700. Holding stocks from 1982 to 2000 paid a handsome return.

## A Lot of Money Is Poised to Enter the Market

It is important to note that there were about 20 million people in the United States who owned stocks in 1982. By 2000, that number had grown to 100 million, and that wall of liquidity pouring into the stock market helped drive prices higher. Recently, we have once again seen increased investor interest in the stock market as mutual funds have experienced net inflows every month during the period 2007 through 2009. This represents only a small fraction of potential investment as money market fund investments have stayed close to the $4 trillion level during the latter half of 2009.

## Unsustainable Investments Undermine the Economy

At the same time, investors have purchased emerging market ETFs (particularly funds that invest in China, Brazil, and India), foreign currency ETFs, precious metals funds, and ETFs that own oil and natural gas. The amount invested in these categories far exceeds the total invested in domestic equities.

At the beginning of 2010, two new ETFs were created that invest in platinum and palladium (symbols PPLT and PALL). The demand for these metals comes mostly from the automobile industry for pollution control equipment, which accounts for more than 50% of the demand for both of them. Between 2008 and 2009, the prices of both of these metals were in free fall, dropping more than 50%. In late 2009, prices began to firm in anticipation of the launch of these ETFs. The demand for platinum is 6 million ounces per year (as compared to 100 million ounces for gold and 900 million ounces for silver). As the new ETFs started to trade, investors bought up millions of shares requiring the ETFs to purchase large quantities of the metals. Prices rose more than 5% in the first week of trading. Note that this is not based upon the demand for automobiles, but rather on a speculative bet on the metals. A buyer of these ETFs may see them rise in value based upon the fund's accumulation of the metal but ultimately, if the automobile industry doesn't recover, the price will simply collapse. Meantime, the increased cost of platinum and palladium (used in catalytic converters) will make autos more expensive, which of course will dampen demand for them and reduce further the auto makers' appetite for these metals.

Investors are being given a variety of ways to bet against the U.S. economy, and are seizing upon them without regard to the fundamentals. Millions of investors have purchased gold and silver, oil and gas, and emerging market securities without having any idea about the underlying economics of these investments and how these commodities, and other countries, affect the U.S. economy. Energy experts are baffled by the high prices for oil and gas in the face of a slumping worldwide economy. Ultimately, if there is insufficient end user demand for these products (as opposed to investor demand) the price must fall.

There is no denying the globalization of the world economy. In recognition of the fact, fund companies have created ETFs to allow us to invest directly in virtually every emerging market and every major commodity and energy product. All these securities have been created in the past five years. Because they are new, they are the focus of much attention by professional investors, and they have been highlighted in the financial press.

We focus so much attention on the new securities that we tend to overlook the fact that the biggest player in globalization is the United States. The $14 trillion U.S. economy still represents 30% of the total world GDP. The U.S. consumes about 25% of the world's resources. If investors drive up the cost of those resources and do not invest in the innovation that will drive our prosperity, our economy is doomed to fail.

## Innovation Is Still Happening

The United States is still far and away the leader in innovation. Yes we have been through some difficult times and our financial industry has been greedy and destructive, but, as detailed in this book, some of the most compelling technology in our history is ready to burst on the scene. During the past 100 years, there have been a number of times when it seemed a good idea to bet against prosperity in the United States. But those who did lost while those who bet on an ever brighter future have created vast fortunes. There perhaps has never been a time when the U.S. economy looked more vulnerable. Equally, there has never been a better time to invest in the future.

It can be difficult to envision change in technology, even as it is about to occur. In 1980, there were few of us who understood that the personal computer was about to change our lives. Virtually nobody owned one. Nobody had a mobile phone, either, and most homes did not get cable TV. During the 1980s, all these products became ubiquitous, and investors in the relevant industries did very well. At the same time, commodity prices dropped, and oil went back to $12 per barrel. Investors were not speculating on hard assets, and nobody wanted to invest in emerging markets, even if that had been possible. We had a strong sense that our economy was growing and prospering as we watched the information age unfold before our eyes. It took most of the decade before the entire investing community embraced the new economy, but once the trend took hold it was inexorable.

# Look Ahead—Not Backward—to See Where to Invest

Because we invest on a legacy basis, wanting to look back at how stocks have performed to determine which ones we want in our portfolio, we tend not to see the newer companies that have not yet established a suitable track record. In 1980, General Motors certainly appeared to be a "better" investment than Apple Computer based upon their relative track records. If a poll had been conducted asking the question, "Which stock will perform better over the next 30 years?" General Motors would have been the overwhelming choice. But General Motors was part of the old economy, and Apple represented the new.

When we view the world through the rear view mirror, we may have a clear view of where we have been, but, unless we look through the windshield, we cannot see where we are going, no matter how obvious it may be. And because most investors who have been paying attention for the past 30 years have seen more innovation than they can fathom, there is a tendency to believe there will not be any more. But nothing could be further from the truth. We are in a position to completely revolutionize medicine, create a green environment, end our dependence on fossil fuels, and rebuild our infrastructure in the next 20 years. The technology is in place, there are ample investor funds sitting on the sidelines, and, as this book goes to press, more than 60 IPOs are in the queue. The only other ingredient required is a shift of the pendulum away from fear and toward greed. We must try to avoid the temptation of becoming too greedy, investing instead in innovation while mitigating risk by buying companies in baskets. Exchange traded funds will be the vehicle that allows us to sensibly invest to get that exposure and participate in the coming prosperity.

# A

# Healthcare and Biotech ETFs

## Pharmaceuticals

**TABLE A.1   iShares S&P Global Healthcare Sector Index Fund (IXJ)
Expense Ratio (0.48%)   Holdings (30 November 2009)**

| Ticker Symbol | Name | Weight | Sector |
|---|---|---|---|
| JNJ | Johnson & Johnson | 8.48% | Pharmaceuticals |
| NOVN | Novartis AG-REG | 7.19% | Pharmaceuticals |
| PFE | Pfizer Inc. | 7.18% | Pharmaceuticals |
| ROG | Roche Holding AG-Genusschein | 5.63% | Pharmaceuticals |
| MRK | Merck & Co. Inc. | 5.41% | Pharmaceuticals |
| GSK | GlaxoSmithKline Plc. | 5.25% | Pharmaceuticals |
| ABT | Abbott Laboratories | 4.13% | Pharmaceuticals |
| SAN | Sanofi-Aventis | 3.96% | Pharmaceuticals |
| AZN | Astrazeneca Plc. | 3.17% | Pharmaceuticals |
| BAYN | Bayer AG | 3.1% | Pharmaceuticals |
| AMGN | Amgen Inc. | 2.8% | Biotechnology |
| BMY | Bristol-Myers Squibb Co. | 2.46% | Pharmaceuticals |
| MDT | Medtronic Inc. | 2.3% | Medical Devices |
| GILD | Gilead Sciences Inc. | 2.04% | Biotechnology |
| LLY | Eli Lilly & Co. | 1.82% | Pharmaceuticals |
| UNH | United Health Group Inc. | 1.63% | HMO |

**TABLE A.1   iShares S&P Global Healthcare Sector Index Fund (IXJ)
Expense Ratio (0.48%)   Holdings (30 November 2009) (cont.)**

| Ticker Symbol | Name | Weight | Sector |
|---|---|---|---|
| NOVOB | Novo Nordisk A/S-B | 1.62% | Pharmaceuticals |
| BAX | Baxter International Inc. | 1.61% | Medical Products |
| MHS | Medco Health Solutions Inc. | 1.46% | Pharmacy Services |
| 4502 | Takeda Pharmaceutical Co. Ltd. | 1.39% | Pharmaceuticals |
| CELG | Celgene Corp. | 1.25% | Biotechnology |
| WLP | Wellpoint Inc. | 1.22% | HMO |
| ESRX | Express Scripts Inc. | 1.15% | Pharmacy Services |
| TMO | Thermo Fisher Scientific Inc. | 0.94% | Medical Equipment |
| BDX | Becton Dickinson & Co. | 0.88% | Medical Products |
| AGN | Allergan Inc. | 0.87% | Pharmaceuticals |
| CSL | CSL Limited | 0.85% | Biotechnology |
| MCK | McKesson Corp. | 0.81% | Wholesale Drug Distribution |
| 4503 | Astellas Pharma Inc. | 0.73% | Pharmaceuticals |
| SYK | Stryker Corp. | 0.7% | Medical Equipment |
| GENZ | Genzyme Corp. | 0.67% | Biotechnology |
| BIIB | Biogen Idec Inc. | 0.66% | Biotechnology |
| STJ | St Jude Medical Inc. | 0.63% | Medical Equipment |
| AET | Aetna Inc. | 0.62% | HMO |
| ZMH | Zimmer Holdings Inc. | 0.62% | Medical Equipment |
| BSX | Boston Scientific Corp. | 0.62% | Medical Equipment |

**TABLE A.1　iShares S&P Global Healthcare Sector Index Fund (IXJ)
Expense Ratio (0.48%)　Holdings (30 November 2009) (cont.)**

| Ticker Symbol | Name | Weight | Sector |
|---|---|---|---|
| 4568 | Daiichi Sankyo Co Ltd. | 0.62% | Pharmaceuticals |
| EI | Essilor International | 0.6% | Optical Supplies |
| CAH | Cardinal Health Inc. | 0.57% | Wholesale Drug Distributor |
| SHP | Shire PLC | 0.53% | Pharmaceuticals |
| ISRG | Intuitive Surgical Inc. | 0.52% | Medical Equipment |
| FME | Fresenius Medical Care Ag | 0.49% | Dialysis Centers |
| FRX | Forest Laboratories Inc. | 0.45% | Pharmaceuticals |
| 4543 | Terumo Corp. | 0.44% | Medical Products |
| DGX | Quest Diagnostics | 0.44% | Medical Labs & Testing Services |
| 4523 | Eisai Co Ltd. | 0.43% | Pharmaceuticals |
| LIFE | Life Technologies Corp. | 0.43% | Biotechnology |
| CI | Cigna Corp. | 0.43% | HMO |
| SNN | Smith & Nephew Plc | 0.41% | Medical Products |
| BCR | Bard (C.R.) Inc. | 0.4% | Disposable Medical Products |
| LH | Laboratory Crp Of Amer Hldgs | 0.39% | Medical Labs & Testing Services |
| HSP | Hospira Inc. | 0.37% | Pharmaceuticals |
| ABC | Amerisourcebergen Corp. | 0.36% | Wholesale Drug Distributor |
| HUM | Humana Inc. | 0.34% | HMO |

**TABLE A.1   iShares S&P Global Healthcare Sector Index Fund (IXJ)
Expense Ratio (0.48%)   Holdings (30 November 2009) (cont.)**

| Ticker Symbol | Name | Weight | Sector |
|---|---|---|---|
| ATLN | Actelion Ltd-Reg | 0.31% | Pharmaceuticals |
| DVA | Davita Inc | 0.3% | Dialysis Centers |
| MRK | Merck Kgaa | 0.3% | Pharmaceuticals |
| VAR | Varian Medical Systems Inc. | 0.29% | Medical Equipment |
| WAT | Waters Corp. | 0.27% | Medical Equipment |
| MYL | Mylan Inc. | 0.27% | Pharmaceuticals |
| QIA | Qiagen N.V. | 0.25% | Diagnostic Kits |
| XRAY | Dentsply International Inc. | 0.24% | Dental Supplies & Equipment |
| SHL | Sonic Healthcare Ltd. | 0.24% | MRI/Medical Diagnostic Imaging |
| CFN | Carefusion Corp. | 0.23% | Medical Products |
| RO | Roche Holding Ag-Br | 0.22% | Pharmaceuticals |
| UCB | Ucb Sa | 0.2% | Pharmaceuticals |
| CEPH | Cephalon Inc. | 0.2% | Pharmaceuticals |
| LONN | Lonza Group Ag-Reg | 0.19% | Chemicals—Specialty |
| RX | Ims Health Inc. | 0.19% | Medical Information Systems |
| WPI | Watson Pharmaceuticals Inc. | 0.19% | Pharmaceuticals |
| ELN | Elan Corp Plc | 0.19% | Pharmaceuticals |
| MIL | Millipore Corp. | 0.18% | Medical Equipment |
| NOBN | Nobel Biocare Holding Ag-Br | 0.18% | Medical Products |

**TABLE A.1   iShares S&P Global Healthcare Sector Index Fund (IXJ) Expense Ratio (0.48%)   Holdings (30 November 2009) (cont.)**

| Ticker Symbol | Name | Weight | Sector |
|---|---|---|---|
| CVH | Coventry Health Care Inc. | 0.17% | HMO |
| | Bgif Treasury Money Market Sl Agency Shares | 0.16% | S-T Securities |
| KG | King Pharmaceuticals Inc. | 0.14% | Pharmaceuticals |
| 4535 | Taisho Pharmaceutical Co Ltd. | 0.13% | Pharmaceuticals |
| PDCO | Patterson Cos Inc. | 0.12% | Dental Supplies & Equipment |
| BVF | Biovail Corporation | 0.11% | Pharmaceuticals |
| PKI | Perkinelmer Inc. | 0.11% | Instruments— Scientific |
| THC | Tenet Healthcare Corp. | 0.1% | Hospitals |

**TABLE A.2   iShares Dow Jones U.S. Pharmaceuticals Index Fund (IHE) Expense Ratio (0.48%)   Holdings (30 November 2009)**

| Ticker Symbol | Name | Weight | Sector |
|---|---|---|---|
| MRK | Merck & Co. Inc. | 10.33% | Pharmaceuticals |
| PFE | Pfizer Inc. | 9.77% | Pharmaceuticals |
| JNJ | Johnson & Johnson | 8.67% | Pharmaceuticals |
| ABT | Abbott Laboratories | 7.49% | Pharmaceuticals |
| BMY | Bristol-Myers Squibb Co. | 6.22% | Pharmaceuticals |
| LLY | Eli Lilly & Co. | 5.55% | Pharmaceuticals |
| AGN | Allergan Inc. | 4.25% | Pharmaceuticals |

**TABLE A.2   iShares Dow Jones U.S. Pharmaceuticals Index Fund (IHE) Expense Ratio (0.48%)   Holdings (30 November 2009) (cont.)**

| Ticker Symbol | Name | Weight | Sector |
|---|---|---|---|
| HSP | Hospira Inc. | 3.57% | Pharmaceuticals |
| FRX | Forest Laboratories Inc. | 3.55% | Pharmaceuticals |
| MYL | Mylan Inc. | 3.22% | Pharmaceuticals |
| PRGO | Perrigo Co. | 2.99% | Pharmaceuticals |
| SLXP | Salix Pharmaceuticals Ltd. | 2.68% | Pharmaceuticals |
| WPI | Watson Pharmaceuticals Inc. | 2.66% | Pharmaceuticals |
| KG | King Pharmaceuticals Inc. | 2.56% | Pharmaceuticals |
| CEPH | Cephalon Inc. | 2.55% | Pharmaceuticals |
| VRX | Valeant Pharmaceuticals Inte | 2.51% | Pharmaceuticals |
| ENDP | Endo Pharmaceutical Holdings Inc. | 2.15% | Pharmaceuticals |
| MRX | Medicis Pharmaceutical-Cl A | 2.12% | Pharmaceuticals |
| AUXL | Auxilium Pharmaceuticals Inc. | 2.07% | Pharmaceuticals |
| MDVN | Medivation Inc. | 1.91% | Pharmaceuticals |
| PRX | Par Pharmaceutical Cos Inc. | 1.67% | Pharmaceuticals |
| ALKS | Alkermes Inc. | 1.54% | Drug Delivery Systems |
| RIGL | Rigel Pharmaceuticals Inc. | 1.51% | Pharmaceuticals |
| AMAG | Amag Pharmaceuticals Inc. | 1.36% | Biotechnology |
| VPHM | Viropharma Inc. | 1.33% | Pharmaceuticals |
| VVUS | Vivus Inc. | 1.21% | Pharmaceuticals |

**TABLE A.2   iShares Dow Jones U.S. Pharmaceuticals Index Fund (IHE)**
**Expense Ratio (0.48%)   Holdings (30 November 2009) (cont.)**

| Ticker Symbol | Name | Weight | Sector |
|---------------|------|--------|--------|
| THRX | Theravance Inc. | 1.19% | Therapeutics |
| XNPT | Xenoport Inc. | 1.16% | Pharmaceuticals |
| PBH | Prestige Brands Holdings Inc. | 1% | Pharmaceuticals |
| MDCO | Medicines Company | 0.95% | Biotechnology |
| | BGIF Treasury Money Market SL Agency Shares | 0.17% | S-T Securities |

# Healthcare

**TABLE A.3   Vanguard Healthcare ETF (VHT)**
**Expense Ratio (0.25%)   Holdings (30 September 2009)**

| Ticker Symbol | Name | Weight | Sector |
|---------------|------|--------|--------|
| JNJ | Johnson & Johnson | 11.3% | Pharmaceuticals |
| PFE | Pfizer Inc. | 7.5% | Pharmaceuticals |
| ABT | Abbott Laboratories | 5.2% | Pharmaceuticals |
| MRK | Merck & Co. Inc. | 4.5% | Pharmaceuticals |
| WYE | Wyeth (now part of Pfizer) | 4.4% | Pharmaceuticals |
| AMGN | Amgen Inc. | 4.1% | Biotechnology |
| | Schering-Plough Corp. (now part of Merck) | 3.1% | Pharmaceuticals |
| BMY | Bristol-Myers Squibb Co. | 3.0% | Pharmaceuticals |
| GILD | Gilead Sciences Inc. | 2.8% | Biotechnology |

**TABLE A.3   Vanguard Healthcare ETF (VHT)**
**Expense Ratio (0.25%)   Holdings (30 September 2009) (cont.)**

| Ticker Symbol | Name | Weight | Sector |
|---|---|---|---|
| MDT | Medtronic Inc. | 2.8% | Medical Equipment |
| BAX | Baxter International Inc. | 2.3% | Medical Products |
| LLY | Eli Lilly & Co. | 2.3% | Pharmaceuticals |
| UNH | UnitedHealth Group Inc. | 2.0% | HMO |
| MHS | Medco Health Solutions Inc. | 1.8% | Pharmacy Services |
| CELG | Celgene Corp. | 1.7% | Biotechnology |
| WLP | WellPoint Inc. | 1.5% | HMO |
| COV | Covidien PLC | 1.5% | Medical Products |
| ESRX | Express Scripts Inc. | 1.3% | Pharmacy Services |
| TMO | Thermo Fisher Scientific Inc. | 1.2% | Medical Equipment |
| AGN | Allergan Inc./United States | 1.2% | Pharmaceuticals |
| BDX | Becton Dickinson & Co. | 1.1% | Medical Products |
| MCK | McKesson Corp. | 1.1% | Wholesale Drug Distribution |
| BSX | Boston Scientific Corp. | 1.1% | Medical Equipment |
| GENZ | Genzyme Corp. | 1.0% | Biotechnology |
| BIIB | Biogen Idec Inc. | 1.0% | Biotechnology |
| SYK | Stryker Corp. | 0.9% | Medical Equipment |
| STJ | St Jude Medical Inc. | 0.9% | Medical Equipment |
| AET | Aetna Inc. | 0.8% | HMO |
| ZMH | Zimmer Holdings Inc. | 0.8% | Medical Equipment |

**TABLE A.3   Vanguard Healthcare ETF (VHT)**
**Expense Ratio (0.25%)   Holdings (30 September 2009) (cont.)**

| Ticker Symbol | Name | Weight | Sector |
|---|---|---|---|
| ISRG | Intuitive Surgical Inc. | 0.7% | Medical Equipment |
| CAH | Cardinal Health Inc. | 0.7% | Wholesale Drug Distributor |
| FRX | Forest Laboratories Inc. | 0.6% | Pharmaceuticals |
| DGX | Quest Diagnostics Inc./DE | 0.6% | Medical Labs & Testing Services |
| LIFE | Life Technologies Corp. | 0.6% | Biotechnology |
| BCR | CR Bard Inc. | 0.5% | Disposable Medical Products |
| CI | CIGNA Corp. | 0.5% | HMO |
| HSP | Hospira Inc. | 0.5% | Medical Products |
| LH | Laboratory Corp. of America Holdings | 0.5% | Medical Labs & Testing Services |
| ABC | AmerisourceBergen Corp. Class A | 0.5% | Wholesale Drug Distributor |
| VRTX | Vertex Pharmaceuticals Inc. | 0.4% | Biotechnology |
| HUM | Humana Inc. | 0.4% | HMO |
| DVA | DaVita Inc. | 0.4% | Dialysis Centers |
| WAT | Waters Corp. | 0.4% | Medical Equipment |
| VAR | Varian Medical Systems Inc. | 0.4% | Medical Equipment |
| ILMN | Illumina Inc. | 0.4% | Biotechnology |
| CERN | Cerner Corp. | 0.3% | Medical Information Systems |
| HSIC | Henry Schein Inc. | 0.3% | Medical Products |
| XRAY | DENTSPLY International Inc. | 0.3% | Dental Supplies & Equipment |

**TABLE A.3   Vanguard Healthcare ETF (VHT)**
**Expense Ratio (0.25%)    Holdings (30 September 2009) (cont.)**

| Ticker Symbol | Name | Weight | Sector |
|---|---|---|---|
| MYL | Mylan Inc./PA | 0.3% | Pharmaceuticals |
| BEC | Beckman Coulter Inc. | 0.3% | Medical Equipment |
| CEPH | Cephalon Inc. | 0.3% | Pharmaceuticals |
| HOLX | Hologic Inc. | 0.3% | Medical Equipment |
| EW | Edwards LifeSciences Corp. | 0.3% | Medical Equipment |
| CFN | CareFusion Corp. | 0.3% | Medical Products |
| MIL | Millipore Corp. | 0.3% | Medical Equipment |
| WPI | Watson Pharmaceuticals Inc. | 0.2% | Pharmaceuticals |
| ALXN | Alexion Pharmaceuticals Inc. | 0.2% | Biotechnology |
| CVD | Covance Inc. | 0.2% | Medical Labs & Testing Services |
| RMD | ResMed Inc. | 0.2% | Medical Equipment |
| DNDN | Dendreon Corp. | 0.2% | Biotechnology |
| MTD | Mettler-Toledo International Inc. | 0.2% | Instruments— Controls |
| HGSI | Human Genome Sciences Inc. | 0.2% | Biotechnology |
| CVH | Coventry Health Care Inc. | 0.2% | HMO |
| CYH | Community Health Systems Inc. | 0.2% | Hospitals |
| IDXX | Idexx Laboratories Inc. | 0.2% | Diagnostic Kits |
| IMA | Inverness Medical Innovations Inc. | 0.2% | Diagnostic Kits |
| UHS | Universal Health Services Inc. Class B | 0.2% | Hospitals |
| THC | Tenet Healthcare Corp. | 0.2% | Hospitals |

**TABLE A.3   Vanguard Healthcare ETF (VHT)
Expense Ratio (0.25%)    Holdings (30 September 2009) (cont.)**

| Ticker Symbol | Name | Weight | Sector |
|---|---|---|---|
| RX | IMS Health Inc. | 0.2% | Medical Information Systems |
| PRGO | Perrigo Co. | 0.2% | Pharmaceuticals |
| KG | King Pharmaceuticals Inc. | 0.2% | Pharmaceuticals |
| OCR | Omnicare Inc. | 0.2% | Pharmacy Services |
| ENDP | Endo Pharmaceuticals Holdings Inc. | 0.2% | Pharmaceuticals |
| MYGN | Myriad Genetics Inc. | 0.2% | Biotechnology |
| MD | Mednax Inc. | 0.2% | Physician Practice Management |
| | Sepracor Inc. (now part of Dainippon Sumitomo Pharma Co., Ltd. | 0.2% | Pharmaceuticals |
| PDCO | Patterson Cos. Inc. | 0.2% | Dental Supplies & Equipment |
| CRL | Charles River Laboratories International Inc. | 0.2% | Biotechnology |
| UTHR | United Therapeutics Corp. | 0.2% | Biotechnology |
| PPDI | Pharmaceutical Product Development Inc. | 0.2% | Research and Development |
| WOOF | VCA Antech Inc. | 0.2% | Veterinary Diagnostics |
| PKI | PerkinElmer Inc. | 0.2% | Instruments— Scientific |
| LNCR | Lincare Holdings Inc. | 0.2% | Outpatient/Home Medical Care |
| TECH | Techne Corp. | 0.2% | Medical Instruments |
| VRX | Valeant Pharmaceuticals International | 0.1% | Pharmaceuticals |

**TABLE A.3    Vanguard Healthcare ETF (VHT)**
**Expense Ratio (0.25%)    Holdings (30 September 2009) (cont.)**

| Ticker Symbol | Name | Weight | Sector |
|---|---|---|---|
| WCRX | Warner Chilcott PLC Class A | 0.1% | Therapeutics |
| GPRO | Gen-Probe Inc. | 0.1% | Diagnostic Equipment |
| OSIP | OSI Pharmaceuticals Inc. | 0.1% | Biotechnology |
| KCI | Kinetic Concepts Inc. | 0.1% | Medical Equipment |
| AMLN | Amylin Pharmaceuticals Inc. | 0.1% | Biotechnology |
| TFX | Teleflex Inc. | 0.1% | Diversified Manufacturing |
| OMI | Owens & Minor Inc. | 0.1% | Distribution/Wholesale |
| HMA | Health Management Associates Inc. Class A | 0.1% | Hospitals |
| ONXX | Onyx Pharmaceuticals Inc. | 0.1% | Therapeutics |
| BMRN | BioMarin Pharmaceutical Inc. | 0.1% | Therapeutics |
| STE | STERIS Corp. | 0.1% | Medical Equipment |
| BIO | Bio-Rad Laboratories Inc. Class A | 0.1% | Medical Equipment |
| THOR | Thoratec Corp. | 0.1% | Medical Equipment |
| HNT | Health Net Inc. | 0.1% | HMO |
| AUXL | Auxilium Pharmaceuticals Inc. | 0.1% | Pharmaceuticals |
| NUVA | NuVasive Inc. | 0.1% | Medical Equipment |
| VARI | Varian Inc. | 0.1% | Medical Equipment |
| HLTH | HLTH Corp. (now part of WebMD) | 0.1% | Health Information Services |
| HAE | Haemonetics Corp. | 0.1% | Medical Products |

**TABLE A.3   Vanguard Healthcare ETF (VHT)
Expense Ratio (0.25%)   Holdings (30 September 2009) (cont.)**

| Ticker Symbol | Name | Weight | Sector |
|---|---|---|---|
| PSYS | Psychiatric Solutions Inc. | 0.1% | Physical Therapy/Rehab Centers |
| LPNT | LifePoint Hospitals Inc. | 0.1% | Hospitals |
| HLS | Healthsouth Corp. | 0.1% | Physical Therapy/Rehab Centers |
| COO | Cooper Cos. Inc. | 0.1% | Medical Products |
| ISIS | Isis Pharmaceuticals Inc. | 0.1% | Therapeutics |
| WST | West Pharmaceutical Services Inc. | 0.1% | Medical Products |
| MDRX | Allscripts-Misys Healthcare Solutions Inc. | 0.1% | Medical Information Systems |
| HRC | Hill-Rom Holdings Inc. | 0.1% | Medical Equipment |
| PSSI | PSS World Medical Inc. | 0.1% | Medical Products |
| MASI | Masimo Corp. | 0.1% | Patient Monitoring Equip |
| MRX | Medicis Pharmaceutical Corp. Class A | 0.1% | Pharmaceuticals |
| BLUD | Immucor Inc. | 0.1% | Medical Equipment |
| AMMD | American Medical Systems Holdings Inc. | 0.1% | Medical Equipment |
| REGN | Regeneron Pharmaceuticals Inc. | 0.1% | Biotechnology |
| AMED | Amedisys Inc. | 0.1% | Outpatient/Home Medical Care |
| AGP | AMERIGROUP Corp. | 0.1% | HMO |
| SGEN | Seattle Genetics Inc. | 0.1% | Biotechnology |

**TABLE A.3  Vanguard Healthcare ETF (VHT)
Expense Ratio (0.25%)   Holdings (30 September 2009) (cont.)**

| Ticker Symbol | Name | Weight | Sector |
|---|---|---|---|
| CBST | Cubist Pharmaceuticals Inc. | 0.1% | Biotechnology |
| DNX | Dionex Corp. | 0.1% | Instruments—Scientific |
| QSII | Quality Systems Inc. | 0.1% | Medical Information Systems |
| MGLN | Magellan Health Services Inc. | 0.1% | HMO |
| ECLP | Eclipsys Corp. | 0.1% | Medical Information Systems |
| CHSI | Catalyst Health Solutions Inc. | 0.1% | Pharmacy Services |
| WCG | WellCare Health Plans Inc. | 0.1% | HMO |
| SLXP | Salix Pharmaceuticals Ltd. | 0.1% | Pharmaceuticals |
| VIVO | Meridian Bioscience Inc. | 0.1% | Diagnostic Kits |
| CHE | Chemed Corp. | 0.1% | Diversified Operations/ Commercial Services |
| HMSY | HMS Holdings Corp. | 0.1% | Commercial Services |
| BKD | Brookdale Senior Living Inc. | 0.1% | Retirement/Aged Care |
| PDLI | PDL BioPharma Inc. | 0.1% | Biotechnology |
| SVNT | Savient Pharmaceuticals Inc. | 0.1% | Pharmaceuticals |
| NKTR | Nektar Therapeutics | 0.1% | Drug Delivery Systems |
| ACOR | Acorda Therapeutics Inc. | 0.1% | Biotechnology |
| ALKS | Alkermes Inc. | 0.1% | Drug Delivery Systems |
| EMS | Emergency Medical Services Corp. Class A | 0.1% | Human Resources |
| ATHN | athenahealth Inc. | 0.1% | Medical Information Systems |

**TABLE A.3   Vanguard Healthcare ETF (VHT)**
**Expense Ratio (0.25%)   Holdings (30 September 2009) (cont.)**

| Ticker Symbol | Name | Weight | Sector |
|---|---|---|---|
| CNC | Centene Corp. | 0.1% | HMO |
| ALGN | Align Technology Inc. | 0.1% | Dental Supplies & Equipment |
| ALNY | Alnylam Pharmaceuticals Inc. | 0.1% | Biotechnology |
| VVUS | Vivus Inc. | 0.1% | Pharmaceuticals |
| PRXL | Parexel International Corp. | 0.1% | Research & Development |
| EVVV | ev3 Inc. | 0.1% | Medical Equipment |
| CPHD | Cepheid Inc. | 0.1% | Diagnostic Equipment |
| MDVN | Medivation Inc. | 0.1% | Pharmaceuticals |
| VPHM | Viropharma Inc. | 0.1% | Pharmaceuticals |
| MATK | Martek Biosciences Corp. | 0.1% | Biotechnology |
| PRX | Par Pharmaceutical Cos. Inc. | 0.1% | Pharmaceuticals |
| AMAG | AMAG Pharmaceuticals Inc. | 0.1% | Biotechnology |
| SIRO | Sirona Dental Systems Inc. | 0.1% | Medical Equipment |
| VOLC | Volcano Corp. | 0.0% | Medical Equipment |
| IART | Integra LifeSciences Holdings Corp. | 0.0% | Medical Equipment |
| INCY | Incyte Corp. Ltd. | 0.0% | Biotechnology |
| BRKR | Bruker Corp. | 0.0% | Medical Equipment |
| THRX | Theravance Inc. | 0.0% | Therapeutics |
| GTIV | Gentiva Health Services Inc. | 0.0% | Outpatient/Home Medical Care |
| WMGI | Wright Medical Group Inc. | 0.0% | Medical Equipment |

**TABLE A.3   Vanguard Healthcare ETF (VHT)**
**Expense Ratio (0.25%)   Holdings (30 September 2009) (cont.)**

| Ticker Symbol | Name | Weight | Sector |
|---|---|---|---|
| LMNX | Luminex Corp. | 0.0% | Medical Products |
| | Exelixis Inc. | 0.0% | Biotechnology |
| IVC | Invacare Corp. | 0.0% | Medical Equipment |
| MNKD | MannKind Corp. | 0.0% | Therapeutics |
| AMSG | Amsurg Corp. Class A | 0.0% | Outpatient/Home Medical Care |
| ITMN | InterMune Inc. | 0.0% | Biotechnology |
| AFFX | Affymetrix Inc. | 0.0% | Diagnostic Equipment |
| MDAS | MedAssets Inc. | 0.0% | Enterprise Software/Services |
| HS | Healthspring Inc. | 0.0% | HMO |
| HALO | Halozyme Therapeutics Inc. | 0.0% | Biotechnology |
| PFWD | Phase Forward Inc. | 0.0% | Medical Information Systems |
| ABAX | Abaxis Inc. | 0.0% | Medical Instruments |
| GERN | Geron Corp. | 0.0% | Biotechnology |
| MDCO | Medicines Co. | 0.0% | Biotechnology |
| XNPT | XenoPort Inc. | 0.0% | Pharmaceuticals |
| IPCM | IPC The Hospitalist Co. Inc. | 0.0% | Physician Practice Management |
| BABY | Natus Medical Inc. | 0.0% | Medical Equipment |
| HGR | Hanger Orthopedic Group Inc. | 0.0% | Medical Products |
| FACT | Facet Biotech Corp. | 0.0% | Biotech |
| ODSY | Odyssey HealthCare Inc. | 0.0% | Nursing Homes |

**TABLE A.3    Vanguard Healthcare ETF (VHT)**
**Expense Ratio (0.25%)    Holdings (30 September 2009) (cont.)**

| Ticker Symbol | Name | Weight | Sector |
|---|---|---|---|
| ARNA | Arena Pharmaceuticals Inc. | 0.0% | Biotechnology |
| RIGL | Rigel Pharmaceuticals Inc. | 0.0% | Pharmaceuticals |
| BRLI | Bio-Reference Labs Inc. | 0.0% | Medical Labs/Testing Services |
| CPSI | Computer Programs & Systems Inc. | 0.0% | Medical Information Systems |
| RHB | RehabCare Group Inc. | 0.0% | Physical Therapy/Rehab Centers |
| SRDX | SurModics Inc. | 0.0% | Medical Instruments |
| SUNH | Sun Healthcare Group Inc. | 0.0% | Nursing Homes |
| MNTA | Momenta Pharmaceuticals Inc. | 0.0% | Biotechnology |
| SMA | Symmetry Medical Inc. | 0.0% | Medical Equipment |
| ENZN | Enzon Pharmaceuticals Inc. | 0.0% | Biotechnology |
| RSCR | Res-Care Inc. | 0.0% | Outpatient/Home Medical Care |
| AIRM | Air Methods Corp. | 0.0% | Outpatient/Home Medical Care |
| GXDX | Genoptix Inc. | 0.0% | Medical Labs & Testing Services |
| ISPH | Inspire Pharmaceuticals Inc. | 0.0% | Therapeutics |
| GTS | Triple-S Management Corp. Class B | 0.0% | HMO |
| OMCL | Omnicell Inc. | 0.0% | Medical Equipment |
| QCOR | Questcor Pharmaceuticals Inc. | 0.0% | Therapeutics |
| AHS | AMN Healthcare Services Inc. | 0.0% | Human Resources |

**TABLE A.3   Vanguard Healthcare ETF (VHT)
Expense Ratio (0.25%)   Holdings (30 September 2009)  (cont.)**

| Ticker Symbol | Name | Weight | Sector |
| --- | --- | --- | --- |
| AFFY | Affymax Inc. | 0.0% | Biotechnology |
| GHDX | Genomic Health Inc. | 0.0% | Medical Instruments |
| CYPB | Cypress Bioscience Inc. | 0.0% | Therapeutics |
| DXCM | DexCom Inc. | 0.0% | Medical Instruments |
| ABMD | ABIOMED Inc. | 0.0% | Medical Equipment |
| KNSY | Kensey Nash Corp. | 0.0% | Medical Instruments |
| ERES | eResearchTechnology Inc. | 0.0% | Internet Application Software |
| VITA | Orthovita Inc. | 0.0% | Medical Products |
| ABII | Abraxis Bioscience Inc. | 0.0% | Biotechnology |
| ARAY | Accuray Inc. | 0.0% | Medical Equipment |
| MITI | Micromet Inc. | 0.0% | Biotechnology |
| SGMO | Sangamo Biosciences Inc. | 0.0% | Biotechnology |
| PMTI | Palomar Medical Technologies Inc. | 0.0% | Medical Laser Systems |
| CADX | Cadence Pharmaceuticals Inc. | 0.0% | Pharmaceuticals |
| MOH | Molina Healthcare Inc. | 0.0% | HMO |
| OREX | Orexigen Therapeutics Inc. | 0.0% | Pharmaceuticals |
| CCRN | Cross Country Healthcare Inc. | 0.0% | Human Resources |
| NHC | National Healthcare Corp. | 0.0% | Nursing Homes |
| LGND | Ligand Pharmaceuticals Inc. Class B | 0.0% | Biotechnology |
| CRVL | Corvel Corp. | 0.0% | Healthcare Cost Containment |
| ENZ | Enzo Biochem Inc. | 0.0% | Biotechnology |

**TABLE A.3  Vanguard Healthcare ETF (VHT)**
**Expense Ratio (0.25%)  Holdings (30 September 2009) (cont.)**

| Ticker Symbol | Name | Weight | Sector |
|---|---|---|---|
| EBS | Emergent Biosolutions Inc. | 0.0% | Biotechnology |
| KNDL | Kendle International Inc. | 0.0% | Research & Development |
| RTIX | RTI Biologics Inc. | 0.0% | Biotechnology |
| ZGEN | Zymogenetics Inc. | 0.0% | Biotechnology |
| SIGA | SIGA Technologies Inc. | 0.0% | Pharmaceuticals |
| CRY | CryoLife Inc. | 0.0% | Medical Instruments |
| AFAM | Almost Family Inc. | 0.0% | Outpatient/Home Medical Care |
| ATRI | Atrion Corp. | 0.0% | Medical Products |
| CLDA | Clinical Data Inc. | 0.0% | Biotechnology |
| CMN | Cantel Medical Corp. | 0.0% | Medical Products |
| GTXI | GTx Inc. | 0.0% | Biotechnology |
| IRIS | IRIS International Inc. | 0.0% | Medical Imaging Systems |
| ALC | Assisted Living Concepts Inc. Class A | 0.0% | Nursing Homes |
| PODD | Insulet Corp. | 0.0% | Patient Monitoring Equipment |
| CLRT | Clarient Inc. | 0.0% | Pharmacy Services |
| DRRX | Durect Corp. | 0.0% | Pharmaceuticals |
| SMTS | Somanetics Corp. | 0.0% | Patient Monitoring Equipment |
| AMRI | Albany Molecular Research Inc. | 0.0% | Research & Development |
| NABI | Nabi Biopharmaceuticals | 0.0% | Therapeutics |
| ARQL | Arqule Inc. | 0.0% | Biotechnology |

**TABLE A.3   Vanguard Healthcare ETF (VHT)**
**Expense Ratio (0.25%)   Holdings (30 September 2009) (cont.)**

| Ticker Symbol | Name | Weight | Sector |
|---|---|---|---|
| NPSP | NPS Pharmaceuticals Inc. | 0.0% | Biotechnology |
| POZN | Pozen Inc. | 0.0% | Pharmaceuticals |
| VTAL | Vital Images Inc. | 0.0% | Medical Imaging Systems |
| SQNM | Sequenom Inc. | 0.0% | Biotechnology |
| MAXY | Maxygen Inc. | 0.0% | Biotechnology |
| PTIE | Pain Therapeutics Inc. | 0.0% | Pharmaceuticals |
| NHWK | Nighthawk Radiology Holdings Inc. | 0.0% | MRI/Medical Diagnostic Imaging |
| LXRX | Lexicon Pharmaceuticals Inc. | 0.0% | Biotechnology |
| SKH | Skilled Healthcare Group Inc. | 0.0% | Nursing Homes |
| CHDX | Chindex International Inc. | 0.0% | Distribution/Wholesale |
| PGNX | Progenics Pharmaceuticals Inc. | 0.0% | Pharmaceuticals |
| SYNO | Synovis Life Technologies Inc. | 0.0% | Medical Products |
| ENSG | Ensign Group Inc. | 0.0% | Nursing Homes |
| TOMO | TomoTherapy Inc. | 0.0% | Medical Products |
| AIQ | Alliance HealthCare Services Inc. | 0.0% | MRI/Medical Diagnostic Imaging |
| MDTH | Medcath Corp. | 0.0% | Hospitals |
| OPK | Opko Health Inc. | 0.0% | Pharmaceuticals |
| MAPP | MAP Pharmaceuticals Inc. | 0.0% | Pharmaceuticals |
| MAKO | MAKO Surgical Corp. | 0.0% | Surgical Instruments |
| STXS | Stereotaxis Inc. | 0.0% | Medical Instruments |

**TABLE A.3   Vanguard Healthcare ETF (VHT)**
**Expense Ratio (0.25%)   Holdings (30 September 2009) (cont.)**

| Ticker Symbol | Name | Weight | Sector |
|---|---|---|---|
| SRZ | Sunrise Senior Living Inc. | 0.0% | Retirement/Aged Care |
| MYRX | Myriad Pharmaceuticals Inc. | 0.0% | Pharmaceuticals |
| OSUR | OraSure Technologies Inc. | 0.0% | Diagnostic Kits |
| EXAC | Exactech Inc. | 0.0% | Medical Products |
| ATSI | ATS Medical Inc. | 0.0% | Medical Products |
| CYNO | Cynosure Inc. Class A | 0.0% | Medical Laser Systems |
| NBIX | Neurocrine Biosciences Inc. | 0.0% | Therapeutics |
| XOMA | XOMA Ltd. | 0.0% | Biotechnology |
| ARRY | Array Biopharma Inc. | 0.0% | Pharmaceuticals |
| KV/a | KV Pharmaceutical Co. Class A | 0.0% | Pharmaceuticals |
| OSIR | Osiris Therapeutics Inc. | 0.0% | Therapeutics |
| VRAD | Virtual Radiologic Corp. | 0.0% | MRI/Medical Diagnostic Imaging |
| BEAT | CardioNet Inc. | 0.0% | Patient Monitoring Equip |
| HNSN | Hansen Medical Inc. | 0.0% | Diagnostic Equipment |
| LIFE | Life Sciences Research Inc. | 0.0% | Biotechnology |
| AKRX | Akorn Inc. | 0.0% | Pharmaceuticals |
| IDIX | Idenix Pharmaceuticals Inc. | 0.0% | Pharmaceuticals |
| FOLD | Amicus Therapeutics Inc. | 0.0% | Pharmaceuticals |
| CPD | Caraco Pharmaceutical Laboratories Ltd. | 0.0% | Pharmaceuticals |
| SCMP | Sucampo Pharmaceuticals Inc. Class A | 0.0% | Pharmaceuticals |

**TABLE A.4   Healthcare Select Sector SPDR (XLV)**
**Expense Ratio (0.22%)   Holdings (18 December 2009)**

| Ticker Symbol | Name | Weight | Sector |
|---|---|---|---|
| JNJ | Johnson & Johnson | 14.16% | Pharmaceuticals |
| PFE | Pfizer Inc. | 11.77% | Pharmaceuticals |
| MRK | Merck & Co Inc. | 9.11% | Pharmaceuticals |
| ABT | Abbott Labs | 5.58% | Pharmaceuticals |
| AMGN | Amgen Inc. | 4.5% % | Biotechnology |
| MDT | Medtronic Inc. | 3.83% | Medical Equipment |
| BMY | Bristol-Myers Squibb Co. | 3.59% | Pharmaceuticals |
| GILD | Gilead Sciences Inc. | 3.07% | Biotechnology |
| UNH | Unitedhealth Group Inc. | 2.95% | HMO |
| LLY | Eli Lilly & Co. | 2.88% | Pharmaceuticals |
| BAX | Baxter Intl Inc. | 2.81% | Medical Products |
| MHS | Medco Health Solutions Inc. | 2.47% | Wholesale Drug Distribution |
| WLP | Wellpoint Inc. | 2.2% | HMO |
| CELG | Celgene Corp. | 2.05% | Biotechnology |
| ESRX | Express Scripts Inc. | 1.95% | Pharmacy Services |
| TMO | Thermo Fisher Scientific Inc. | 1.57% | Medical Equipment |
| AGN | Allergan Inc. | 1.53% | Pharmaceuticals |
| BDX | Becton Dickinson & Co. | 1.46% | Medical Products |
| MCK | Mckesson Corp. | 1.39% | Wholesale Drug Distribution |
| BIIB | Biogen Idec Inc. | 1.18% | Biotechnology |

**TABLE A.4  Healthcare Select Sector SPDR (XLV)
Expense Ratio (0.22%)  Holdings (18 December 2009) (cont.)**

| Ticker Symbol | Name | Weight | Sector |
|---|---|---|---|
| SYK | Stryker Corp. | 1.16% | Medical Equipment |
| AET | Aetna Inc. | 1.15% | HMO |
| BSX | Boston Scientific Corp. | 1.08% | Medical Equipment |
| GENZ | Genzyme Corp. | 1.06% | Biotechnology |
| STJ | St Jude Med Inc. | 1.01% | Medical Equipment |
| ZMH | Zimmer Hldgs Inc. | 1.01% | Medical Equipment |
| CAH | Cardinal Health Inc. | 0.94% | Wholesale Drug Distributor |

**TABLE A.5  iShares Dow Jones U.S. Healthcare Sector Index Fund (IYH)
Expense Ratio (0.48%)  Holdings (30 November 2009)**

| Ticker Symbol | Name | Weight | Sector |
|---|---|---|---|
| JNJ | Johnson & Johnson | 12.54% | Pharmaceuticals |
| PFE | Pfizer Inc. | 10.56% | Pharmaceuticals |
| MRK | Merck & Co. Inc. | 7.96% | Pharmaceuticals |
| ABT | Abbott Laboratories | 6.05% | Pharmaceuticals |
| AMGN | Amgen Inc. | 4.11% | Biotechnology |
| BMY | Bristol-Myers Squibb Co. | 3.59% | Pharmaceuticals |
| MDT | Medtronic Inc. | 3.4% | Medical Equipment |
| GILD | Gilead Sciences Inc. | 3.02% | Biotechnology |
| LLY | Eli Lilly & Co. | 2.6% | Pharmaceuticals |

**TABLE A.5    iShares Dow Jones U.S. Healthcare Sector Index Fund (IYH)
Expense Ratio (0.48%)    Holdings (30 November 2009) (cont.)**

| Ticker Symbol | Name | Weight | Sector |
|---|---|---|---|
| UNH | UnitedHealth Group Inc. | 2.4% | HMO |
| BAX | Baxter International Inc. | 2.38% | Medical Products |
| MHS | Medco Health Solutions Inc. | 2.16% | Pharmacy Services |
| WLP | Wellpoint Inc. | 1.85% | HMO |
| CELG | Celgene Corp. | 1.84% | Biotechnology |
| COV | Covidien Plc. | 1.7% | Medical Products |
| ESRX | Express Scripts Inc. | 1.57% | Pharmacy Services |
| TMO | Thermo Fisher Scientific Inc. | 1.39% | Medical Equipment |
| AGN | Allergan Inc. | 1.29% | Pharmaceuticals |
| BDX | Becton Dickinson & Co. | 1.22% | Medical Products |
| SYK | Stryker Corp. | 1.11% | Healthcare Equipment & Services |
| GENZ | Genzyme Corp. | 0.99% | Biotechnology |
| BIIB | Biogen Idec Inc. | 0.98% | Biotechnology |
| ZMH | Zimmer Holdings Inc. | 0.92% | Medical Equipment |
| AET | Aetna Inc. | 0.92% | HMO |
| STJ | St Jude Medical Inc. | 0.91% | Medical Equipment |
| BSX | Boston Scientific Corp. | 0.91% | Medical Equipment |
| ACL | Alcon Inc. | 0.81% | Optical Supplies |
| ISRG | Intuitive Surgical Inc. | 0.77% | Medical Equipment |

# Biotechnology

**TABLE A.6   iShares Nasdaq Biotech Index Fund (IBB)**
**Expense Ratio (0.48%)   Holdings (30 November 2009)**

| Ticker Symbol | Name | Weight | Sector |
|---|---|---|---|
| AMGN | Amgen Inc. | 10.58% | Biotechnology |
| GILD | Gilead Sciences Inc. | 8.48% | Biotechnology |
| TEVA | Teva Pharmaceutical-SP ADR | 7.78% | Pharmaceuticals |
| CELG | Celgene Corp. | 6.52% | Biotechnology |
| VRTX | Vertex Pharmaceuticals Inc. | 3.96% | Biotechnology |
| BIIB | Biogen Idec Inc. | 3.08% | Biotechnology |
| GENZ | Genzyme Corp. | 2.78% | Biotechnology |
| ALXN | Alexion Pharmaceuticals Inc. | 2.48% | Biotechnology |
| MYL | Mylan Inc. | 2.28% | Pharmaceuticals |
| WCRX | Warner Chilcott Plc-Class A | 2.27% | Therapeutics |
| LIFE | Life Technologies Corp. | 2.27% | Biotechnology |
| PRGO | Perrigo Co. | 2.16% | Pharmaceuticals |
| ILMN | Illumina Inc. | 1.95% | Biotechnology |
| DNDN | Dendreon Corp. | 1.89% | Biotechnology |
| QGEN | Qiagen N.V. | 1.8% | Diagnostic Kits |
| SHPGY | Shire Plc-ADR | 1.75% | Pharmaceuticals |
| UTHR | United Therapeutics Corp. | 1.67% | Biotechnology |
| HGSI | Human Genome Sciences Inc. | 1.48% | Biotechnology |
| ONXX | Onyx Pharmaceuticals Inc. | 1.46% | Therapeutics |
| REGN | Regeneron Pharmaceuticals | 1.27% | Biotechnology |

**TABLE A.6   iShares Nasdaq Biotech Index Fund (IBB)**
**Expense Ratio (0.48%)   Holdings (30 November 2009) (cont.)**

| Ticker Symbol | Name | Weight | Sector |
|---|---|---|---|
| MYGN | Myriad Genetics Inc. | 1.25% | Biotechnology |
| BMRN | Biomarin Pharmaceutical Inc. | 1.21% | Therapeutics |
| CEPH | Cephalon Inc. | 1.09% | Pharmaceuticals |
| OSIP | OSI Pharmaceuticals Inc. | 1.04% | Biotechnology |
| TECH | Techne Corp. | 0.96% | Medical Instruments |
| AUXL | Auxilium Pharmaceuticals Inc. | 0.95% | Pharmaceuticals |
| GPRO | Gen-Probe Inc. | 0.83% | Diagnostic Equipment |
| VRUS | Pharmasset Inc. | 0.81% | Pharmaceuticals |
| ENDP | Endo Pharmaceutical Holdings Inc. | 0.75% | Pharmaceuticals |
| SLXP | Salix Pharmaceuticals Ltd. | 0.74% | Pharmaceuticals |
| INCY | Incyte Corp. | 0.69% | Biotechnology |
| CBST | Cubist Pharmaceuticals Inc. | 0.68% | Biotechnology |
| MDVN | Medivation Inc. | 0.63% | Pharmaceuticals |
| ISIS | Isis Pharmaceuticals Inc. | 0.62% | Therapeutics |
| NKTR | Nektar Therapeutics | 0.61% | Drug Delivery Systems |
| EXEL | Exelixis Inc. | 0.59% | Biotechnology |
| AMLN | Amylin Pharmaceuticals Inc. | 0.58% | Biotechnology |
| MNKD | Mannkind Corp. | 0.57% | Therapeutics |
| ACOR | Acorda Therapeutics Inc. | 0.54% | Biotechnology |

**TABLE A.6   iShares Nasdaq Biotech Index Fund (IBB)**
**Expense Ratio (0.48%)   Holdings (30 November 2009) (cont.)**

| Ticker Symbol | Name | Weight | Sector |
|---|---|---|---|
| SGEN | Seattle Genetics Inc. /WA | 0.53% | Biotechnology |
| SVNT | Savient Pharmaceuticals Inc. | 0.49% | Pharmaceuticals |
| IPXL | Impax Laboratories Inc. | 0.47% | Pharmaceuticals |
| ITMN | Intermune Inc. | 0.46% | Biotechnology |
| THRX | Theravance Inc. | 0.45% | Therapeutics |
| ALKS | Alkermes Inc. | 0.45% | Drug Delivery Systems |
| ALNY | Alnylam Pharmaceuticals Inc. | 0.43% | Biotechnology |
| AMAG | Amag Pharmaceuticals Inc. | 0.4% | Biotechnology |
| ISPH | Inspire Pharmaceuticals Inc. | 0.38% | Therapeutics |
| ALTH | Allos Therapeutics Inc. | 0.37% | Therapeutics |
| GERN | Geron Corp. | 0.36% | Biotechnology |
| ENZN | Enzon Pharmaceuticals Inc. | 0.35% | Biotechnology |
| PDLI | PDL BioPharma Inc. | 0.35% | Biotechnology |
| LMNX | Luminex Corp. | 0.35% | Medical Products |
| GHDX | Genomic Health Inc. | 0.35% | Medical Instruments |
| TRGT | Targacept Inc. | 0.34% | Pharmaceuticals |
| VPHM | Viropharma Inc. | 0.34% | Pharmaceuticals |
| VVUS | Vivus Inc. | 0.33% | Pharmaceuticals |
| XNPT | Xenoport Inc | 0.31% | Pharmaceuticals |
| CRA | Celera Corp. | 0.31% | Biotechnology |

**TABLE A.6   iShares Nasdaq Biotech Index Fund (IBB)**
**Expense Ratio (0.48%)   Holdings (30 November 2009) (cont.)**

| Ticker Symbol | Name | Weight | Sector |
|---|---|---|---|
| ZGEN | Zymogenetics Inc. | 0.3% | Biotechnology |
| HALO | Halozyme Therapeutics Inc. | 0.3% | Biotechnology |
| MNTA | Momenta Pharmaceuticals Inc. | 0.28% | Biotechnology |
| MITI | Micromet Inc. | 0.27% | Biotechnology |
| FACT | Facet Biotech Corp. | 0.25% | Biotechnology |
| RIGL | Rigel Pharmaceuticals Inc. | 0.24% | Pharmaceuticals |
| CADX | Cadence Pharmaceuticals Inc. | 0.24% | Pharmaceuticals |
| OPTR | Optimer Pharmaceuticals Inc. | 0.23% | Pharmaceuticals |
| NABI | Nabi Biopharmaceuticals | 0.22% | Therapeutics |
| IMGN | Immunogen Inc. | 0.21% | Biotechnology |
| CRXL | Crucell-ADR | 0.21% | Biotechnology |
| OREX | Orexigen Therapeutics Inc. | 0.19% | Pharmaceuticals |
| AMRI | Albany Molecular Research | 0.19% | Research & Development |
| BCRX | Biocryst Pharmaceuticals Inc. | 0.19% | Biotechnology |
| MDCO | Medicines Company | 0.18% | Biotechnology |
| QCOR | Questcor Pharmaceuticals | 0.18% | Therapeutics |
| AFFX | Affymetrix Inc. | 0.18% | Diagnostic Equipment |
| QLTI | QLT Inc. | 0.18% | Therapeutics |
| DYAX | Dyax Corp. | 0.18% | Therapeutics |

**TABLE A.6 iShares Nasdaq Biotech Index Fund (IBB)**
**Expense Ratio (0.48%) Holdings (30 November 2009) (cont.)**

| Ticker Symbol | Name | Weight | Sector |
|---|---|---|---|
| OMPI | Obagi Medical Products Inc. | 0.17% | Wound, Burn, & Skin Care |
| CRME | Cardiome Pharma Corporation | 0.17% | Pharmaceuticals |
| NVAX | Novavax Inc. | 0.17% | Biotechnology |
| ARNA | Arena Pharmaceuticals Inc. | 0.16% | Biotechnology |
| SQNM | Sequenom Inc. | 0.16% | Biotechnology |
| LGND | Ligand Pharmaceuticals-Cl B | 0.15% | Biotechnology |
| ARIA | Ariad Pharmaceuticals Inc. | 0.15% | Biotechnology |
| SIGA | SIGA Technologies Inc. | 0.15% | Pharmaceuticals |
| IMMU | Immunomedics Inc. | 0.15% | Biotechnology |
| OSIR | Osiris Therapeutics Inc. | 0.15% | Therapeutics |
| SGMO | Sangamo Biosciences Inc. | 0.14% | Biotechnology |
| POZN | Pozen Inc. | 0.14% | Pharmaceuticals |
| CYPB | Cypress Bioscience Inc. | 0.14% | Therapeutics |
| BMTI | Biomimetic Therapeutics Inc. | 0.14% | Medical Products |
| SNTS | Santarus Inc. | 0.14% | Pharmaceuticals |
| LXRX | Lexicon Pharmaceuticals Inc. | 0.12% | Biotechnology |
| VNDA | Vanda Pharmaceuticals Inc. | 0.12% | Pharmaceuticals |
| MAXY | Maxygen Inc. | 0.12% | Biotechnology |
| FLML | Flamel Technologies-Sp ADR | 0.11% | Drug Delivery Systems |
| CSKI | China Sky One Medical Inc. | 0.11% | Pharmaceuticals |

**TABLE A.6   iShares Nasdaq Biotech Index Fund (IBB)**
**Expense Ratio (0.48%)   Holdings (30 November 2009) (cont.)**

| Ticker Symbol | Name | Weight | Sector |
|---|---|---|---|
| DRRX | Durect Corporation | 0.11% | Pharmaceuticals |
| DEPO | Depomed Inc. | 0.11% | Drug Delivery Systems |
| CYTK | Cytokinetics Inc. | 0.11% | Biotechnology |
| PTIE | Pain Therapeutics Inc. | 0.11% | Pharmaceuticals |
| AKRX | Akorn Inc. | 0.09% | Pharmaceuticals |
| SUPG | Supergen Inc. | 0.09% | Biotechnology |
| BJGP | BMP Sunstone Corp. | 0.09% | Distribution/Wholesale |
| XOMA | Xoma Ltd. | 0.09% | Biotechnology |
| GTXI | GTx Inc. | 0.09% | Biotechnology |
| HITK | Hi-Tech Pharmacal Co Inc. | 0.09% | Pharmaceuticals |
| SPPI | Spectrum Pharmaceuticals Inc. | 0.09% | Therapeutics |
| NPSP | NPS Pharmaceuticals Inc. | 0.09% | Biotechnology |
| ARQL | Arqule Inc. | 0.08% | Biotechnology |
| PGNX | Progenics Pharmaceuticals | 0.08% | Pharmaceuticals |
| STEM | StemCells Inc. | 0.07% | Biotechnology |
| ADLR | Adolor Corporation | 0.07% | Pharmaceuticals |
| IDIX | Idenix Pharmaceuticals Inc. | 0.06% | Pharmaceuticals |
| DSCO | Discovery Laboratories Inc. | 0.06% | Biotechnology |
| BIOD | Biodel Inc. | 0.06% | Pharmaceuticals |
| PARD | Poniard Pharmaceuticals Inc. | 0.05% | Pharmaceuticals |
| VICL | Vical Inc. | 0.04% | Biotechnology |

**TABLE A.6  iShares Nasdaq Biotech Index Fund (IBB)**
**Expense Ratio (0.48%)  Holdings (30 November 2009) (cont.)**

| Ticker Symbol | Name | Weight | Sector |
|---|---|---|---|
| ALXA | Alexza Pharmaceuticals Inc. | 0.04% | Therapeutics |
| | BGIF Treasury Money Market SL Agency Shares | 0.04% | S-T Securities |
| ARRY | Array Biopharma Inc. | 0.04% | Pharmaceuticals |
| SNTA | Synta Pharmaceuticals Corp. | 0.04% | Pharmaceuticals |
| NBIX | Neurocrine Biosciences Inc. | 0.03% | Therapeutics |
| CBRX | Columbia Laboratories Inc. | 0.03% | Feminine Healthcare Prd. |
| MBRK | Middlebrook Pharmaceuticals | 0.01% | Pharmaceuticals |

**TABLE A.7  SPDR S&P Biotech ETF (XBI)**
**Expense Ratio (0.35%)  Holdings (18 December 2009)**

| Ticker Symbol | Name | Weight | Sector |
|---|---|---|---|
| REGN | Regeneron Pharmaceuticals | 4.22% | Biotechnology |
| UTHR | United Therapeutics Corp. | 4.17% | Biotechnology |
| INCY | Incyte Corp. | 4.10% | Biotechnology |
| BMRN | Biomarin Pharmaceutical Inc. | 4.07% | Therapeutics |
| MDVN | Medivation Inc. | 4.00% | Pharmaceuticals |
| AMLN | Amylin Pharmaceuticals Inc. | 3.99% | Biotechnology |
| VRTX | Vertex Pharmaceuticals Inc. | 3.97% | Biotechnology |
| CELG | Celgene Corp. | 3.97% | Biotechnology |

**TABLE A.7    SPDR S&P Biotech ETF (XBI)**
**Expense Ratio (0.35%)    Holdings (18 December 2009) (cont.)**

| Ticker Symbol | Name | Weight | Sector |
|---|---|---|---|
| SGEN | Seattle Genetics Inc. | 3.92% | Biotechnology |
| CBST | Cubist Pharmaceuticals Inc. | 3.89% | Biotechnology |
| ACOR | Acorda Therapeutics Inc. | 3.87% | Biotechnology |
| BIIB | Biogen Idec Inc. | 3.85% | Biotechnology |
| ALXN | Alexion Pharmaceuticals Inc. | 3.82% | Biotechnology |
| DNDN | Dendreon Corp. | 3.81% | Biotechnology |
| ALKS | Alkermes Inc. | 3.78% | Drug Delivery Systems |
| HGSI | Human Genome Sciences Inc. | 3.75% | Biotechnology |
| CEPH | Cephalon Inc. | 3.75% | Pharmaceuticals |
| MYGN | Myriad Genetics Inc. | 3.73% | Biotechnology |
| ISIS | Isis Pharmaceuticals Inc. | 3.72% | Therapeutics |
| SVNT | Savient Pharmaceuticals Inc. | 3.72% | Pharmaceuticals |
| AMGN | Amgen Inc. | 3.71% | Biotechnology |
| GENZ | Genzyme Corp. | 3.67% | Biotechnology |
| EXEL | Exelixis Inc. | 3.63% | Biotechnology |
| ONXX | Onyx Pharmaceuticals Inc. | 3.52% | Therapeutics |
| GILD | Gilead Sciences Inc. | 3.45% | Biotechnology |
| OSIP | OSI Pharmaceuticals Inc. | 3.34% | Biotechnology |
| CASH_USD | U.S. Dollar | 0.52% | Unassigned |
| 85749P9A | State Street Institutional Liquid Reserves | 0.08% | Unassigned |

**TABLE A.8  PowerShares Dynamic Biotechnology and Genome Portfolio (PBE)**
**Expense Ratio (0.63%)  Holdings (21 December 2009)**

| Ticker Symbol | Name | Weight | Sector |
|---|---|---|---|
| BIIB | Biogen Idec Inc. | 5.17% | Biotechnology |
| ALXN | Alexion Pharmaceuticals Inc. | 5.08% | Biotechnology |
| MIL | Millipore Corp. | 5.00% | Medical Equipment |
| LIFE | Life Technologies Corp. | 4.91% | Biotechnology |
| WAT | Waters Corp. | 4.90% | Medical Equipment |
| AMGN | Amgen Inc. | 4.76% | Biotechnology |
| GILD | Gilead Sciences Inc. | 4.40% | Biotechnology |
| AFFX | Affymetrix Inc. | 3.15% | Diagnostic Equipment |
| REGN | Regeneron Pharmaceuticals Inc. | 3.14% | Biotechnology |
| AFFY | Affymax Inc. | 3.07% | Biotechnology |
| ITMN | InterMune Inc. | 3.00% | Biotechnology |
| ISPH | Inspire Pharmaceuticals Inc. | 2.98% | Therapeutics |
| EXEL | Exelixis Inc. | 2.94% | Biotechnology |
| CBST | Cubist Pharmaceuticals Inc. | 2.92% | Biotechnology |
| AMLN | Amylin Pharmaceuticals Inc. | 2.87% | Biotechnology |
| VPHM | ViroPharma Inc. | 2.87% | Pharmaceuticals |
| ZGEN | ZymoGenetics Inc. | 2.84% | Biotechnology |
| NEOG | Neogen Corp. | 2.83% | Veterinary Diagnostics |
| ALKS | Alkermes Inc. | 2.81% | Drug Delivery Systems |
| BRKR | Bruker Corp. | 2.73% | Medical Equipment |

**TABLE A.8   PowerShares Dynamic Biotechnology and Genome Portfolio (PBE)**
**Expense Ratio (0.63%)   Holdings (21 December 2009) (cont.)**

| Ticker Symbol | Name | Weight | Sector |
|---|---|---|---|
| INCY | Incyte Corp. | 2.69% | Biotechnology |
| DNEX | Dionex Corp. | 2.66% | Instruments - Scientific |
| PDLI | PDL BioPharma Inc. | 2.65% | Biotechnology |
| VRUS | Pharmasset Inc. | 2.65% | Pharmaceuticals |
| TECH | Techne Corp. | 2.62% | Medical Instruments |
| NKTR | Nektar Therapeutics | 2.62% | Drug Delivery Systems |
| TRGT | Targacept Inc. | 2.50% | Pharmaceuticals |
| OSIP | OSI Pharmaceuticals Inc. | 2.38% | Biotechnology |
| EBS | Emergent Biosolutions Inc. | 2.30% | Biotechnology |
| SIAL | Sigma-Aldrich Corp. | 4.56% | Materials |

# Medical Devices

**TABLE A.9   iShares Dow Jones U.S. Medical Devices Index Fund (IHI)**
**Total Expense Ratio (0.48%)   Holdings (30 November 2009)**

| Ticker Symbol | Name | Weight | Sector |
|---|---|---|---|
| MDT | Medtronic Inc. | 12.1% | Medical Equipment |
| TMO | Thermo Fisher Scientific Inc. | 7.52% | Medical Equipment |
| SYK | Stryker Corp. | 6.83% | Medical Equipment |
| ZMH | Zimmer Holdings Inc. | 6.34% | Medical Equipment |
| STJ | St Jude Medical Inc. | 5.69% | Medical Equipment |
| ISRG | Intuitive Surgical Inc. | 5.62% | Medical Equipment |

**TABLE A.9   iShares Dow Jones U.S. Medical Devices Index Fund (IHI)
Total Expense Ratio (0.48%)   Holdings (30 November 2009) (cont.)**

| Ticker Symbol | Name | Weight | Sector |
| --- | --- | --- | --- |
| BSX | Boston Scientific Corp. | 5.09% | Medical Equipment |
| VAR | Varian Medical Systems Inc. | 3.97% | Medical Equipment |
| WAT | Waters Corp. | 3.92% | Medical Equipment |
| BEC | Beckman Coulter Inc. | 3.18% | Medical Equipment |
| RMD | Resmed Inc. | 3.13% | Medical Equipment |
| MIL | Millipore Corp. | 3.00% | Medical Equipment |
| KCI | Kinetic Concepts Inc. | 2.13% | Medical Equipment |
| BIO | Bio-Rad Laboratories-CL A | 2.08% | Medical Equipment |
| STE | Steris Corp. | 2.07% | Medical Equipment |
| THOR | Thoratec Corp. | 1.98% | Medical Equipment |
| VARI | Varian Inc. | 1.79% | Medical Equipment |
| AMMD | American Medical Sys Holdings | 1.70% | Medical Equipment |
| HRC | Hill-Rom Holdings | 1.70% | Medical Equipment |
| MASI | Masimo Corporation | 1.68% | Medical Equipment |
| BLUD | Immucor Inc. | 1.65% | Medical Equipment |
| NUVA | Nuvasive Inc. | 1.41% | Medical Equipment |
| EVVV | Ev3 Inc. | 1.31% | Medical Equipment |
| IVC | Invacare Corp. | 1.31% | Medical Equipment |
| WMGI | Wright Medical Group Inc. | 1.17% | Medical Equipment |
| IART | Integra LifeSciences Holding | 1.13% | Medical Equipment |

**TABLE A.9   iShares Dow Jones U.S. Medical Devices Index Fund (IHI)**
**Total Expense Ratio (0.48%)   Holdings (30 November 2009) (cont.)**

| Ticker Symbol | Name | Weight | Sector |
|---|---|---|---|
| CPHD | Cepheid Inc. | 1.13% | Medical Equipment |
| ZOLL | Zoll Medical Corp. | 1.07% | Medical Equipment |
| BRKR | Bruker Biosciences Corp. | 1.06% | Medical Equipment |
| VOLC | Volcano Corp. | 1.03% | Medical Equipment |
| ALOG | Analogic Corp. | 1.01% | Medical Equipment |
| SIRO | Sirona Dental Systems Inc. | 0.99% | Medical Equipment |
| SONO | Sonosite Inc. | 0.80% | Medical Equipment |
| BABY | Natus Medical Inc. | 0.77% | Medical Equipment |
| OMCL | Omnicell Inc. | 0.71% | Medical Equipment |
| ABMD | Abiomed Inc. | 0.69% | Medical Equipment |
| SMA | Symmetry Medical Inc. | 0.57% | Medical Equipment |
| ARAY | Accuray Inc. | 0.52% | Medical Equipment |
|  | BGIF Treasury Money Market SL Agency Shares | 0.05% | S-T Securities |

# B

# Green ETFs

## Clean Energy

**TABLE B.1    PowerShares WilderHill Clean Energy Portfolio (PBW)
Expense Ratio (0.69%)    Holdings (24 December 2009)**

| Ticker Symbol | Name | Weight | Sector |
|---|---|---|---|
| FSYS | Fuel Systems Solutions Inc. | 1.99% | Auto/Truck Parts & Equipment—Original |
| BLDP | Ballard Power Systems Inc. | 1.16% | Consumer Discretionary |
| ARGN | Amerigon Inc. | 0.59% | Consumer Discretionary |
| QTWW | Quantum Fuel Systems Technologies Worldwide Inc. | 0.32% | Consumer Discretionary |
| RZ | Raser Technologies Inc. | 0.31% | Consumer Discretionary |
| CZZ | Cosan Ltd. (Cl A) | 2.21% | Consumer Staples |
| GU | Gushan Environmental Energy Ltd. | 0.35% | Energy |
| JASO | JA Solar Holdings Co. Ltd. (ADS) | 3.78% | Industrials |
| AMSC | American Superconductor Corp. | 3.51% | Industrials |
| YGE | Yingli Green Energy Holding Co. Ltd. (ADS) | 3.25% | Industrials |
| BWEN | Broadwind Energy Inc. | 2.93% | Industrials |
| STP | Suntech Power Holdings Co. Ltd. (ADS) | 2.68% | Industrials |
| SOLR | GT Solar International Inc. | 2.50% | Industrials |
| PWR | Quanta Services Inc. | 2.45% | Industrials |

**TABLE B.1    PowerShares WilderHill Clean Energy Portfolio (PBW)
Expense Ratio (0.69%)    Holdings (24 December 2009) (cont.)**

| Ticker Symbol | Name | Weight | Sector |
|---|---|---|---|
| ENER | Energy Conversion Devices Inc. | 2.22% | Industrials |
| FSLR | First Solar Inc. | 2.21% | Industrials |
| ESLR | Evergreen Solar Inc. | 2.17% | Industrials |
| HEV | Ener1 Inc. | 1.88% | Industrials |
| ABAT | Advanced Battery Technologies Inc. | 1.76% | Industrials |
| CBAK | China BAK Battery Inc. | 1.15% | Industrials |
| FCEL | FuelCell Energy Inc. | 1.11% | Industrials |
| VLNC | Valence Technology Inc. | 1.06% | Industrials |
| OPTT | Ocean Power Technologies Inc. | 0.87% | Industrials |
| SPIR | Spire Corp. | 0.48% | Industrials |
| UQM | UQM Technologies Inc. | 0.47% | Industrials |
| PLUG | Plug Power Inc. | 0.41% | Industrials |
| BCON | Beacon Power Corp. | 0.32% | Industrials |
| ASTI | Ascent Solar Technologies Inc. | 0.30% | Industrials |
| CREE | Cree Inc. | 3.95% | Information Technology |
| RBCN | Rubicon Technology Inc. | 3.66% | Information Technology |
| IRF | International Rectifier Corp. | 2.89% | Information Technology |
| PANL | Universal Display Corp. | 2.84% | Information Technology |
| ITRI | Itron Inc. | 2.74% | Information Technology |
| AMAT | Applied Materials Inc. | 2.68% | Information Technology |
| COMV | Comverge Inc. | 2.42% | Information Technology |
| ELON | Echelon Corp. | 2.42% | Information Technology |
| SOL | ReneSola Ltd. (ADS) | 2.38% | Information Technology |
| SPWRA | SunPower Corp. (Cl A) | 2.01% | Information Technology |

**TABLE B.1    PowerShares WilderHill Clean Energy Portfolio (PBW) Expense Ratio (0.69%)   Holdings (24 December 2009) (cont.)**

| Ticker Symbol | Name | Weight | Sector |
|---|---|---|---|
| WFR | MEMC Electronic Materials Inc. | 1.97% | Information Technology |
| MXWL | Maxwell Technologies Inc. | 1.90% | Information Technology |
| EMKR | EMCORE Corp. | 0.38% | Information Technology |
| APD | Air Products & Chemicals Inc. | 2.30% | Materials |
| ZOLT | Zoltek Cos. | 2.27% | Materials |
| OMG | OM Group Inc. | 2.13% | Materials |
| SQM | Sociedad Quimica y Minera de Chile S.A. (ADS) | 1.95% | Materials |
| TSL | Trina Solar Ltd. (ADS) | 4.41% | Energy—Alternate Sources |
| ORA | Ormat Technologies Inc. | 2.52% | Independent Power Producer |
| CPL | CPFL Energia S.A. (ADS) | 1.95% | Utilities |
| IDA | IDACORP Inc. | 1.92% | Utilities |
| POR | Portland General Electric Co. | 1.74% | Utilities |
| CPN | Calpine Corp. | 1.65% | Utilities |
| HTM | U.S. Geothermal Inc. | 0.50% | Utilities |

**TABLE B.2    Market Vectors Global Alternative Energy ETF (GEX) Expense Ratio (0.62%)   Holdings (24 December 2009)**

| Ticker Symbol | Name | Weight | Sector |
|---|---|---|---|
| VWS DC | Vestas Wind Systems A/S | 9.11% | Industrials |
| FSLR | First Solar Inc. | 6.62% | Industrials |
| CREE | Cree Inc. | 5.99% | Information Technology |
| IBR SM | Iberdrola Renovables S.A. | 4.93% | Utilities |
| 6370 JP | Kurita Water Industries Ltd. | 4.70% | Industrials |

**TABLE B.2  Market Vectors Global Alternative Energy ETF (GEX)**
**Expense Ratio (0.62%)  Holdings (24 December 2009) (cont.)**

| Ticker Symbol | Name | Weight | Sector |
|---|---|---|---|
| WFR | MEMC Electronic Materials Inc. | 4.28% | Information Technology |
| GAM SM | Gamesa Corp Tecnologica S.A. | 4.26% | Industrials |
| VER AV | Verbund - Oesterreichische Elektrizitaetswirtschafts AG | 4.05% | Energy—Alternate Sources |
| ITRI | Itron Inc. | 4.01% | Information Technology |
| REC NO | Renewable Energy Corp AS | 3.64% | Industrials |
| CVA | Covanta Holding Corp. | 3.63% | Energy-Alternate Sources |
| EDPR PL | EDP Renovaveis S.A. | 3.31% | Energy-Alternate Sources |
| STP | Suntech Power Holdings Co. Ltd. | 3.26% | Industrials |
| TSL | Trina Solar Ltd. | 3.08% | Energy—Alternate Sources |
| AMSC | American Superconductor Corp. | 3.02% | Industrials |
| SWV GR | Solarworld AG | 2.98% | Electronic Components— Semiconductors |
| IRF | International Rectifier Corp. | 2.81% | Information Technology |
| YGE | Yingli Green Energy Holding Co. Ltd. | 2.69% | Industrials |
| CZZ | Cosan Ltd. | 2.60% | Consumer Staples |
| SPWRA | Sunpower Corp. | 2.55% | Information Technology |
| VECO US | Veeco Instruments Inc. | 2.52% | Semiconductor Equipment |
| S92 GR | SMA Solar Technology A.G. | 2.22% | Power Conversion/Supply Equipment |
| EEN FP | EDF Energies Nouvelles S.A. | 2.06% | Energy—Alternate Sources |

**TABLE B.2    Market Vectors Global Alternative Energy ETF (GEX)
Expense Ratio (0.62%)    Holdings (24 December 2009) (cont.)**

| Ticker Symbol | Name | Weight | Sector |
|---|---|---|---|
| 1072 HK | Dongfang Electric Corp Ltd. | 2.00% | Power Conversion/Supply Equipment |
| ENS US | EnerSys | 1.95% | Industrials |
| QCE GR | Q-Cells AG | 1.92% | Power Conversion/Supply Equipment |
| ORA | Ormat Technologies Inc. | 1.58% | Independent Power Producer |
| FSYS | Fuel Systems Solutions Inc. | 1.42% | Auto/Truck Parts & Equipment - Original |
| NDX1 GR | Nordex AG | 1.38% | Energy-Alternate Sources |
| ENER | Energy Conversion Devices Inc. | 1.27% | Power Conversion/Supply Equipment |
| | Cash | 0.36% | |

# Natural Gas

**TABLE B.3    Market Vectors Nuclear Energy ETF (FCG)
Expense Ratio (0.60%)    Holdings (24 December 2009)**

| Ticker Symbol | Name | Weight | Sector |
|---|---|---|---|
| DPTR | Delta Petroleum Corporation | 4.44% | Oil Companies—Exploration and Production |
| BEXP | Brigham Exploration Company | 3.82% | Oil Companies—Exploration and Production |
| NFX | Newfield Exploration Company | 3.55% | Oil Companies—Exploration and Production |

**TABLE B.3   Market Vectors Nuclear Energy ETF (FCG)**
**Expense Ratio (0.60%)   Holdings (24 December 2009) (cont.)**

| Ticker Symbol | Name | Weight | Sector |
|---|---|---|---|
| RRC | Range Resources Corporation | 3.54% | Oil Companies—Exploration and Production |
| SWN | Southwestern Energy Company | 3.54% | Oil Companies—Exploration and Production |
| PQ | PetroQuest Energy, Inc. | 3.52% | Oil Companies—Exploration and Production |
| PXD | Pioneer Natural Resources Company | 3.52% | Oil Companies—Exploration and Production |
| KWK | Quicksilver Resources Inc. | 3.52% | Oil Companies—Exploration and Production |
| CHK | Chesapeake Energy Corporation | 3.50% | Oil Companies—Exploration and Production |
| COG | Cabot Oil & Gas Corporation | 3.46% | Oil Companies—Exploration and Production |
| EOG | EOG Resources, Inc. | 3.39% | Oil Companies—Exploration and Production |
| FST | Forest Oil Corporation | 3.39% | Oil Companies—Exploration and Production |
| ECA | EnCana Corp. | 3.36% | Oil Companies—Exploration and Production |
| HK | PetroHawk Energy Corporation | 3.31% | Oil Companies—Exploration and Production |
| DVN | Devon Energy Corporation | 3.31% | Oil Companies—Exploration and Production |
| XCO | EXCO Resources, Inc. | 3.31% | Oil Companies—Exploration and Production |
| UPL | Ultra Petroleum Corp. | 3.29% | Oil Companies—Exploration and Production |
| XTO | XTO Energy, Inc. | 3.29% | Oil Companies—Exploration and Production |
| XEC | Cimarex Energy Co. | 3.28% | Oil Companies—Exploration and Production |

**TABLE B.3   Market Vectors Nuclear Energy ETF (FCG)**
**Expense Ratio (0.60%)   Holdings (24 December 2009) (cont.)**

| Ticker Symbol | Name | Weight | Sector |
|---|---|---|---|
| AAV | Advantage Oil & Gas Ltd. | 3.26% | Oil Companies—Exploration and Production |
| APA | Apache Corporation | 3.21% | Oil Companies—Exploration and Production |
| APC | Anadarko Petroleum Corporation | 3.21% | Oil Companies—Exploration and Production |
| LINE | Linn Energy, LLC | 3.21% | Oil Companies—Exploration and Production |
| TLM | Talisman Energy Inc. | 3.19% | Oil Companies—Exploration and Production |
| NBL | Noble Energy, Inc. | 3.18% | Oil Companies—Exploration and Production |
| STR | Questar Corporation | 3.16% | Oil Companies—Exploration and Production |
| SGY | Stone Energy Corporation | 3.15% | Oil Companies—Exploration and Production |
| RDS/A | Royal Dutch Shell Plc. (ADR) | 2.98% | Oil Companies—Integrated |
| CVX | Chevron Corporation | 2.89% | Oil Companies—Integrated |
| ME | Mariner Energy Inc. | 2.75% | Oil Companies—Exploration and Production |
| MISXX | Morgan Stanley Institutional Liquidity Fund | 1.46% | |

# Wind Power

**TABLE B.4　FirstTrust Global Wind Energy ETF (FAN)
Expense Ratio (0.60%)　Holdings (24 December 2009)**

| Ticker Symbol | Name | Weight | Sector |
|---|---|---|---|
| EDPR.PL | EDP Renovaveis SA | 7.79% | Energy—Alternate Sources |
| IBR.SM | Iberdrola Renovables | 7.30% | Utilities |
| VWS.DC | Vestas Wind Systems | 6.75% | Industrials |
| RPW.GY | REpower Systems AG | 5.92% | Power Conversion/Supply Equipment |
| GAM.SM | Gamesa Corporacion Tecnologica, S.A. (Gamesa) | 5.58% | Industrials |
| HSN.LN | Hansen Transmissions | 5.53% | Industrials |
| BWEN | Broadwind Energy, Inc. | 5.16% | Industrials |
| IFN.AU | Infigen Energy | 4.61% | Energy—Alternate Sources |
| NDX1.GY | Nordex AG | 4.39% | Energy—Alternate Sources |
| FRS.SM | Fersa Energias Renovables SA | 3.08% | Energy—Alternate Sources |
| CWP.LN | Clipper Windpower PLC | 2.89% | Energy—Alternate Sources |
| 2766.JP | Japan Wind Development Co., Ltd. | 2.82% | Energy—Alternate Sources |
| PNE3.GY | PNE Wind | 1.77% | Energy—Alternate Sources |
| WIND.LN | Renewable Energy Generation | 1.75% | Energy—Alternate Sources |
| ELE.SM | Endesa, S.A. | 1.46% | Electric Utilities |
| BP | BP Plc (ADR) | 1.44% | Oil Companies—Integrated |
| TEO.FP | Theolia S.A. | 1.44% | Energy—Alternate Sources |
| RDS/A | Royal Dutch Shell Plc (ADR) | 1.43% | Oil Companies—Integrated |
| SI | Siemens AG (ADR) | 1.42% | Industrials |
| EOAN.GY | E.ON AG | 1.42% | Electric Utilities |

**TABLE B.4   FirstTrust Global Wind Energy ETF (FAN)
Expense Ratio (0.60%)   Holdings (24 December 2009) (cont.)**

| Ticker Symbol | Name | Weight | Sector |
|---|---|---|---|
| 8031.JP | Mitsui & Co., Ltd. | 1.41% | Import/Export |
| GES.DC | Greentech Energy Systems | 1.39% | Energy—Alternate Sources |
| GE | General Electric Company | 1.35% | Diversified Manufacturing |
| DE | Deere & Company | 1.20% | Machinery—Farm |
| AES | The AES Corporation | 1.19% | Electric Utilities |
| ANA.SM | Acciona S.A. | 1.19% | Building—Heavy Construction |
| ALO.FP | Alstom | 1.11% | Machinery—General Industry |
| EDP.PL | Energias De Portugal S.A. | 1.09% | Gas, Water, & Multiutilities |
| DUK | Duke Energy Corporation | 1.08% | Gas, Water, & Multiutilities |
| FPL | FPL Group, Inc. | 1.05% | Electric Utilities |
| ATI | Allegheny Technologies, Inc. | 1.05% | Machinery—General Industry |
| EBR | Centrais Eletricas Brasileiras S.A. | 1.04% | Electric Utilities |
| LNT | Alliant Energy Corporation | 0.86% | Energy—Alternate Sources |
| SKFB.SS | AB SKF | 0.85% | Metal Processors & Fabricators |
| BKWN.SW | BKW FMB Energie Ag | 0.84% | Electric Utilities |
| AGK.AU | AGL Energy Limited | 0.84% | Electric Utilities |
| 658.HK | China High Speed Transmission Equipment Group Co., Ltd. | 0.83% | Power Conversion/Supply Equipment |
| EEN.FP | EDF Energies Nouvelles S.A. | 0.83% | Energy—Alternate Sources |
| NRG | NRG Energy Inc. | 0.82% | Electric Utilities |

**TABLE B.4    FirstTrust Global Wind Energy ETF (FAN)**
**Expense Ratio (0.60%)    Holdings (24 December 2009) (cont.)**

| Ticker Symbol | Name | Weight | Sector |
|---|---|---|---|
| MISXX | Morgan Stanley Institutional Liquidity Fund | 0.72% | |
| FDML | Federal-Mogul Corporation | 0.67% | Auto/Truck Parts & Equipment—Original |
| AMSC | American Superconductor Corporation | 0.62% | Industrials |
| WGOV | Woodward Governor Company | 0.60% | Instruments—Controls |
| KDN | Kaydon Corporation | 0.56% | Metal Processors & Fabricators |
| BRC-U.CN | Brookfield Renewable Power Fund | 0.56% | Electric—Generation |
| TRN | Trinity Industries, Inc. | 0.55% | Diversified Manufacturing |
| 182.HK | China WindPower Group Limited | 0.54% | Energy—Alternate Sources |
| TENERGY.GA | Terna Energy S.A. | 0.52% | Energy—Alternate Sources |
| ZOLT | Zoltek Companies, Inc. | 0.25% | Chemicals—Fibers |
| AMN | Ameron International Corporation | 0.25% | Diversified Manufacturing |
| BLX.CN | Boralex Inc. | 0.25% | Electric—Transmission |
| OTTR | Otter Tail Corporation | 0.24% | Electric Utilities |
| CPST | Capstone Turbine Corporation | 0.22% | Power Conversion/Supply Equipment |
| GUR.SW | Gurit Holding AG | 0.22% | Chemicals—Specialty |
| 1133.HK | Harbin Power Equipment Company Ltd. | 0.21% | Power Conversion/Supply Equipment |
| CGY.GY | Conergy AG | 0.20% | Power Conversion/Supply Equipment |

# Solar Energy

**TABLE B.5   Claymore/MAC Global Solar Energy Index ETF (TAN)
Expense Ratio (0.70%)   Holdings (24 December 2009)**

| Ticker Symbol | Name | Weight | Sector |
|---|---|---|---|
| FSLR | First Solar Inc. | 8.17% | Industrials |
| REC | Renewable Energy Corp. AS | 6.08% | Industrials |
| STP | Suntech Power Holdings ADR | 5.46% | Industrials |
| TSL | Trina Solar Ltd-Spon ADR | 5.42% | Energy—Alternate Sources |
| SWV | Solarworld AG | 4.98% | Electronic Components—Semiconductors |
| WFR | Memc Electronic Materials Inc. | 4.91% | Information Technology |
| YGE | Yingli Green Energy - ADR | 4.82% | Industrials |
| SPWRA | Sunpower Corp-A | 4.62% | Information Technology |
| CSIQ | Canadian Solar Inc. | 4.08% | Power Conversion/Supply Equipment |
| JASO | JA Solar Holdings Co. Ltd. | 4.07% | Industrials |
| S92 | SMA Solar Technology | 4.02% | Power Conversion/Supply Equipment |
| QCE | Q-Cells AG | 3.59% | Power Conversion/Supply |
| MBTN | Meyer Burger Technology AG | 3.36% | Industrials |
| S2M | Solar Millennium AG | 3.21% | Energy—Alternate Sources |
| R8R | Roth & Rau AG | 3.01% | Industrials |
| CTN | Centrotherm Photovoltaics | 2.89% | Industrials |
| ENER | Energy Conversion Devices | 2.67% | Power Conversion/Supply Equipment |
| PS4 | Phoenix Solar AG | 2.64% | Power Conversion/Supply Equipment |
| SOL | Renesola Ltd. - ADR | 2.48% | Information Technology |
| ESLR | Evergreen Solar Inc. | 2.28% | Industrials |

**TABLE B.5   Claymore/MAC Global Solar Energy Index ETF (TAN)
Expense Ratio (0.70%)   Holdings (24 December 2009) (cont.)**

| Ticker Symbol | Name | Weight | Sector |
|---|---|---|---|
| PVCS | PV Crystalox Solar Plc. | 2.20% | Electronic Components—Semiconductors |
| M5Z | Manz Automation AG | 2.14% | Industrial Automation/Robotics |
| SOLF | Solarfun Power Holdings Co. | 1.86% | Energy—Alternate Sources |
| LDK | LDK Solar Co. Ltd.-ADR | 1.85% | Electronic Components—Semiconductors |
| SOLR | GT Solar Int. Inc. | 1.72% | Electronic Components—Semiconductors |
| CGY | Conergy AG | 1.61% | Power Conversion/Supply Equipment |
| SLR | Solaria Energia Y Medio Ambiente SA | 1.59% | Power Conversion/Supply Equipment |
| CSUN | China Sunergy Co. Ltd. | 1.56% | Energy—Alternate Sources |
| 757 | Solargiga Energy Holdings Ltd. | 1.42% | Electronic Components—Semiconductors |
| SOO1 | Solon SE | 1.28% | Power Conversion/Supply Equipment |

# Nuclear Energy

**TABLE B.6   Market Vectors Nuclear Energy ETF (NLR)
Expense Ratio (0.61%)   Holdings (24 December 2009)**

| Ticker Symbol | Name | Weight | Sector |
|---|---|---|---|
| CEG | Constellation Energy Group Inc. | 8.47% | Electric Utilities |
| CCJ | Cameco Corp. | 8.44% | Non-Ferrous Metals |
| 7011 JP | Mitsubishi Heavy Industries Ltd. | 7.98% | Machinery—General Industry |
| EDF FP | EDF | 7.90% | Electric Utilities |

**TABLE B.6    Market Vectors Nuclear Energy ETF (NLR)
Expense Ratio (0.61%)    Holdings (24 December 2009) (cont.)**

| Ticker Symbol | Name | Weight | Sector |
|---|---|---|---|
| EXC | Exelon Corp. | 7.60% | Electric Utilities |
| PDN AU | Paladin Energy Ltd. | 4.52% | Non-Ferrous Metals |
| ERA AU | Energy Resources of Australia Ltd. | 4.48% | Non-Ferrous Metals |
| 1963 JP | JGC Corp. | 4.44% | Engineering/R&D Services |
| UUU CN | Uranium One Inc. | 4.40% | Non-Ferrous Metals |
| CEI FP | Areva SA | 4.36% | Energy—Alternate Sources |
| U CN | Uranium Participation Corp. | 4.22% | Sector Fund—Energy |
| FRG CN | Fronteer Development Group Inc. | 3.69% | Diversified Minerals |
| DML CN | Denison Mines Corp. | 3.48% | Non-Ferrous Metals |
| USU | USEC Inc. | 3.45% | Non-Ferrous Metals |
| 7013 JP | IHI Corp. | 3.05% | Machinery—General Industry |
| 1968 JP | Taihei Dengyo Kaisha Ltd. | 2.99% | Engineering/R&D Services |
| 1812 JP | Kajima Corp. | 2.81% | Building & Construction—Miscellaneous |
| FIU CN | First Uranium Corp. | 2.69% | Metal-Diversfied |
|  | Cash | 2.51% |  |
| ECOL | American Ecology Corp. | 2.40% | Hazardous Waste Disposal |
| FSY CN | Forsys Metals Corp. | 2.38% | Non-Ferrous Metals |
| CV | Central Vermont Public Service Corp. | 1.88% | Electric Utilities |
| 1983 JP | Toshiba Plant Systems & Services Corp. | 1.65% | Engineering/R&D Services |
| UEX CN | Uex Corp. | 1.52% | Non-Ferrous Metals |
| HAT CN | Hathor Exploration Ltd. | 1.11% | Non-Ferrous Metals |

# Clean Tech

**TABLE B.7   PowerShares Cleantech Portfolio (PZD)**
**Expense Ratio (0.67%)   Holdings (24 December 2009)**

| Ticker Symbol | Name | Weight | Sector |
|---|---|---|---|
| FSYS | Fuel Systems Solutions Inc. | 0.80% | Auto/Truck Parts & Equipment—Original |
| °WPT | Westport Innovations Inc. | 0.33% | Consumer Discretionary |
| DNEX | Dionex Corp. | 1.24% | Healthcare |
| MATK | Martek Biosciences Corp. | 0.61% | Healthcare |
| 483410 | Schneider Electric S.A. | 2.93% | Industrials |
| 572797 | Siemens AG | 2.86% | Industrials |
| 710889 | ABB Ltd. | 2.74% | Industrials |
| ROP | Roper Industries Inc. | 2.34% | Industrials |
| DCI | Donaldson Co. Inc. | 2.28% | Industrials |
| PLL | Pall Corp. | 2.28% | Industrials |
| FSLR | First Solar Inc. | 2.12% | Industrials |
| 6370 | Kurita Water Industries Ltd. | 2.05% | Industrials |
| 596465 | Vestas Wind Systems A/S | 1.99% | Industrials |
| STP | Suntech Power Holdings Co. Ltd. (ADS) | 1.93% | Industrials |
| SPW | SPX Corp. | 1.85% | Industrials |
| B01VHW | Renewable Energy Corp. ASA | 1.77% | Industrials |
| B1YC2B | China High Speed Transmission Equipment Group Co. Ltd. | 1.64% | Industrials |
| B01CP2 | Gamesa Corporacion Tecnologica S.A. | 1.64% | Industrials |
| WGOV | Woodward Governor Co. | 1.55% | Instruments-Controls |
| AMSC | American Superconductor Corp. | 1.55% | Industrials |
| CLC | CLARCOR Inc. | 1.48% | Industrials |

**TABLE B.7 PowerShares Cleantech Portfolio (PZD)**
**Expense Ratio (0.67%) Holdings (24 December 2009) (cont.)**

| Ticker Symbol | Name | Weight | Sector |
|---|---|---|---|
| TTEK | Tetra Tech Inc. | 1.48% | Industrials |
| BEZ | Baldor Electric Co. | 1.46% | Industrials |
| 576920 | ARCADIS N.V. | 1.36% | Industrials |
| 449123 | Kingspan Group PLC | 1.27% | Industrials |
| HXL | Hexcel Corp. | 1.26% | Industrials |
| ENS | EnerSys Inc. | 1.10% | Industrials |
| B2885W | centrotherm photovoltaics AG | 1.06% | Industrials |
| ESE | ESCO Technologies Inc. | 1.04% | Industrials |
| INSU | Insituform Technologies Inc. (Cl A) | 0.93% | Industrials |
| B09YFD | Saft Groupe S.A. | 0.90% | Industrials |
| B0FBSD | Solar Millennium AG | 0.83% | Industrials |
| 473087 | Tomra Systems ASA | 0.77% | Industrials |
| 19520 | Chloride Group PLC | 0.76% | Industrials |
| SOLR | GT Solar International Inc. | 0.75% | Industrials |
| 597264 | Eurofins Scientific SE | 0.74% | Industrials |
| B142TD | Roth & Rau AG | 0.72% | Industrials |
| B1HDMD | Meyer Burger Technology AG | 0.69% | Industrials |
| LNN | Lindsay Corp. | 0.67% | Industrials |
| BMI | Badger Meter Inc. | 0.66% | Industrials |
| ERII | Energy Recovery Inc. | 0.63% | Industrials |
| B291RX | Hansen Transmissions International N.V. | 0.58% | Industrials |
| IFSIA | Interface Inc. (Cl A) | 0.58% | Industrials |
| KAI | Kadant Inc. | 0.56% | Industrials |
| 411905 | BWT AG | 0.55% | Industrials |

**TABLE B.7   PowerShares Cleantech Portfolio (PZD)**
**Expense Ratio (0.67%)   Holdings (24 December 2009) (cont.)**

| Ticker Symbol | Name | Weight | Sector |
|---|---|---|---|
| PPO | Polypore International Inc. | 0.55% | Industrials |
| 5857 | Asahi Holdings Inc. | 0.55% | Industrials |
| ENOC | EnerNOC Inc. | 0.52% | Industrials |
| °WFI | WaterFurnace Renewable Energy Inc. | 0.50% | Industrials |
| B1Y4GT | Grontmij N.V. | 0.50% | Industrials |
| ENER | Energy Conversion Devices Inc. | 0.48% | Power Conversion/Supply Equipment |
| FTEK | Fuel Tech Inc. | 0.36% | Industrials |
| AONE | A123 Systems Inc. | 0.27% | Industrials |
| GLW | Corning Inc. | 3.47% | Information Technology |
| CREE | Cree Inc. | 3.16% | Information Technology |
| ADSK | Autodesk Inc. | 2.44% | Information Technology |
| ANSS | Ansys Inc. | 2.39% | Information Technology |
| 728344 | Tandberg ASA | 2.27% | Information Technology |
| ITRI | Itron Inc. | 1.99% | Information Technology |
| TRMB | Trimble Navigation Ltd. | 1.99% | Information Technology |
| WFR | MEMC Electronic Materials Inc. | 1.57% | Information Technology |
| SPWRA | SunPower Corp. (Cl A) | 1.45% | Information Technology |
| TLVT | Telvent GIT S.A. | 1.06% | Information Technology |
| 6856 | Horiba Ltd. | 1.01% | Information Technology |
| POWI | Power Integrations Inc. | 0.94% | Information Technology |
| 593235 | Vaisala Oyj | 0.42% | Information Technology |
| °RCM | RuggedCom Inc. | 0.42% | Information Technology |
| 465853 | Novozymes A/S | 2.50% | Materials |

**TABLE B.7  PowerShares Cleantech Portfolio (PZD)**
**Expense Ratio (0.67%)  Holdings (24 December 2009)  (cont.)**

| Ticker Symbol | Name | Weight | Sector |
|---|---|---|---|
| NLC | Nalco Holding Co. | 2.37% | Materials |
| ZOLT | Zoltek Cos. | 0.46% | Materials |
| 570379 | Gurit Holding AG | 0.43% | Materials |
| B01JC5 | Plant Health Care PLC | 0.22% | Materials |
| B0LMC5 | Accsys Technologies PLC | 0.17% | Materials |
| B29NWR | Iberdrola Renovables S.A. | 2.54% | Utilities |
| ORA | Ormat Technologies Inc. | 1.38% | Independent Power Producer |
| B1GHQN | Energy Development Corp. | 1.37% | Utilities |
| 632005 | Hyflux Ltd. | 0.91% | Utilities |

# C

## Infrastructure ETFs

Note: We recommend using Bloomberg.com to look up ticker symbols.

## Utilities

**TABLE C.1    Utilities Select SPDR Fund (XLU)**
**Expense Ratio (0.22%)   Holdings (23 December 2009)**

| Ticker Symbol | Name | Weight | Sector |
|---|---|---|---|
| EXC | Exelon Corp. | 8.8% | Electric Utilities |
| SO | Southern Co. | 7.2% | Electric Utilities |
| D | Dominion Res. Inc. | 6.32% | Electric Utilities |
| FPL | FPL Group Inc. | 5.91% | Electric Utilities |
| DUK | Duke Energy Corp. | 5.61% | Gas, Water, & Multiutilities |
| PEG | Public Svc. Enterprise Group | 4.54% | Electric Utilities |
| PCG | PG&E Corp. | 4.51% | Electric Utilities |
| AEP | American Elec. Pwr. Inc. | 4.5% | Electric Utilities |
| ETR | Entergy Corp. | 4.23% | Electric Utilities |
| FE | FirstEnergy Corp. | 3.9% | Electric Utilities |
| SRE | Sempra Energy | 3.76% | Gas, Water, & Multiutilities |
| ED | Consolidated Edison Inc. | 3.47% | Electric Utilities |
| PPL | PPL Corp. | 3.31% | Electric Utilities |

**TABLE C.1    Utilities Select SPDR Fund (XLU)**
**Expense Ratio (0.22%)    Holdings (23 December 2009) (cont.)**

| Ticker Symbol | Name | Weight | Sector |
|---|---|---|---|
| EIX | Edison Intl. | 3.12% | Electric Utilities |
| PGN | Progress Energy Inc. | 3.12% | Electric Utilities |
| XEL | Xcel Energy Inc. | 2.66% | Electric Utilities |
| AES | AES Corp. | 2.52% | Electric Utilities |
| STR | Questar Corp. | 2.02% | Gas, Water, & Multiutilities |
| DTE | DTE Energy Co. | 1.98% | Electric Utilities |
| CEG | Constellation Energy Group | 1.96% | Electric Utilities |
| AEE | Ameren Corp. | 1.82% | Gas, Water, & Multiutilities |
| CNP | Centerpoint Energy Inc. | 1.57% | Gas, Water, & Multiutilities |
| EQT | EQT Corp. | 1.57% | Gas, Water, & Multiutilities |
| WEC | Wisconsin Energy Corp. | 1.56% | Gas, Water, & Multiutilities |
| NU | Northeast Utils. | 1.23% | Electric Utilities |
| NI | Nisource Inc. | 1.18% | Gas, Water, & Multiutilities |
| SCG | SCANA Corp. | 1.13% | Gas, Water, & Multiutilities |
| AYE | Allegheny Energy Inc. | 1.11% | Electric Utilities |
| PNW | Pinnacle West Cap Corp. | 1.04% | Electric Utilities |
| POM | Pepco Holdings Inc. | 1.03% | Electric Utilities |
| CMS | CMS Energy Corp. | 1% | Electric Utilities |
| TE | Teco Energy Inc. | 0.98% | Electric Utilities |
| 85749P9A | State Street Instl. Liquid Resvs. | 0.97% | Unassigned |
| TEG | Integrys Energy Group Inc. | 0.89% | Gas, Water, & Multiutilities |
| GAS | Nicor Inc. | 0.54% | Gas, Water, & Multiutilities |
| CASH_ USD | U.S. Dollar | -1.11% | Unassigned |

**TABLE C.2  iShares DJ U.S. Utility Sector Index Fund (IDU)**
**Expense Ratio (0.48%)   Holdings (30 November 2009)**

| Ticker Symbol | Name | Weight | Sector |
|---|---|---|---|
| EXC | Exelon Corp. | 7.26% | Electric Utilities |
| SO | Southern Co. | 5.83% | Electric Utilities |
| DUK | Duke Energy Corp. | 4.9% | Gas, Water, & Multiutilities |
| D | Dominion Resources Inc./Va | 4.9% | Electric Utilities |
| FPL | FPL Group Inc. | 4.46% | Electric Utilities |
| PEG | Public Service Enterprise GP | 3.64% | Electric Utilities |
| PCG | PG&E Corp. | 3.58% | Electric Utilities |
| ETR | Entergy Corp. | 3.52% | Electric Utilities |
| AEP | American Electric Power | 3.5% | Electric Utilities |
| FE | FirstEnergy Corp. | 3% | Electric Utilities |
| SE | Spectra Energy Corp. | 2.8% | Gas, Water, & Multiutilities |
| SRE | Sempra Energy | 2.75% | Gas, Water, & Multiutilities |
| ED | Consolidated Edison Inc. | 2.68% | Electric Utilities |
| PPL | PPL Corporation | 2.59% | Electric Utilities |
| PGN | Progress Energy Inc. | 2.49% | Electric Utilities |
| EIX | Edison International | 2.33% | Electric Utilities |
| XEL | Xcel Energy Inc. | 2.11% | Electric Utilities |
| AES | AES Corp. | 1.94% | Electric Utilities |
| STR | Questar Corp. | 1.56% | Gas, Water, & Multiutilities |
| DTE | DTE Energy Company | 1.5% | Electric Utilities |
| NRG | NRG Energy Inc. | 1.45% | Electric Utilities |
| CEG | Constellation Energy Group | 1.31% | Electric Utilities |
| AEE | Ameren Corporation | 1.27% | Gas, Water, & Multiutilities |
| WEC | Wisconsin Energy Corp. | 1.21% | Gas, Water, & Multiutilities |

**TABLE C.2   iShares DJ U.S. Utility Sector Index Fund (IDU)**
**Expense Ratio (0.48%)   Holdings (30 November 2009) (cont.)**

| Ticker Symbol | Name | Weight | Sector |
|---|---|---|---|
| EQT | EQT Corp. | 1.16% | Gas, Water, & Multiutilities |
| CNP | Centerpoint Energy Inc. | 0.98% | Gas, Water, & Multiutilities |
| NU | Northeast Utilities | 0.96% | Electric Utilities |
| CPN | Calpine Corp. | 0.95% | Independent Power Producer |
| OKE | Oneok Inc. | 0.9% | Gas, Water, & Multiutilities |
| NI | Nisource Inc. | 0.89% | Gas, Water, & Multiutilities |
| SCG | SCANA Corp. | 0.88% | Gas, Water, & Multiutilities |
| AYE | Allegheny Energy Inc. | 0.85% | Electric Utilities |
| POM | Pepco Holdings Inc. | 0.82% | Electric Utilities |
| NST | NSTAR | 0.81% | Electric Utilities |
| PNW | Pinnacle West Capital | 0.81% | Electric Utilities |
| CMS | CMS Energy Corp. | 0.74% | Electric Utilities |
| NFG | National Fuel Gas Co. | 0.72% | Gas, Water, & Multiutilities |
| DPL | DPL Inc. | 0.71% | Electric Utilities |
| LNT | Alliant Energy Corp. | 0.69% | Electric Utilities |
| TEG | Integrys Energy Group Inc. | 0.67% | Gas, Water, & Multiutilities |
| TE | Teco Energy Inc. | 0.67% | Electric Utilities |
| NVE | NV Energy Inc. | 0.62% | Electric Utilities |
| AGL | AGL Resources Inc. | 0.6% | Gas, Water, & Multiutilities |
| UGI | UGI Corp. | 0.58% | Gas, Water, & Multiutilities |
| ATO | Atmos Energy Corp. | 0.57% | Gas, Water, & Multiutilities |
| GXP' | Great Plains Energy Inc. | 0.55% | Electric Utilities |
| WR | Westar Energy Inc. | 0.51% | Electric Utilities |

**TABLE C.2   iShares DJ U.S. Utility Sector Index Fund (IDU)
Expense Ratio (0.48%)   Holdings (30 November 2009) (cont.)**

| Ticker Symbol | Name | Weight | Sector |
|---|---|---|---|
| CVA | Covanta Holding Corp. | 0.51% | Electric Utilities |
| WTR | Aqua America Inc. | 0.51% | Gas, Water, & Multiutilities |
| ITC | ITC Holdings Corp. | 0.5% | Electric Utilities |
| MIR | Mirant Corp. | 0.47% | Independent Power Producer |
| AWK | American Water Works Co. Inc. | 0.46% | Gas, Water, & Multiutilities |
| VVC | Vectren Corporation | 0.44% | Gas, Water, & Multiutilities |
| HE | Hawaiian Electric Inds. | 0.42% | Electric Utilities |
| GAS | Nicor Inc. | 0.4% | Gas, Water, & Multiutilities |
| RRI | RRI Energy Inc. | 0.39% | Electric Utilities |
| PNY | Piedmont Natural Gas Co. | 0.37% | Gas, Water, & Multiutilities |
| WGL | WGL Holdings Inc. | 0.36% | Gas, Water, & Multiutilities |
| CNL | Cleco Corporation | 0.35% | Electric Utilities |
| NJR | New Jersey Resources Corp. | 0.34% | Gas, Water, & Multiutilities |
| POR | Portland General Electric Co. | 0.34% | Electric Utilities |
| IDA | Idacorp Inc. | 0.32% | Electric Utilities |
| SWX | Southwest Gas Corp. | 0.27% | Gas, Water, & Multiutilities |
| NWN | Northwest Natural Gas Co. | 0.26% | Gas, Water, & Multiutilities |
| AVA | Avista Corp. | 0.26% | Gas, Water, & Multiutilities |
| SJI | South Jersey Industries | 0.25% | Gas, Water, & Multiutilities |
| UNS | Unisource Energy Corp. | 0.24% | Electric Utilities |
| ALE | Allete Inc. | 0.22% | Electric Utilities |
| NWE | Northwestern Corp. | 0.21% | Electric Utilities |
| BKH | Black Hills Corp. | 0.21% | Electric Utilities |

**TABLE C.2   iShares DJ U.S. Utility Sector Index Fund (IDU)**
**Expense Ratio (0.48%)   Holdings (30 November 2009) (cont.)**

| Ticker Symbol | Name | Weight | Sector |
|---|---|---|---|
| DYN | Dynegy Inc-Cl A | 0.21% | Electric Utilities |
| EE | El Paso Electric Co. | 0.21% | Electric Utilities |
| PNM | PNM Resources Inc. | 0.2% | Gas, Water, & Multiutilities |
| CWT | California Water Service Grp. | 0.16% | Gas, Water, & Multiutilities |
| LG | Laclede Group Inc./The | 0.15% | Gas, Water, & Multiutilities |
| | BGIF Treasury Money Market Sl Agency Shares | 0.12% | S-T Securities |

**TABLE C.3   Vanguard Utilities ETF (VPU)**
**Expense Ratio (0.25%)   Holdings (30 September 2009)**

| Ticker Symbol | Name | Weight | Sector |
|---|---|---|---|
| EXC | Exelon Corp. | 7.50% | Electric Utilities |
| SO | Southern Co. | 5.70% | Electric Utilities |
| FPL | FPL Group Inc. | 4.90% | Electric Utilities |
| D | Dominion Resources Inc. | 4.60% | Electric Utilities |
| DUK | Duke Energy Corp. | 4.60% | Gas, Water, & Multiutilities |
| PEG | Public Service Enterprise Group Inc. | 3.60% | Electric Utilities |
| ETR | Entergy Corp. | 3.60% | Electric Utilities |
| PCG | PG&E Corp. | 3.40% | Electric Utilities |
| AEP | American Electric Power Co. Inc. | 3.40% | Electric Utilities |
| FE | FirstEnergy Corp. | 3.20% | Electric Utilities |
| SRE | Sempra Energy | 2.60% | Gas, Water, & Multiutilities |
| PPL | PPL Corp. | 2.60% | Electric Utilities |

**TABLE C.3    Vanguard Utilities ETF (VPU)**
**Expense Ratio (0.25%)   Holdings (30 September 2009) (cont.)**

| Ticker Symbol | Name | Weight | Sector |
|---|---|---|---|
| ED | Consolidated Edison Inc. | 2.60% | Electric Utilities |
| PGN | Progress Energy Inc. | 2.50% | Electric Utilities |
| EIX | Edison International | 2.40% | Electric Utilities |
| AES | AES Corp. | 2.30% | Electric Utilities |
| XEL | Xcel Energy Inc. | 2.00% | Electric Utilities |
| NRG | NRG Energy Inc. | 1.70% | Electric Utilities |
| STR | Questar Corp. | 1.50% | Gas, Water, & Multiutilities |
| AEE | Ameren Corp. | 1.30% | Gas, Water, & Multiutilities |
| CEG | Constellation Energy Group Inc. | 1.30% | Electric Utilities |
| DTE | DTE Energy Co. | 1.30% | Electric Utilities |
| EQT | EQT Corp. | 1.20% | Gas, Water, & Multiutilities |
| WEC | Wisconsin Energy Corp. | 1.20% | Gas, Water, & Multiutilities |
| CNP | Centerpoint Energy Inc. | 1.00% | Gas, Water, & Multiutilities |
| AYE | Allegheny Energy Inc. | 1.00% | Electric Utilities |
| NU | Northeast Utilities | 0.90% | Electric Utilities |
| SCG | SCANA Corp. | 0.90% | Gas, Water, & Multiutilities |
| CPN | Calpine Corp. | 0.90% | Electric Utilities |
| NI | NiSource Inc. | 0.90% | Gas, Water & Multiutilities |
| OKE | Oneok Inc. | 0.80% | Gas, Water & Multiutilities |
| MDU | MDU Resources Group Inc. | 0.80% | Electric Utilities |
| NST | NSTAR | 0.80% | Electric Utilities |
| PNW | Pinnacle West Capital Corp. | 0.80% | Electric Utilities |
| NFG | National Fuel Gas Co. | 0.70% | Gas, Water, & Multiutilities |
| POM | Pepco Holdings Inc. | 0.70% | Electric Utilities |

**TABLE C.3   Vanguard Utilities ETF (VPU)**
**Expense Ratio (0.25%)   Holdings (30 September 2009) (cont.)**

| Ticker Symbol | Name | Weight | Sector |
|---|---|---|---|
| OGE | OGE Energy Corp. | 0.70% | Electric Utilities |
| LNT | Alliant Energy Corp. | 0.70% | Electric Utilities |
| CMS | CMS Energy Corp. | 0.70% | Electric Utilities |
| DPL | DPL Inc. | 0.70% | Electric Utilities |
| EGN | Energen Corp. | 0.70% | Gas, Water, & Multiutilities |
| TE | TECO Energy Inc. | 0.70% | Electric Utilities |
| TEG | Integrys Energy Group Inc. | 0.60% | Gas, Water, & Multiutilities |
| AGL | AGL Resources Inc. | 0.60% | Gas, Water, & Multiutilities |
| NVE | NV Energy Inc. | 0.60% | Electric Utilities |
| UGI | UGI Corp. | 0.60% | Gas, Water, & Multiutilities |
| AWK | American Water Works Co. Inc. | 0.60% | Gas, Water, & Multiutilities |
| ATO | Atmos Energy Corp. | 0.60% | Gas, Water, & Multiutilities |
| RRI | RRI Energy Inc. | 0.60% | Electric Utilities |
| GXP | Great Plains Energy Inc. | 0.50% | Electric Utilities |
| WTR | Aqua America Inc. | 0.50% | Gas, Water & Multiutilities |
| MIR | Mirant Corp. | 0.50% | Independent Power Producers |
| ITC | ITC Holdings Corp. | 0.50% | Electric Utilities |
| WR | Westar Energy Inc. | 0.50% | Electric Utilities |
| VVC | Vectren Corp. | 0.40% | Gas, Water, & Multiutilities |
| PNY | Piedmont Natural Gas Co. Inc. | 0.40% | Gas, Water, & Multiutilities |
| WGL | WGL Holdings Inc. | 0.40% | Gas, Water, & Multiutilities |
| HE | Hawaiian Electric Industries Inc. | 0.40% | Electric Utilities |
| GAS | Nicor Inc. | 0.40% | Gas, Water, & Multiutilities |

**TABLE C.3    Vanguard Utilities ETF (VPU)**
**Expense Ratio (0.25%)    Holdings (30 September 2009) (cont.)**

| Ticker Symbol | Name | Weight | Sector |
|---|---|---|---|
| NJR | New Jersey Resources Corp. | 0.30% | Gas, Water, & Multiutilities |
| CNL | Cleco Corp. | 0.30% | Electric Utilities |
| POR | Portland General Electric Co. | 0.30% | Electric Utilities |
| IDA | IDACORP Inc. | 0.30% | Electric Utilities |
| DYN | Dynegy Inc. Class A | 0.30% | Electric Utilities |
| SWX | Southwest Gas Corp. | 0.30% | Gas, Water, & Multiutilities |
| AVA | Avista Corp. | 0.30% | Gas, Water, & Multiutilities |
| NWN | Northwest Natural Gas Co. | 0.30% | Gas, Water, & Multiutilities |
| UNS | Unisource Energy Corp. | 0.30% | Electric Utilities |
| SJI | South Jersey Industries Inc. | 0.20% | Gas, Water, & Multiutilities |
| PNM | PNM Resources Inc. | 0.20% | Gas, Water, & Multiutilities |
| BKH | Black Hills Corp. | 0.20% | Electric Utilities |
| ALE | Allete Inc. | 0.20% | Electric Utilities |
| NEW | NorthWestern Corp. | 0.20% | Electric Utilities |
| MGEE | MGE Energy Inc. | 0.20% | Electric Utilities |
| ORA | Ormat Technologies Inc. | 0.20% | Independent Power Producer |
| EE | El Paso Electric Co. | 0.20% | Electric Utilities |
| CWT | California Water Service Group | 0.20% | Gas, Water, & Multiutilities |
| UIL | UIL Holdings Corp. | 0.20% | Electric Utilities |
| CHG | CH Energy Group Inc. | 0.20% | Gas, Water, & Multiutilities |
| LG | Laclede Group Inc. | 0.20% | Gas, Water, & Multiutilities |
| AWR | American States Water Co. | 0.20% | Gas, Water, & Multiutilities |
| EDE | Empire District Electric Co. | 0.10% | Gas, Water, & Multiutilities |

TABLE C.3    Vanguard Utilities ETF (VPU)
Expense Ratio (0.25%)    Holdings (30 September 2009) (cont.)

| Ticker Symbol | Name | Weight | Sector |
|---|---|---|---|
| SJW | SJW Corp. | 0.10% | Gas, Water, & Multiutilities |
| CWCO | Consolidated Water Co. Inc. | 0.10% | Gas, Water, & Multiutilities |
| CV | Central Vermont Public Service Corp. | 0.10% | Electric Utilities |
|  | Chesapeake Utilities Corp. | 0.00% | Gas, Water, & Multiutilities |
| MSEX | Middlesex Water Co. | 0.00% | Gas, Water, & Multiutilities |
| CTWS | Connecticut Water Service Inc. | 0.00% | Gas, Water, & Multiutilities |

TABLE C.4    iShares S&P Global Utilities Sector Index Fund (JXI)
Expense Ratio (0.48%)    Holdings (30 November 2009)

| Ticker Symbol | Name | Weight | Sector |
|---|---|---|---|
| EOAN | E.ON AG | 7.97% | Electric Utilities |
| GSZ | GDF Suez | 6.42% | Gas, Water, & Multiutilities |
| ENEL | Enel SPA | 4.03% | Electric Utilities |
| IBE | Iberdrola SA | 4.01% | Gas, Water, & Multiutilities |
| RWE | RWE AG | 3.98% | Gas, Water, & Multiutilities |
| EXC | Exelon Corp. | 3.36% | Electric Utilities |
| 9501 | Tokyo Electric Power Co. Inc. | 3.23% | Electric Utilities |
| NG/ | National Grid Plc. | 2.83% | Electric Utilities |
| SO | Southern Co. | 2.71% | Electric Utilities |
| DUK | Duke Energy Corp. | 2.29% | Gas, Water, & Multiutilities |
| D | Dominion Resources Inc/Va | 2.29% | Utilities |
| CNA | Centrica Plc. | 2.27% | Gas, Water & Multiutilities |
| FPL | FPL Group Inc. | 2.27% | Electric Utilities |

**TABLE C.4    iShares S&P Global Utilities Sector Index Fund (JXI)
Expense Ratio (0.48%)    Holdings (30 November 2009) (cont.)**

| Ticker Symbol | Name | Weight | Sector |
|---|---|---|---|
| 9503 | Kansai Electric Power Co. Inc. | 1.92% | Electric Utilities |
| SSE | Scottish & Southern Energy | 1.79% | Gas, Water, & Multiutilities |
| VIE | Veolia Environnement | 1.76% | Gas, Water, & Multiutilities |
| 9502 | Chubu Electric Power Co. Inc. | 1.75% | Electric Utilities |
| EDF | Electricite De France | 1.69% | Electric Utilities |
| PEG | Public Service Enterprise Gp. | 1.68% | Electric Utilities |
| PCG | PG&E Corp. | 1.66% | Electric Utilities |
| ETR | Entergy Corp. | 1.63% | Electric Utilities |
| AEP | American Electric Power | 1.63% | Electric Utilities |
| FE | FirstEnergy Corp. | 1.39% | Electric Utilities |
| SRE | Sempra Energy | 1.38% | Gas, Water, & Multiutilities |
| 000 | CLP Holdings Ltd. | 1.3% | Electric Utilities |
| ED | Consolidated Edison Inc. | 1.25% | Electric Utilities |
| PPL | PPL Corporation | 1.22% | Utilities |
| FUM1V | Fortum Oyj | 1.17% | Electric Utilities |
| EIX | Edison International | 1.17% | Electric Utilities |
| PGN | Progress Energy Inc. | 1.16% | Electric Utilities |
| EDP | Energias De Portugal SA | 1.1% | Gas, Water, & Multiutilities |
| 9531 | Tokyo Gas Co .Ltd. | 1.06% | Gas, Water, & Multiutilities |
| 3 | Hong Kong & China Gas | 1.02% | Gas, Water, & Multiutilities |
| XEL | Xcel Energy Inc. | 0.98% | Electric Utilities |
| 9508 | Kyushu Electric Power Co. Inc. | 0.94% | Electric Utilities |

**TABLE C.4    iShares S&P Global Utilities Sector Index Fund (JXI)
Expense Ratio (0.48%)    Holdings (30 November 2009) (cont.)**

| Ticker Symbol | Name | Weight | Sector |
|---|---|---|---|
| SRG | Snam Rete Gas | 0.94% | Gas, Water, & Multiutilities |
| AES | AES Corp. | 0.9% | Electric Utilities |
| 9532 | Osaka Gas Co. Ltd. | 0.78% | Gas, Water, & Multiutilities |
| KEP | Korea Elec Power Corp.-Sp ADR | 0.76% | Electric Utilities |
| IPR | International Power Plc. | 0.73% | Electric Utilities |
| STR | Questar Corp. | 0.73% | Gas, Water, & Multiutilities |
| DTE | DTE Energy Company | 0.69% | Electric Utilities |
| CEG | Constellation Energy Group | 0.68% | Electric Utilities |
| CIG | Cemig SA -Spons ADR | 0.67% | Electric Utilities |
| GAS | Gas Natural Sdg. SA | 0.66% | Gas, Water, & Multiutilities |
| AEE | Ameren Corporation | 0.64% | Gas, Water, & Multiutilities |
| SEV | Suez Environnement SA | 0.63% | Gas, Water, & Multiutilities |
| REE | Red Electrica Corporacion SA | 0.62% | Electric Utilities |
| AGK | AGL Energy Ltd. | 0.6% | Gas, Water, & Multiutilities |
| TRN | Terna SPA | 0.58% | Electric Utilities |
| EQT | EQT Corp. | 0.57% | Gas, Water, & Multiutilities |
| EOC | Empresa Nac Elec-Chil-Sp ADR | 0.57% | Electric Utilities |
| UU/ | United Utilities Group Plc. | 0.56 | Gas, Water, & Multiutilities |
| WEC | Wisconsin Energy Corp. | 0.55 | Gas, Water, & Multiutilities |
| CNP | Centerpoint Energy Inc. | 0.54 | Gas, Water, & Multiutilities |
| ENI | Enersis S.A. -Spons ADR | 0.53 | Electric Utilities |
| FTS | Fortis Inc. | 0.45 | Gas, Water, & Multiutilities |
| NU | Northeast Utilities | 0.44 | Electric Utilities |

**TABLE C.4   iShares S&P Global Utilities Sector Index Fund (JXI)
Expense Ratio (0.48%)   Holdings (30 November 2009) (cont.)**

| Ticker Symbol | Name | Weight | Sector |
|---|---|---|---|
| TA | Transalta Corp. | 0.44 | Electric Utilities |
| ENG | Enagas | 0.44 | Gas, Water, & Multiutilities |
| SVT | Severn Trent Plc. | 0.43 | Gas, Water, & Multiutilities |
| EBR | Centrais Elec Bras-Sp ADR Cm | 0.43 | Electric Utilities |
| IBR | Iberdrola Renovables | 0.43 | Green Power |
| NI | Nisource Inc. | 0.41 | Gas, Water, & Multiutilities |
| SCG | SCANA Corp. | 0.41 | Gas, Water, & Multiutilities |
| AYE | Allegheny Energy Inc. | 0.39 | Electric Utilities |
| POM | Pepco Holdings Inc. | 0.38 | Electric Utilities |
| PNW | Pinnacle West Capital | 0.37 | Electric Utilities |
| ANA | Acciona SA | 0.37 | Green Power |
| CMS | CMS Energy Corp. | 0.34 | Electric Utilities |
| TE | Teco Energy Inc. | 0.33 | Electric Utilities |
| TEG | Integrys Energy Group Inc. | 0.31 | Gas, Water, & Multiutilities |
| DRX | Drax Group Plc. | 0.26 | Electric Utilities |
| ELP | CIA Paranaense Ener-Sp ADR P | 0.22 | Electric Utilities |
| GAS | Nicor Inc. | 0.18 | Gas, Water, & Multiutilities |
| DYN | Dynegy Inc-Cl A | 0.1 | Electric Utilities |
| — | BGIF Treasury Money Market Sl Agency Shares | 0.05 | S-T Securities |

# Water

**TABLE C.5    PowerShares Water Resources Portfolio (PHO)**
**Expense Ratio (0.64%)    Holdings (23 December 2009)**

| Ticker Symbol | Name | Weight | Sector |
|---|---|---|---|
| URS | URS Corp. | 5.15% | Industrials |
| ACM | AECOM Technology Corp. | 5.11% | Industrials |
| TTEK | Tetra Tech Inc. | 5.08% | Industrials |
| DHR | Danaher Corp. | 4.92% | Industrials |
| VMI | Valmont Industries Inc. | 4.71% | Industrials |
| ROP | Roper Industries Inc. | 4.15% | Industrials |
| BMI | Badger Meter Inc. | 3.96% | Industrials |
| FLS | Flowserve Corp. | 3.87% | Industrials |
| INSU | Insituform Technologies Inc. (Cl A) | 3.85% | Industrials |
| IEX | IDEX Corp. | 3.65% | Industrials |
| LNN | Lindsay Corp. | 3.47% | Industrials |
| LAYN | Layne Christensen Co. | 3.46% | Industrials |
| AMN | Ameron International Corp. | 3.41% | Industrials |
| PNR | Pentair Inc. | 3.34% | Industrials |
| WTS | Watts Water Technologies Inc. (Cl A) | 3.32% | Industrials |
| PLL | Pall Corp. | 3.30% | Industrials |
| MWA | Mueller Water Products Inc. | 3.22% | Industrials |
| GRC | Gorman-Rupp Co. | 3.06% | Industrials |
| FELE | Franklin Electric Co. Inc. | 3.02% | Industrials |
| ITT | ITT Corp. | 2.89% | Industrials |
| NWPX | Northwest Pipe Co. | 1.67% | Industrials |
| ITRI | Itron Inc. | 4.71% | Information Technology |

**TABLE C.5    PowerShares Water Resources Portfolio (PHO)
Expense Ratio (0.64%)    Holdings (23 December 2009) (cont.)**

| Ticker Symbol | Name | Weight | Sector |
|---|---|---|---|
| NLC | Nalco Holding Co. | 3.84% | Water Treatment Systems |
| CCC | Calgon Carbon Corp. | 2.80% | Materials |
| VE | Veolia Environnement (ADS) | 4.15% | Gas, Water, & Multiutilities |
| AWK | American Water Works Co. | 1.34% | Gas, Water, & Multiutilities |
| WTR | Aqua America Inc. | 1.25% | Gas, Water, & Multiutilities |
| AWR | American States Water Co. | 1.20% | Gas, Water, & Multiutilities |
| SBS | Companhia de Saneamento Basico do Estado de Sao Paulo (ADS) | 1.19% | Gas, Water, & Multiutilities |
| CWCO | Consolidated Water Co. Inc. | 0.90% | Gas, Water, & Multiutilities |

**TABLE C.6    PowerShares Global Water Portfolio (PIO)
Expense Ratio (0.75%)    Holdings (23 December 2009)**

| Ticker Symbol | Name | Weight | Sector |
|---|---|---|---|
| ARCAD | ARCADIS N.V. | 5.99% | Industrials |
| STN | Stantec Inc. | 5.68% | Industrials |
| TTEK | Tetra Tech Inc. | 5.14% | Industrials |
| VMI | Valmont Industries Inc. | 4.67% | Industrials |
| 6370 | Kurita Water Industries Ltd. | 4.40% | Industrials |
| 6368 | Organo Corp. | 4.00% | Industrials |
| UNR1 | Uponor Oyj | 3.45% | Industrials |

**TABLE C.6   PowerShares Global Water Portfolio (PIO)
Expense Ratio (0.75%)   Holdings (23 December 2009) (cont.)**

| Ticker Symbol | Name | Weight | Sector |
|---|---|---|---|
| GEBN | Geberit AG | 3.28% | Industrials |
| DHR | Danaher Corp. | 3.26% | Industrials |
| PNR | Pentair Inc. | 3.18% | Industrials |
| ITT | ITT Corp. | 2.79% | Industrials |
| KSB | KSB AG | 2.67% | Machinery—Pumps |
| EBCOY | Ebara Corp. | 2.66% | Machinery—Pumps |
| | GLV Inc. (Cl A) | 0.74% | Industrials |
| HLMA | Halma PLC | 3.31% | Information Technology |
| ITRI | Itron Inc. | 3.11% | Information Technology |
| NLC | Nalco Holding Co. | 6.18% | Water Treatment Systems |
| KRA1 | Kemira Oyj | 4.49% | Materials |
| HYF | Hyflux Ltd. | 5.73% | Gas, Water, & Multiutilities |
| SEV | Suez Environnement S.A. | 4.87% | Gas, Water, & Multiutilities |
| VIE | Veolia Environnement S.A. | 4.07% | Gas, Water, & Multiutilities |
| SVT | Severn Trent PLC | 3.21% | Gas, Water, & Multiutilities |
| 270.HK | Guangdong Investment Ltd. | 1.84% | Gas, Water, & Multiutilities |
| AWK | American Water Works Co. | 1.81% | Gas, Water, & Multiutilities |
| UU/ | United Utilities Group PLC | 1.75% | Gas, Water, & Multiutilities |
| WTR | Aqua America Inc. | 1.68% | Gas, Water, & Multiutilities |
| AGS | Sociedad General de Aguas de Barcelona S.A. | 1.63% | Gas, Water, & Multiutilities |
| PNH | Puncak Niaga Holdings Bhd. | 1.56% | Gas, Water, & Multiutilities |
| SBS | Companhia de Saneamento Basico do Estado de Sao Paulo | 1.55% | Gas, Water, & Multiutilities |
| ACE | Acea S.P.A. | 1.28% | Gas, Water, & Multiutilities |

**TABLE C.7  Claymore S&P Global Water Index (CGW)
Expense Ratio (0.70%)  Holdings (24 December 2009)**

| Ticker Symbol | Name | Weight | Sector |
|---|---|---|---|
| GEBN | Geberit AG | 10.05% | Industrials |
| VIE | Veolia Environnement | 7.62% | Gas, Water, & Multiutilities |
| UU/ | United Utilities Grp. PLC | 6.45% | Gas, Water & Multiutilities |
| 6370 | Kurita Water Industries Ltd. | 5.21% | Industrials |
| DHR | Danaher Corp. | 5.09% | Industrials |
| SVT | Severn Trent PLC | 4.99% | Gas, Water, & Multiutilities |
| NLC | Nalco Holding Co. | 4.81% | Water Treatment Systems |
| ITT | ITT Industries Inc. | 4.41% | Industrials |
| WOR | Worleyparsons Ltd. | 3.56% | Engineering/R&D Services |
| PNN | Pennon Group PLC | 3.48% | Gas, Water, & Multiutilities |
| SEV | Suez Environnement SA | 3.42% | Gas, Water, & Multiutilities |
| WTR | Aqua America Inc. | 2.90% | Gas, Water, & Multiutilities |
| SBS | Companhia De Saneamento Basico Do Estado De Sao Paulo | 2.57% | Gas, Water, & Multiutilities |
| PNR | Pentair Inc. | 2.32% | Industrials |
| TTEK | Tetra Tech Inc. | 2.24% | Industrials |
| AWK | American Water Works Co. Inc | 1.90% | Gas, Water, & Multiutilities |
| NWG | Northumbrian Water Group | 1.90% | Gas, Water, & Multiutilities |
| IEX | Idex Corp. | 1.84% | Industrials |
| ITRI | Itron Inc. | 1.76% | Information Technology |
| 270.HK | Guangdong Investment Ltd. | 1.71% | Gas, Water, & Multiutilities |
| WAVIN | Wavin NV | 1.49% | Building & Construction Products—Miscellaneous |
| ANDR | Andritz AG | 1.45% | Machinery—General Industrial |
| WTS | Watts Water Technologies | 1.39% | Industrials |

**TABLE C.7   Claymore S&P Global Water Index (CGW)
Expense Ratio (0.70%)   Holdings (24 December 2009) (cont.)**

| Ticker Symbol | Name | Weight | Sector |
|---|---|---|---|
| ARJ | Arch Chemicals Inc. | 1.11% | Chemicals |
| INSU | Insituform Tech | 1.08% | Industrials |
| VMI | Valmont Industries | 1.05% | Industrials |
| HLMA | Halma PLC | 1.01% | Information Technology |
| 6361 | Ebara Corp. | 0.99% | Industrials |
| FCC | FOM Const Y Contraeur1 | 0.93% | Construction |
| CWT | California Water Service | 0.91% | Gas, Water, & Multiutilities |
| HYF | Hyflux Ltd. | 0.87% | Gas, Water, & Multiutilities |
| UNR1 | Uponor Oyj | 0.85% | Industrials |
| KRA1 | Kemira Oyj | 0.82% | Materials |
| MWA | Mueller Water-A | 0.81% | Industrials |
| 257 | China Everbright Hkd0.10 | 0.76% | Alternative Waste Technology |
| AWR | American States Water Co. | 0.74% | Gas, Water, & Multiutilities |
| HER | Hera SPA | 0.60% | Gas, Water, & Multiutilities |
| CCC | Calgon Carbon Corp. | 0.54% | Alternative Waste Technology |
| LAYN | Layne Christensen Co. | 0.54% | Building & Construction— Miscellaneous |
| ACE | ACEA SPA | 0.50% | Gas, Water, & Multiutilities |
| AGS | Sociedad General De Aguas De Barcelona SA | 0.50% | Gas, Water, & Multiutilities |
| FELE | Franklin Electric Co. Inc. | 0.49% | Machinery—Eelctrical |
| EPUR | Epure International Ltd. | 0.43% | Water Treatment Systems |
| BMI | Badger Meter Inc. | 0.41% | Electronic Measuring Instruments |
| IP | Interpump Group SPA | 0.39% | Machinery—Pumps |

**TABLE C.7   Claymore S&P Global Water Index (CGW)**
**Expense Ratio (0.70%)   Holdings (24 December 2009) (cont.)**

| Ticker Symbol | Name | Weight | Sector |
|---|---|---|---|
| BWT | BWT AG | 0.36% | Water Treatment Systems |
| SJW | SJW Corp. | 0.35% | Gas, Water, & Multiutilities |
| 6368 | Organo Corp. | 0.26% | Water Treatment Equipment |
| 4997 | Nihon Nohyaku Co. Ltd. | 0.17% | Agricultural Chemicals |

# Infrastructure

**TABLE C.8   iShares S&P Global Infrastructure Index Fund (IGF)**
**Expense Ratio (0.48%)   Holdings (30 November 2009)**

| Ticker Symbol | Name | Weight | Sector |
|---|---|---|---|
| TRP | Transcanada Corp. | 4.84% | Energy |
| ENB | Enbridge Inc. | 4.48% | Energy |
| ABE | Abertis Infraestructuras SA | 4.39% | Industrials |
| EOAN | E.ON AG | 3.93% | Utilities |
| TCL | Transurban Group | 3.77% | Industrials |
| GSZ | GDF SUEZ | 3.69% | Utilities |
| ATL | Atlantia SPA | 3.69% | Industrials |
| SE | Spectra Energy Corp. | 3.55% | Energy |
| WMB | Williams Cos Inc. | 2.99% | Energy |
| IBE | Iberdrola SA | 2.85% | Utilities |
| RWE | RWE AG | 2.6% | Utilities |
| ENEL | Enel SPA | 2.27% | Utilities |
| EXC | Exelon Corp. | 2.03% | Electric Utilities |

**TABLE C.8   iShares S&P Global Infrastructure Index Fund (IGF)
Expense Ratio (0.48%)   Holdings (30 November 2009) (cont.)**

| Ticker Symbol | Name | Weight | Sector |
|---|---|---|---|
| MAP | MAP Group | 2.03% | Industrials |
| 144 | China Merchants Hldgs. Intl. | 2% | Industrials |
| 9501 | Tokyo Electric Power Co. Inc. | 1.9% | Utilities |
| BRI | BRISA | 1.91% | Industrials |
| EP | El Paso Corp. | 1.71% | Energy |
| NG/ | National Grid Plc. | 1.64% | Utilities |
| VPK | Vopak | 1.61% | Industrials |
| SO | Southern Co. | 1.59% | Utilities |
| ADP | ADP | 1.51% | Industrials |
| FPL | FPL Group Inc. | 1.44% | Utilities |
| SATS | Singapore Airport Terminal S | 1.4% | Industrials |
| 9364 | Kamigumi Co. Ltd. | 1.39% | Industrials |
| DUK | Duke Energy Corp. | 1.36% | Utilities |
| D | Dominion Resources Inc./Va | 1.34% | Utilities |
| CNA | Centrica Plc. | 1.32% | Utilities |
| FRA | Fraport AG | 1.3% | Industrials |
| MIG | Macquarie Infrastructure Grp. | 1.24% | Industrials |
| 9503 | Kansai Electric Power Co. Inc. | 1.17% | Utilities |
| CIN | Cintra Concesiones De Infrae | 1.09% | Industrials |
| ARR | Societe Des Autoroutes Paris | 1.08% | Industrials |
| SSE | Scottish & Southern Energy | 1.05% | Utilities |
| PEG | Public Service Enterprise GP | 1.04% | Utilities |
| PCG | PG&E Corp. | 0.99% | Utilities |
| AEP | American Electric Power | 0.99% | Utilities |
| ETR | Entergy Corp. | 0.98% | Utilities |

**TABLE C.8   iShares S&P Global Infrastructure Index Fund (IGF)
Expense Ratio (0.48%)   Holdings (30 November 2009) (cont.)**

| Ticker Symbol | Name | Weight | Sector |
|---|---|---|---|
| SMIT | Smit International NV | 0.98% | Industrials |
| 576 | Zhejiang Expressway Co-H | 0.97% | Industrials |
| 9301 | Mitsubishi Logistics Corp. | 0.93% | Industrials |
| CEU | Connecteast Group | 0.93% | Industrials |
| EDF | Electricite De France | 0.91% | Utilities |
| GET | Groupe Eurotunnel SA | 0.91% | Industrials |
| 1199 | Cosco Pacific Limited | 0.9% | Industrials |
| FE | FirstEnergy Corp. | 0.82% | Utilities |
| 2 | CLP Holdings Ltd. | 0.79% | Utilities |
| STS | Ansaldo Sts SPA | 0.75% | Industrials |
| 694 | Beijing Capital Intl. Airpo-H | 0.73% | Industrials |
| SUG | Southern Union Co. | 0.72% | Energy |
| AIA | Auckland Intl Airport Ltd. | 0.71% | Industrials |
| 177 | Jiangsu Express Co. Ltd.-H | 0.67% | Industrials |
| PAC | Grupo Aeroportuario Pac-ADR | 0.66% | Industrials |
| BBA | BBA Aviation Plc. | 0.65% | Industrials |
| ASR | Grupo Aeroportuario Sur-ADR | 0.65% | Industrials |
| 9706 | Japan Airport Terminal Co. | 0.56% | Industrials |
| HHFA | Hamburger Hafen Und Logistik | 0.55% | Industrials |
| FPT | Forth Ports Plc. | 0.54% | Industrials |
| FRO | Frontline Ltd. | 0.44% | Energy |
| CIG | Cemig Sa -Spons ADR | 0.4% | Utilities |
| NAT | Nordic Amer Tanker Shipping | 0.39% | Energy |
| PIF-U | Pembina Pipeline Inc-Tr Uts | 0.33% | Energy |
| EOC | Empresa Nac Elec-Chil-Sp ADR | 0.33% | Utilities |

**TABLE C.8   iShares S&P Global Infrastructure Index Fund (IGF)
Expense Ratio (0.48%)   Holdings (30 November 2009) (cont.)**

| Ticker Symbol | Name | Weight | Sector |
|---|---|---|---|
| ENI | Enersis S.A. -Spons ADR | 0.3% | Utilities |
| TK | Teekay Corp. | 0.24% | Energy |
| 836 | China Resources Power Holdings | 0.24% | Utilities |
| ALA-U | Altagas Income Trust | 0.18% | Energy |
| SFL | Ship Finance Intl. Ltd. | 0.17% | Energy |
| CPL | CPFL Energia SA - ADR | 0.13% | Utilities |
| SBS | CIA Saneamento Basico De-ADR | 0.13% | Utilities |
| HNP | Huaneng Power Intl-Spons ADR | 0.12% | Utilities |
| EURN | Euronav SA | 0.12% | Energy |
| GMR | General Maritime Corp. | 0.12% | Energy |
| TNP | Tsakos Energy Navigation Ltd. | 0.11% | Energy |
| 991 | Datang Intl. Power Gen. Co-H | 0.08% | Utilities |
| — | BGIF Treasury Money Market SL Agency Shares | 0.04% | S-T Securities |

**TABLE C.9   PowerShares Emerging Infrastructure Portfolio (PXR)
Expense Ratio (0.75%)   Holdings (23 December 2009)**

| Ticker Symbol | Name | Weight | Sector |
|---|---|---|---|
| ABB | ABB Ltd. | 3.75% | Industrials |
| CAT | Caterpillar Inc. | 3.63% | Industrials |
| DG | Vinci S.A. | 3.51% | Industrials |
| FWLT | Foster Wheeler AG | 3.06% | Industrials |
| RLO | Reunert Ltd. | 2.86% | Industrials |
| 2727:HK | Shanghai Electric Group Co. Ltd. | 2.61% | Industrials |

**TABLE C.9    PowerShares Emerging Infrastructure Portfolio (PXR)
Expense Ratio (0.75%)    Holdings (23 December 2009) (cont.)**

| Ticker Symbol | Name | Weight | Sector |
|---|---|---|---|
| LTOD | Larsen And Toubro Ltd. Gdr. Reg. S | 2.56% | Industrials |
| KBR | KBR Inc. | 2.49% | Industrials |
| WBO | Wilson Bayly Holmes-Ovcon Ltd. | 2.27% | Industrials |
| 1072:HK | Dongfang Electric Corp. Ltd. | 2.22% | Industrials |
| 3339:HK | Lonking Holdings Ltd. | 2.10% | Industrials |
| ALO | Alstom S.A. | 1.95% | Industrials |
| UNTR | United Tractors | 1.74% | Industrials |
| PBG | PBG S.A. | 1.74% | Industrials |
| SMM | SembCorp Marine Ltd. | 1.66% | Industrials |
| AEG | Aveng Ltd. | 1.62% | Industrials |
| 1133:HK | Harbin Power Equipment Co. Ltd. | 1.41% | Industrials |
| ATLCY | Atlas Copco AB | 1.28% | Industrials |
| ITT | ITT Corp. | 1.25% | Industrials |
| ORA | Ormat Industries Ltd. | 1.17% | Industrials |
| FLR | Fluor Corp. | 1.10% | Industrials |
| ICA | Empresas ICA S.A.B. de C.V. | 1.08% | Industrials |
| 9933:TT | CTCI Corp. | 1.05% | Industrials |
| GAM:MK | Gamuda Bhd. | 1.04% | Industrials |
| IJM:MK | IJM Corp. Bhd. | 0.97% | Industrials |
| GRF:SJ | Group Five Ltd. | 0.93% | Industrials |
| MIDAS:SP | Midas Holdings Ltd. | 0.87% | Industrials |
| RBX | Raubex Group Ltd. | 0.85% | Industrials |
| 983 | Shui On Construction & Materials Ltd. | 0.78% | Industrials |
| LEI | Leighton Holdings Ltd. | 0.66% | Industrials |

**TABLE C.9    PowerShares Emerging Infrastructure Portfolio (PXR)
Expense Ratio (0.75%)   Holdings (23 December 2009) (cont.)**

| Ticker Symbol | Name | Weight | Sector |
|---|---|---|---|
| ORSDF | Orascom Construction Industries S.A.E. | 0.61% | Industrials |
| 1800 | China Communications Construction Co. Ltd. | 0.56% | Industrials |
| 190 | HKC (Holdings) Ltd. | 0.46% | Industrials |
| ARVCY | Areva S.A. | 0.39% | Industrials |
| VALE | Vale S.A. (ADS) | 3.58% | Materials |
| JIXAY | Jiangxi Copper Co. Ltd. | 2.52% | Materials |
| 1101 | Taiwan Cement Corp. | 2.35% | Materials |
| 600585 | Anhui Conch Cement Co. Ltd. | 2.17% | Materials |
| SLT | Sterlite Industries (India) Ltd. (ADS) | 2.09% | Materials |
| CAP | CAP S.A. | 1.95% | Materials |
| THSGG | Tung Ho Steel Enterprise Corp. | 1.94% | Materials |
| 3323 | China National Building Material Co. Ltd. | 1.91% | Materials |
| 2626 | Hunan Nonferrous Metals Corp. Ltd. | 1.87% | Materials |
| ANGGY | Angang Steel Co. Ltd. | 1.86% | Materials |
| ARBWY | African Rainbow Minerals Ltd. | 1.70% | Materials |
| SID | Companhia Siderurgica Nacional (ADS) | 1.67% | Materials |
| LFRGY | Lafarge Malayan Cement Bhd | 1.60% | Materials |
| PPCYY | Pretoria Portland Cement Co. Ltd. | 1.58% | Materials |
| NILSY | Norilsk Nickel Mining & Metallurgical Co. (ADS) | 1.56% | Materials |
| GGB | Gerdau S.A. (ADS) | 1.54% | Materials |
| 2002 | China Steel Corp. | 1.37% | Materials |
| MMK | OJSC Magnitogorsk Iron & Steel Works GDR (Reg S Sh) | 1.33% | Materials |

**TABLE C.9   PowerShares Emerging Infrastructure Portfolio (PXR) Expense Ratio (0.75%)   Holdings (23 December 2009) (cont.)**

| Ticker Symbol | Name | Weight | Sector |
|---|---|---|---|
| 2014 | Chung Hung Steel Corp. | 1.11% | Materials |
| INTP | Indocement Tunggal Prakarsa | 0.91% | Materials |
| SMGR | Semen Gresik (Persero) | 0.88% | Materials |
| 3993 | China Molybdenum Co. Ltd. | 0.83% | Materials |
| LSRG | LSR Group | 0.69% | Materials |
| ANTM | Aneka Tambang | 0.60% | Materials |
| INCO | International Nickel Indonesia | 0.55% | Materials |
| NLMK | NovolipetskIron Spon GDR Reg S | 0.39% | Materials |
| MTL | Mechel OAO (ADS) | 0.37% | Materials |
| CHMF | Severstal JT STK CO SP GDR OCT 06 | 0.23% | Materials |
| HYF | Hyflux Ltd. | 2.16% | Utilities |
| ANA | Acciona S.A. | 0.50% | Utilities |

# Materials

**TABLE C.10   Dow Jones U.S. Basic Materials Sector Index Fund (IYM) Expense Ratio (0.47%)   Holdings (30 November 2009)**

| Ticker Symbol | Name | Weight | Sector |
|---|---|---|---|
| FCX | Freeport-Mcmoran Copper-B | 8.94% | Industrial Metals & Mining |
| DOW | Dow Chemical | 8.33% | Chemicals |
| DD | Du Pont (E.I.) De Nemours | 7.68% | Chemicals |
| NEM | Newmont Mining Corp. | 6.72% | Mining |
| PX | Praxair Inc. | 6.63% | Chemicals |
| APD | Air Products & Chemicals Inc. | 4.29% | Chemicals |

**TABLE C.10　Dow Jones U.S. Basic Materials Sector Index Fund (IYM)
Expense Ratio (0.47%)　Holdings (30 November 2009) (cont.)**

| Ticker Symbol | Name | Weight | Sector |
|---|---|---|---|
| AA | Alcoa Inc. | 3.19% | Industrial Metals & Mining |
| NUE | Nucor Corp. | 3.17% | Industrial Metals & Mining |
| BTU | Peabody Energy Corp. | 3.11% | Mining |
| ECL | Ecolab Inc. | 2.78% | Chemicals |
| IP | International Paper Co. | 2.65% | Forestry & Paper |
| PPG | PPG Industries Inc. | 2.58% | Chemicals |
| CNX | Consol Energy Inc. | 2.17% | Mining |
| MOS | Mosaic Co./THE | 2.12% | Chemicals |
| PCU | Southern Copper Corp. | 1.93% | Industrial Metals & Mining |
| X | United States Steel Corp. | 1.68% | Industrial Metals & Mining |
| ANR | Alpha Natural Resources Inc. | 1.52% | Mining |
| CLF | Cliffs Natural Resources Inc. | 1.51% | Industrial Metals & Mining |
| SIAL | Sigma-Aldrich | 1.46% | Chemicals |
| LZ | Lubrizol Corp. | 1.28% | Chemicals |
| CF | CF Industries Holdings Inc. | 1.26% | Chemicals |
| CE | Celanese Corp-Series A | 1.12% | Chemicals |
| AVY | Avery Dennison Corp. | 1.11% | Chemicals |
| EMN | Eastman Chemical Company | 1.08% | Chemicals |
| FMC | FMC Corp | 1.07% | Chemicals |
| TRA | Terra Industries Inc. | 1.01% | Chemicals |
| STLD | Steel Dynamics Inc. | 0.95% | Industrial Metals & Mining |
| WLT | Walter Energy Inc. | 0.95% | Mining |
| ACI | Arch Coal Inc. | 0.89% | Mining |
| ARG | Airgas Inc. | 0.85% | Chemicals |
| MEE | Massey Energy Co. | 0.84% | Mining |

**TABLE C.10   Dow Jones U.S. Basic Materials Sector Index Fund (IYM)
Expense Ratio (0.47%)   Holdings (30 November 2009) (cont.)**

| Ticker Symbol | Name | Weight | Sector |
|---|---|---|---|
| IFF | Intl. Flavors & Fragrances | 0.84% | Chemicals |
| ATI | Allegheny Technologies Inc. | 0.82% | Industrial Metals & Mining |
| ALB | Albemarle Corp. | 0.81% | Chemicals |
| RS | Reliance Steel & Aluminum | 0.69% | Industrial Metals & Mining |
| RPM | Rpm International Inc. | 0.66% | Chemicals |
| VAL | Valspar Corp. | 0.64% | Chemicals |
| ASH | Ashland Inc. | 0.63% | Chemicals |
| UFS | Domtar Corp. | 0.62% | Forestry & Paper |
| AKS | AK Steel Holding Corp. | 0.57% | Industrial Metals & Mining |
| RGLD | Royal Gold Inc. | 0.57% | Mining |
| CMP | Compass Minerals Internation | 0.55% | Mining |
| CMC | Commercial Metals Co. | 0.47% | Industrial Metals & Mining |
| CDE | Coeur D'alene Mines Corp. | 0.45% | Mining |
| CYT | Cytec Industries Inc. | 0.43% | Chemicals |
| HL | Hecla Mining Co | 0.41% | Mining |
| HUN | Huntsman Corp. | 0.41% | Chemicals |
| GR | WR Grace & Co. | 0.36% | Chemicals |
| IPI | Intrepid Potash Inc. | 0.34% | Industrial Metals & Mining |
| SOA | Solutia Inc. | 0.34% | Chemicals |
| SXT | Sensient Technologies Corp. | 0.32% | Chemicals |
| CBT | Cabot Corp. | 0.3% | Chemicals |
| OLN | Olin Corp. | 0.3% | Chemicals |
| ROC | Rockwood Holdings Inc. | 0.3% | Chemicals |
| NEU | Newmarket Corp. | 0.3% | Chemicals |
| CRS | Carpenter Technology | 0.27% | Industrial Metals & Mining |

**TABLE C.10   Dow Jones U.S. Basic Materials Sector Index Fund (IYM) Expense Ratio (0.47%)   Holdings (30 November 2009) (cont.)**

| Ticker Symbol | Name | Weight | Sector |
|---|---|---|---|
| MTX | Minerals Technologies Inc. | 0.26% | Chemicals |
| FUL | H.B. Fuller Co. | 0.26% | Chemicals |
| PCX | Patriot Coal Corp. | 0.25% | Mining |
| OMG | OM Group Inc. | 0.25% | Chemicals |
| TIE | Titanium Metals Corp. | 0.22% | Industrial Metals & Mining |
| CCC | Calgon Carbon Corp. | 0.2% | Chemicals |
| WOR | Worthington Industries | 0.2% | Industrial Metals & Mining |
|  | BGIF Treasury Money Market Sl Agency Shares | 0.19% | S-T Securities |
| KALU | Kaiser Aluminum Corp. | 0.16% | Industrial Metals & Mining |
| RTI | RTI International Metals Inc. | 0.15% | Industrial Metals & Mining |
| WPP | Wausau Paper Corp. | 0.13% | Forestry & Paper |
| USU | Usec Inc. | 0.11% | Industrial Metals & Mining |
| SHLM | Schulman (A.) Inc. | 0.1% | Chemicals |
| TG | Tredegar Corp. | 0.09% | Chemicals |

**TABLE C.11   iShares S&P Global Materials Sector Index Fund (MXI) Expense Ratio (0.48%)   Holdings (30 November 2009)**

| Ticker Symbol | Name | Weight | Sector |
|---|---|---|---|
| BHP | BHP Billiton Ltd. | 7.91% | Metals & Mining |
| BLT | BHP Billiton Plc. | 4.24% | Metals & Mining |
| RIO | Rio Tinto Plc. | 4.04% | Metals & Mining |
| BAS | BASF SE | 3.67% | Chemicals |
| AAL | Anglo American Plc. | 3.45% | Metals & Mining |
| VALE/P | Vale SA ADR | 3.21% | Metals & Mining |

**TABLE C.11   iShares S&P Global Materials Sector Index Fund (MXI)
Expense Ratio (0.48%)   Holdings (30 November 2009) (cont.)**

| Ticker Symbol | Name | Weight | Sector |
|---|---|---|---|
| MON | Monsanto Co. | 2.83% | Chemicals |
| ABX | Barrick Gold Corp. | 2.40% | Metals & Mining |
| XTA | Xstrata Plc. | 2.15% | Metals & Mining |
| PKX | Posco-ADR | 2.15% | Metals & Mining |
| FCX | Freeport-Mcmoran Copper-B | 2.12% | Metals & Mining |
| POT | Potash Corp Of Saskatchewan | 2.12% | Chemicals |
| DD | Du Pont (E.I.) De Nemours | 2.06% | Chemicals |
| MT | Arcelormittal | 2.06% | Metals & Mining |
| AI | Air Liquide | 1.95% | Chemicals |
| G | Goldcorp Inc. | 1.89% | Metals & Mining |
| DOW | Dow Chemical | 1.88% | Chemicals |
| RIO | Rio Tinto Ltd. | 1.76% | Metals & Mining |
| SYNN | Syngenta Ag-Reg | 1.67% | Chemicals |
| PX | Praxair Inc. | 1.64% | Chemicals |
| NEM | Newmont Mining Corp. | 1.61% | Metals & Mining |
| CNSD | China Steel Corp-Spons Gdr. | 1.26% | Metals & Mining |
| 4063 | Shin-Etsu Chemical Co Ltd. | 1.25% | Chemicals |
| 5401 | Nippon Steel Corp. | 1.23% | Metals & Mining |
| APD | Air Products & Chemicals Inc. | 1.16% | Chemicals |
| LIN | Linde AG | 1.15% | Chemicals |
| HOLN | Holcim Ltd.-Reg | 1.11% | Construction Materials |
| TCK/B | Teck Resources Ltd.-Cl B | 1.09% | Metals & Mining |
| CRH | CRH Plc. | 1.09% | Construction Materials |
| AKZA | Akzo Nobel | 1.01% | Chemicals |
| NCM | Newcrest Mining Limited | 1.01% | Metals & Mining |

**TABLE C.11    iShares S&P Global Materials Sector Index Fund (MXI)
Expense Ratio (0.48%)    Holdings (30 November 2009) (cont.)**

| Ticker Symbol | Name | Weight | Sector |
| --- | --- | --- | --- |
| SID | Cia Siderurgica Nacl-Sp ADR | 0.91% | Metals & Mining |
| 5411 | JFE Holdings Inc. | 0.87% | Metals & Mining |
| K | Kinross Gold Corp. | 0.86% | Metals & Mining |
| LG | Lafarge SA | 0.85% | Construction Materials |
| NUE | Nucor Corp. | 0.82% | Metals & Mining |
| AA | Alcoa Inc. | 0.79% | Metals & Mining |
| TKA | Thyssenkrupp AG | 0.75% | Metals & Mining |
| IP | International Paper Co. | 0.71% | Paper & Forest Products |
| GGB | Gerdau Sa -Spon ADR | 0.69% | Metals & Mining |
| CEMEXCPO | Cemex Sab-CPO | 0.68% | Construction Materials |
| PPG | PPG Industries Inc. | 0.65% | Chemicals |
| DSM | Koninklijke Dsm NV | 0.64% | Chemicals |
| YRI | Yamana Gold Inc. | 0.61% | Metals & Mining |
| AEM | Agnico-Eagle Mines | 0.60% | Metals & Mining |
| ORI | Orica Ltd. | 0.59% | Chemicals |
| AGU | Agrium Inc. | 0.58% | Chemicals |
| 5713 | Sumitomo Metal Mining Co Ltd. | 0.54% | Metals & Mining |
| SCAB | Svenska Cellulosa Ab-B Shs | 0.52% | Paper & Forest Products |
| SDF | K+S AG | 0.52% | Chemicals |
| YAR | Yara International ASA | 0.51% | Chemicals |
| 5405 | Sumitomo Metal Industries | 0.50% | Metals & Mining |
| WY | Weyerhaeuser Co. | 0.50% | Paper & Forest Products |
| ECL | Ecolab Inc. | 0.49% | Chemicals |

**TABLE C.11   iShares S&P Global Materials Sector Index Fund (MXI)
Expense Ratio (0.48%)   Holdings (30 November 2009) (cont.)**

| Ticker Symbol | Name | Weight | Sector |
|---|---|---|---|
| LGL | Lihir Gold Ltd. | 0.48% | Metals & Mining |
| BVN | Cia De Minas Buenaventur-ADR | 0.46% | Metals & Mining |
| SIAL | Sigma-Aldrich | 0.42% | Chemicals |
| GIVN | Givaudan-Reg | 0.42% | Chemicals |
| AMC | Amcor Ltd. | 0.41% | Containers & Packaging |
| X | United States Steel Corp. | 0.40% | Metals & Mining |
| 4005 | Sumitomo Chemical Co. Ltd. | 0.39% | Chemicals |
| UPM1V | UPM-Kymmene Oyj | 0.38% | Paper & Forest Products |
| SOLB | Solvay SA | 0.37% | Chemicals |
| JMAT | Johnson Matthey Plc. | 0.36% | Chemicals |
| OI | Owens-Illinois Inc. | 0.35% | Containers & Packaging |
| 3402 | Toray Industries Inc. | 0.35% | Chemicals |
| VMC | Vulcan Materials Co. | 0.34% | Construction Materials |
| FM | First Quantum Minerals Ltd. | 0.34% | Metals & Mining |
| SQM | Quimica Y Minera Chil-Sp ADR | 0.33% | Chemicals |
| EMN | Eastman Chemical Company | 0.33% | Chemicals |
| 3407 | Asahi Kasei Corp. | 0.32% | Chemicals |
| 6988 | Nitto Denko Corp. | 0.32% | Chemicals |
| IMG | Iamgold Corp. | 0.32% | Metals & Mining |
| BLL | Ball Corp. | 0.30% | Containers & Packaging |
| 4188 | Mitsubishi Chemical Holdings | 0.30% | Chemicals |
| IPL | Incitec Pivot Ltd. | 0.30% | Chemicals |
| NZYMB | Novozymes A/S-B Shares | 0.30% | Chemicals |

**TABLE C.11    iShares S&P Global Materials Sector Index Fund (MXI) Expense Ratio (0.48%)   Holdings (30 November 2009) (cont.)**

| Ticker Symbol | Name | Weight | Sector |
|---|---|---|---|
| BSL | Bluescope Steel Ltd. | 0.29% | Metals & Mining |
| ELD | Eldorado Gold Corporation | 0.29% | Metals & Mining |
| CF | CF Industries Holdings Inc. | 0.29% | Chemicals |
| NHY | Norsk Hydro Asa | 0.29% | Metals & Mining |
| FMG | Fortescue Metals Group Ltd. | 0.29% | Metals & Mining |
| STERV | Stora Enso Oyj-R Shs | 0.28% | Paper & Forest Products |
| 3861 | Oji Paper Co Ltd. | 0.28% | Paper & Forest Products |
| MWV | Meadwestvaco Corp. | 0.28% | Paper & Forest Products |
| UMI | Umicore | 0.27% | Chemicals |
| LMI | Lonmin Plc. | 0.27% | Metals & Mining |
| REX | Rexam Plc. | 0.27% | Containers & Packaging |
| 4185 | JSR Corp. | 0.25% | Chemicals |
| BOL | Boliden AB | 0.25% | Metals & Mining |
| OST | Onesteel Ltd. | 0.24% | Metals & Mining |
| VOE | Voestalpine AG | 0.23% | Metals & Mining |
| SZG | Salzgitter AG | 0.23% | Metals & Mining |
| PTV | Pactiv Corporation | 0.21% | Containers & Packaging |
| 3401 | Teijin Ltd. | 0.21% | Chemicals |
| ATI | Allegheny Technologies Inc. | 0.20% | Metals & Mining |
| SEE | Sealed Air Corp. | 0.20% | Containers & Packaging |
| CLN | Clariant AG-Reg | 0.20% | Chemicals |
| 3405 | Kuraray Co. Ltd. | 0.20% | Chemicals |
| CPR | Cimpor-Cimentos De Portugal | 0.19% | Construction Materials |

**TABLE C.11 iShares S&P Global Materials Sector Index Fund (MXI) Expense Ratio (0.48%)  Holdings (30 November 2009) (cont.)**

| Ticker Symbol | Name | Weight | Sector |
|---|---|---|---|
| IFF | Intl Flavors & Fragrances | 0.19% | Chemicals |
| PCU | Southern Copper Corp. | 0.18% | Metals & Mining |
| 3893 | Nippon Paper Group Inc. | 0.18% | Paper & Forest Products |
| IMN | Inmet Mining Corporation | 0.17% | Metals & Mining |
| SSABA | SSAB Ab-Ser A | 0.17% | Metals & Mining |
| 5406 | Kobe Steel Ltd. | 0.17% | Metals & Mining |
| 4183 | Mitsui Chemicals Inc. | 0.17% | Chemicals |
| 5711 | Mitsubishi Materials Corp. | 0.16% | Metals & Mining |
| 5901 | Toyo Seikan Kaisha Ltd. | 0.15% | Containers & Packaging |
| ACX | Acerinox SA | 0.15% | Metals & Mining |
| AKS | AK Steel Holding Corp. | 0.14% | Metals & Mining |
| FMC | FMC Corp. | 0.14% | Chemicals |
| BMS | Bemis Company | 0.13% | Containers & Packaging |
| FBR | Fibria Celulose SA | 0.08% | Paper & Forest Products |
| 5706 | Mitsui Mining & Smelting Co. | 0.08% | Metals & Mining |
| — | BGIF Treasury Money Market Sl Agency Shares | 0.08% | S-T Securities |
| TIE | Titanium Metals Corp. | 0.06% | Metals & Mining |
| HOLMB | Holmen Ab-B Shares | 0.05% | Paper & Forest Products |
| ARG | Airgas Inc. | 0.03% | Chemicals |
| SDFB | K+S AG-RTS | 0.03% | — |

**TABLE C.12   Materials Select SPDR (XLB)**
**Expense Ratio (0.22%)   Holdings (23 December 2009)**

| Ticker Symbol | Name | Weight | Sector |
|---|---|---|---|
| MON | Monsanto Co. | 12.46% | Agricultural Chemicals |
| FCX | Freeport-McMoRan | 9.71% | Metal—Copper |
| DOW | Dow Chem Co. | 8.89% | Chemicals—Diversified |
| DD | Du Pont E I De Nemours & Co. | 8.34% | Chemicals—Diversified |
| PX | Praxair Inc. | 6.82% | Industrial Gases |
| NEM | Newmont Mining Corp. | 4.75% | Gold Mining |
| AA | Alcoa Inc. | 4.45% | Metal—Aluminum |
| APD | Air Prods & Chems Inc. | 4.40% | Industrial Gases |
| NUE | Nucor Corp. | 4.13% | Steel—Producers |
| IP | Intl Paper Co. | 3.45% | Paper & Related Products |
| ECL | Ecolab Inc. | 3.06% | Chemicals—Specialty |
| PPG | PPG Inds Inc. | 2.85% | Chemicals—Diversified |
| WY | Weyerhaeuser Co. | 2.69% | Forestry |
| X | United States Stl. Corp. | 2.30% | Steel—Producers |
| VMC | Vulcan Matls Co. | 1.93% | Quarrying |
| SIAL | Sigma Aldrich Corp. | 1.82% | Chemicals—Specialty |
| CLF | Cliffs Natural Resources Inc. | 1.72% | Metal—Iron |
| OI | Owens Ill Inc. | 1.66% | Containers-Metal/Glass |
| MWV | Meadwestvaco Corp. | 1.48% | Chemicals—Specialty |
| BLL | Ball Corp. | 1.45% | Containers—Metal/Glass |
| EMN | Eastman Chem Co. | 1.34% | Chemicals—Specialty |
| ATI | Allegheny Technologies Inc. | 1.32% | Steel—Specialty |
| CF | CF Inds Hldgs Inc. | 1.29% | Agricultural Chemicals |

**TABLE C.12 Materials Select SPDR (XLB)**
**Expense Ratio (0.22%) Holdings (23 December 2009) (cont.)**

| Ticker Symbol | Name | Weight | Sector |
|---|---|---|---|
| FMC | F M C Corp. | 1.23% | Chemicals—Diversified |
| ARG | Airgas Inc. | 1.18% | Industrial Gases |
| SEE | Sealed Air Corp. | 1.07% | Containers—Paper/Plastic |
| BMS | Bemis Inc. | 1.00% | Containers—Paper/Plastic |
| IFF | International Flavors & Fragr. | 1.00% | Chemicals—Specialty |
| PTV | Pactiv Corp. | 0.96% | Containers—Paper/Plastic |
| AKS | AK Steel Hldg. Corp. | 0.77% | Steel—Producers |
| 85749P9A | State Street Instl. Liquid Resvs. | 0.53% | Unassigned |
| TIE | Titanium Metals Corp. | 0.41% | Non-ferrous metals |
| CASH_USD | U.S. Dollar | -0.46% | Unassigned |

**TABLE C.13 SPDR S&P Metals & Mining ETF (XME)**
**Expense Ratio (0.35%) Holdings (23 December 2009)**

| Ticker Symbol | Name | Weight | Sector |
|---|---|---|---|
| PCX | Patriot Coal Corp. | 4.62% | Energy |
| ATI | Allegheny Technologies Inc. | 4.48% | Materials |
| TIE | Titanium Metals Corp. | 4.44% | Materials |
| CNX | Consol Energy Inc. | 4.42% | Energy |
| X | United States Steel Corp. | 4.31% | Materials |
| MEE | Massey Energy Corp. | 4.27% | Energy |
| ANR | Alpha Natural Resources Inc. | 4.27% | Energy |
| ACI | Arch Coal Inc. | 4.18% | Energy |

**TABLE C.13    SPDR S&P Metals & Mining ETF (XME)**
**Expense Ratio (0.35%)    Holdings (23 December 2009) (cont.)**

| Ticker Symbol | Name | Weight | Sector |
|---|---|---|---|
| BTU | Peabody Energy Corp. | 4.14% | Energy |
| WLT | Walter Energy Inc. | 4.05% | Materials |
| AA | Alcoa Inc. | 4.04% | Materials |
| CLF | Cliffs Natural Resources In. | 4.04% | Materials |
| NUE | Nucor Corp. | 4.03% | Materials |
| AKS | AK Steel Hldg. Corp. | 3.98% | Materials |
| RS | Reliance Steel & Aluminum Co. | 3.95% | Materials |
| CRS | Carpenter Technology Corp. | 3.93% | Materials |
| FCX | Freeport-Mcmoran Copper & G | 3.89% | Materials |
| CMP | Compass Minerals Intl. Inc. | 3.81% | Materials |
| SCHN | Schnitzer Stl. Inds. | 3.7% | Materials |
| STLD | Steel Dynamics Inc. | 3.67% | Materials |
| HL | Hecla Mng. Co. | 3.62% | Materials |
| RGLD | Royal Gold Inc. | 3.6% | Materials |
| CMC | Commercial Metals Co. | 3.57% | Materials |
| CDE | Coeur D'Alene Mines Corp. ID | 3.5% | Materials |
| NEM | Newmont Mining Corp. | 3.46% | Materials |
| 85749P9A | State Str. Instl. Liquid Resvs. | 0.28% | Unassigned |
| CASH_USD | U.S. Dollar | –0.25% | Unassigned |

**TABLE C.14   Vanguard Materials ETF (VAW)**
**Expense Ratio (0.25%)   Holdings (30 September 2009)**

| Ticker Symbol | Name | Weight | Sector |
|---|---|---|---|
| MON | Monsanto Co. | 9.60% | Agricultural Chemicals |
| DD | EI Du Pont de Nemours & Co. | 6.60% | Chemicals—Diversified |
| FCX | Freeport-McMoRan Copper & Gold Inc. | 6.40% | Metal—Copper |
| DOW | Dow Chemical Co. | 6.40% | Chemicals—Diversified |
| PX | Praxair Inc. | 5.70% | Industrial Gases |
| NEM | Newmont Mining Corp. | 4.80% | Gold Mining |
| APD | Air Products & Chemicals Inc. | 3.70% | Industrial Gases |
| NUE | Nucor Corp. | 3.40% | Steel—Producers |
| AA | Alcoa Inc. | 2.90% | Metal—Aluminum |
| ECL | Ecolab Inc. | 2.50% | Chemicals—Specialty |
| PPG | PPG Industries Inc. | 2.20% | Chemicals—Diversified |
| IP | International Paper Co. | 2.10% | Paper & Related Products |
| WY | Weyerhaeuser Co. | 1.80% | Forestry |
| MOS | Mosaic Co. | 1.70% | Agricultural Chemicals |
| VMC | Vulcan Materials Co. | 1.50% | Quarrying |
| SIAL | Sigma-Aldrich Corp. | 1.50% | Chemicals—Specialty |
| X | United States Steel Corp. | 1.40% | Steel—Producers |
| OI | Owens-Illinois Inc. | 1.40% | Containers—Metal/Glass |
| LZ | Lubrizol Corp. | 1.10% | Chemicals—Specialty |
| BLL | Ball Corp. | 1.00% | Containers—Metal/Glass |
| CCK | Crown Holdings Inc. | 1.00% | Containers—Metal/Glass |
| CLF | Cliffs Natural Resources Inc. | 0.90% | Metal—Iron |
| CF | CF Industries Holdings Inc. | 0.90% | Agricultural Chemicals |

**TABLE C.14   Vanguard Materials ETF (VAW)**
**Expense Ratio (0.25%)    Holdings (30 September 2009) (cont.)**

| Ticker Symbol | Name | Weight | Sector |
|---|---|---|---|
| MLM | Martin Marietta Materials Inc. | 0.90% | Building Products— Cement/Aggregates |
| FMC | FMC Corp. | 0.90% | Chemicals—Diversified |
| EMN | Eastman Chemical Co. | 0.90% | Chemicals—Specialty |
| MWV | MeadWestvaco Corp. | 0.90% | Chemicals—Specialty |
| CE | Celanese Corp. Class A | 0.80% | Chemicals—Diversified |
| ARG | Airgas Inc. | 0.80% | Industrial Gases |
| TRA | Terra Industries Inc. | 0.80% | Agricultural Chemicals |
| PTV | Pactiv Corp. | 0.80% | Containers—Paper/Plastic |
| WLT | Walter Energy Inc. | 0.70% | Coal |
| SEE | Sealed Air Corp. | 0.70% | Containers—Paper/Plastic |
| ATI | Allegheny Technologies Inc. | 0.70% | Steel—Specialty |
| ASH | Ashland Inc. | 0.70% | Chemicals—Specialty |
| IFF | International Flavors & Fragrances Inc. | 0.70% | Chemicals—Specialty |
| STLD | Steel Dynamics Inc. | 0.70% | Steel—Producers |
| NLC | Nalco Holding Co. | 0.60% | Water Treatment Systems |
| RS | Reliance Steel & Aluminum Co. | 0.60% | Steel—Producers |
| BMS | Bemis Co. Inc. | 0.60% | Containers—Paper/Plastic |
| SON | Sonoco Products Co. | 0.60% | Containers—Paper/Plastic |
| VAL | Valspar Corp. | 0.60% | Coatings/Paint |
| ALB | Albemarle Corp. | 0.60% | Chemicals—Specialty |
| ATR | Aptargroup Inc. | 0.60% | Miscellaneous Manufacturing |
| RPM | RPM International Inc. | 0.50% | Coatings/Paint |

**TABLE C.14  Vanguard Materials ETF (VAW)
Expense Ratio (0.25%)   Holdings (30 September 2009) (cont.)**

| Ticker Symbol | Name | Weight | Sector |
|---|---|---|---|
| AKS | AK Steel Holding Corp. | 0.50% | Steel—Producers |
| PKG | Packaging Corp. of America | 0.50% | Containers—Paper/Plastic |
| CMC | Commercial Metals Co. | 0.50% | Metal Processors & Fabricators |
| CMP | Compass Minerals International Inc. | 0.50% | Quarrying |
| SMG | Scotts Miracle-Gro Co. Class A | 0.40% | Consumer Products—Miscellaneous |
| RGLD | Royal Gold Inc. | 0.40% | Gold Mining |
| RKT | Rock-Tenn Co. Class A | 0.40% | Containers—Paper/Plastic |
| TIN | Temple-Inland Inc. | 0.40% | Containers—Paper/Plastic |
| GRA | WR Grace & Co. | 0.40% | Chemicals—Specialty |
| CYT | Cytec Industries Inc. | 0.30% | Chemicals—Specialty |
| CBT | Cabot Corp. | 0.30% | Chemicals—Specialty |
| HUN | Huntsman Corp. | 0.30% | Chemicals—Diversified |
| SLGN | Silgan Holdings Inc. | 0.30% | Containers—Metal/Glass |
| CDE | Coeur d'Alene Mines Corp. | 0.30% | Precious Metals |
| OLN | Olin Corp. | 0.30% | Chemicals—Diversified |
| SXT | Sensient Technologies Corp. | 0.30% | Chemicals—Specialty |
| GEF | Greif Inc. Class A | 0.30% | Containers—Metal/Glass |
| SOA | Solutia Inc. | 0.30% | Chemicals—Diversified |
| EXP | Eagle Materials Inc. | 0.30% | Building Products—Cement/Aggregates |
| SCHN | Schnitzer Steel Industries Inc. | 0.30% | Steel—Producers |
| TIE | Titanium Metals Corp. | 0.30% | Non-ferrous metals |
| NEU | NewMarket Corp. | 0.30% | Chemicals—Specialty |
| IPI | Intrepid Potash Inc. | 0.20% | Agricultural Chemicals |

**TABLE C.14    Vanguard Materials ETF (VAW)**
**Expense Ratio (0.25%)    Holdings (30 September 2009) (cont.)**

| Ticker Symbol | Name | Weight | Sector |
|---|---|---|---|
| CRS | Carpenter Technology Corp. | 0.20% | Steel—Producers |
| FUL | HB Fuller Co. | 0.20% | Chemicals—Specialty |
| TXI | Texas Industries Inc. | 0.20% | Building Products—Cement/Aggregates |
| HL | Hecla Mining Co. | 0.20% | Silver Mining |
| OMG | OM Group Inc. | 0.20% | Chemicals—Specialty |
| ROC | Rockwood Holdings Inc. | 0.20% | Chemicals—Diversified |
| WOR | Worthington Industries Inc. | 0.20% | Metal Processors & Fabricators |
| MTX | Minerals Technologies Inc. | 0.20% | Chemicals—Specialty |
| SWM | Schweitzer-Mauduit International Inc. | 0.20% | Paper & Related Products |
| LPX | Louisiana-Pacific Corp. | 0.20% | Building & Construction Products—Miscellaneous |
| CCC | Calgon Carbon Corp. | 0.20% | Alternative Waste Technology |
| ARJ | Arch Chemicals Inc. | 0.20% | Chemicals—Specialty |
| RTI | RTI International Metals Inc. | 0.20% | Metal Processors & Fabricators |
| KOP | Koppers Holdings Inc. | 0.10% | Diversified Manufacturing |
| ANV | Allied Nevada Gold Corp. | 0.10% | Gold Mining |
| POL | PolyOne Corp. | 0.10% | Chemicals—Plastics |
| KALU | Kaiser Aluminum Corp. | 0.10% | Metal—Aluminum |
| GLAT | Glatfelter | 0.10% | Paper & Related Products |
| ACO | AMCOL International Corp. | 0.10% | Diversified Minerals |
| WLK | Westlake Chemical Corp. | 0.10% | Chemicals—Diversified |
| ZINC | Horsehead Holding Corp. | 0.10% | Non-ferrous metals |
| DEL | Deltic Timber Corp. | 0.10% | Forestry |

**TABLE C.14  Vanguard Materials ETF (VAW)**
**Expense Ratio (0.25%)   Holdings (30 September 2009) (cont.)**

| Ticker Symbol | Name | Weight | Sector |
|---|---|---|---|
| BW | Brush Engineered Materials Inc. | 0.10% | Non-ferrous metals |
| BCPC | Balchem Corp. | 0.10% | Chemicals—Specialty |
| WPP | Wausau Paper Corp. | 0.10% | Paper & Related Products |
| CLW | Clearwater Paper Corp. | 0.10% | Paper & Related Products |
| SHLM | A Schulman Inc. | 0.10% | Chemicals—Plastics |
| SCL | Stepan Co. | 0.10% | Chemicals—Specialty |
| CENX | Century Aluminum Co. | 0.10% | Metal—Aluminum |
| BKI | Buckeye Technologies Inc. | 0.10% | Paper & Related Products |
| FOE | Ferro Corp. | 0.10% | Chemicals—Specialty |
| HAYN | Haynes International Inc. | 0.10% | Metal Processors & Fabricators |

**TABLE C.15  Dow Jones Transportation Average Index Fund (IYT)**
**Expense Ratio (0.48%)   Holdings (30 November 2009)**

| Ticker Symbol | Name | Weight | Sector |
|---|---|---|---|
| BNI | Burlington Northern Santa Fe | 13.36% | Railroads |
| FDX | FedEx Corp. | 11.29% | Delivery Services |
| UNP | Union Pacific Corp. | 8.48% | Railroads |
| UPS | United Parcel Service-Cl B | 8.09% | Delivery Services |
| CHRW | C.H. Robinson Worldwide Inc. | 6.43% | Trucking |
| CSX | CSX Corp. | 4.96% | Railroads |
| NSC | Norfolk Southern Corp. | 4.88% | Railroads |
| GMT | GATX Corp. | 4.68% | Commercial Vehicles & Trucks |

**TABLE C.15  Dow Jones Transportation Average Index Fund (IYT)
Expense Ratio (0.48%)   Holdings (30 November 2009) (cont.)**

| Ticker Symbol | Name | Weight | Sector |
|---|---|---|---|
| JBHT | Hunt (JB) Transport Svcs. Inc. | 4.55% | Trucking |
| LSTR | Landstar System Inc. | 4.53% | Trucking |
| R | Ryder System Inc. | 4.37% | Transportation Services |
| ALEX | Alexander & Baldwin Inc. | 4.33% | Marine Transportation |
| OSG | Overseas Shipholding Group | 4.31% | Marine Transportation |
| CNW | Con-Way Inc. | 4.17% | Trucking |
| EXPD | Expeditors Intl. Wash. Inc. | 4.14% | Delivery Services |
| LUV | Southwest Airlines Co. | 2.38% | Airlines |
| CAL | Continental Airlines-Cl B | 2.27% | Airlines |
| JBLU | JetBlue Airways Corp. | 1.14% | Airlines |
| AMR | AMR Corp. | 1.02% | Airlines |
| YRCW | YRC Worldwide Inc. | 0.24% | Trucking |
| — | BGIF Treasury Money Market Sl Agency Shares | 0.12% | S-T Securities |

**TABLE C.16  Claymore/Delta Global Shipping Index ETF (SEA)
Expense Ratio (0.65%)   Holdings (24 December 2009)**

| Ticker Symbol | Name | Weight | Sector |
|---|---|---|---|
| TNK | Teekay Tank-Cl A | 4.35% | Marine Transportation |
| OSG | Overseas Shipholding Group | 4.22% | Marine Transportation |
| EURN | Euronav NV | 4.22% | Marine Transportation |
| SFL | Ship Finance International Ltd. | 4.17% | Marine Transportation |
| TGP | Teekay Lng. Partners | 4.13% | Marine Transportation |
| GMR | General Maritime Corp. | 4.02% | Marine Transportation |
| TK | Teekay Shipping Corp. | 3.95% | Marine Transportation |

**TABLE C.16   Claymore/Delta Global Shipping Index ETF (SEA)
Expense Ratio (0.65%)   Holdings (24 December 2009) (cont.)**

| Ticker Symbol | Name | Weight | Sector |
|---|---|---|---|
| NMM | Navios Maritime Partners | 3.94% | Marine Transportation |
| SSW | Seaspan Corp. | 3.93% | Marine Transportation |
| 9101 | Nippon Yusen KK | 3.80% | Marine Transportation |
| DNOR | D/S Norden | 3.79% | Marine Transportation |
| 9104 | Mitsui O.S.K. Lines Ltd. | 3.62% | Marine Transportation |
| COS | Cosco Corp. Singapore Ltd. | 3.56% | Shipbuilding |
| NM | Navios Maritime Holdings | 3.55% | Marine Transportation |
| FRO | Frontline Ltd. | 3.51% | Marine Transportation |
| MAERSKB | A P Moller - Maersk A/S | 3.43% | Marine Transportation |
| TNP | Tsakos Energy Navigation | 3.36% | Marine Transportation |
| 2343 | Pacific Basin Shipping Lt. | 3.36% | Marine Transportation |
| 1919 | China Cosco Holdings-H | 3.35% | Marine Transportation |
| 1138.HK | China Shipping Development | 3.24% | Marine Transportation |
| 9107 | Kawasaki Kisen Kaisha Ltd. | 2.70% | Marine Transportation |
| NOL | Neptune Orient Lines Ltd. | 2.53% | Marine Transportation |
| EXM | Excel Maritime Carriers | 2.46% | Marine Transportation |
| DRYS | Dryships Inc. | 2.44% | Marine Transportation |
| EGLE | Eagle Bulk Shipping Inc. | 2.44% | Marine Transportation |
| 2866 | China Shipping Container | 2.43% | Marine Transportation |
| 316 | Orient Overseas Internati | 2.41% | Marine Transportation |
| DSX | Diana Shipping Inc. | 2.36% | Marine Transportation |
| GOGL | Golden Ocean Group Ltd. | 2.36% | Marine Transportation |
| GNK | Genco Shipping & Trading | 2.34% | Marine Transportation |
| 9110 | Shinwa Kaiun Kaisha Ltd. | 0.02% | Marine Transportation |

# Transportation Infrastructure

**TABLE C.17   iShares Cohen & Steers Realty Majors Index Fund (ICF)
Expense Ratio (0.35%)   Holdings (30 November 2009)**

| Ticker Symbol | Name | Weight | Sector |
|---|---|---|---|
| SPG | Simon Property Group Inc. | 7.91% | Regional Malls |
| PSA | Public Storage | 7.65% | Public Storage |
| VNO | Vornado Realty Trust | 7.24% | Diversified |
| BXP | Boston Properties Inc. | 6.58% | Office |
| HCP | HCP Inc. | 6.50% | Healthcare |
| EQR | Equity Residential | 6.26% | Apartments |
| VTR | Ventas Inc. | 4.77% | Healthcare |
| HST | Host Hotels & Resorts Inc. | 4.50% | Hotels |
| PLD | Prologis | 4.11% | Industrial |
| AVB | Avalon Bay Communities | 4.09% | Apartments |
| HCN | Health Care REIT Inc. | 3.79% | Healthcare |
| KIM | Kimco Realty Corp. | 3.29% | Strip Centers |
| FRT | Federal Realty Investment Trust | 2.79% | Strip Centers |
| DLR | Digital Realty Trust Inc. | 2.63% | Industrial |
| AMB | AMB Property Corp. | 2.44% | Industrial |
| SLG | SL Green Realty Corp. | 2.42% | Office |
| LRY | Liberty Property Trust | 2.34% | Mixed Industrial/Office |
| MAC | Macerich Co. | 1.96% | Regional Malls |
| REG | Regency Centers Corp. | 1.90% | Strip Centers |
| DRE | Duke Realty Corp. | 1.78% | Mixed Industrial/Office |
| CPT | Camden Property Trust | 1.76% | Apartments |
| ARE | Alexandria Real Estate Equities Inc. | 1.74% | Office |

**TABLE C.17   iShares Cohen & Steers Realty Majors Index Fund (ICF)**
**Expense Ratio (0.35%)   Holdings (30 November 2009) (cont.)**

| Ticker Symbol | Name | Weight | Sector |
|---|---|---|---|
| CLI | Mack-Cali Realty Corp. | 1.71% | Office |
| UDR | UDR Inc. | 1.60% | Apartments |
| ESS | Essex Property Trust Inc. | 1.59% | Apartments |
| WRI | Weingarten Realty Investors | 1.43% | Strip Centers |
| OFC | Corporate Office Properties | 1.41% | Office |
| BRE | BRE Properties -Class A | 1.18% | Apartments |
| AIV | Apartment Investment & Management Company -A | 1.12% | Apartments |
| DEI | Douglas Emmett Inc. | 1.11% | Office |
| — | BGIF Treasury Money Market SL Agency Shares | 0.11% | — |

**TABLE C.18   SPDR Dow Jones REIT ETF (RWR)**
**Expense Ratio (0.25%)   Holdings (24 December 2009)**

| Ticker Symbol | Name | Weight | Sector |
|---|---|---|---|
| SPG | Simon Property Group Inc. | 10.76% | Regional Malls |
| VNO | Vornado Rlty. Tr. | 5.92% | Diversified |
| PSA | Public Storage | 4.93% | Self-Storage |
| BXP | Boston Properties Inc. | 4.48% | Office |
| EQR | Equity Residential | 4.41% | Apartments |
| HCP | HCP Inc. | 4.22% | Healthcare |
| HST | Host Hotels & Resorts Inc. | 3.46% | Hotels |
| AVB | Avalon Bay Communities | 3.22% | Apartments |
| PLD | Prologis | 3.17% | Industrial |
| VTR | Ventas Inc. | 3.15% | Healthcare |

**TABLE C.18    SPDR Dow Jones REIT ETF (RWR)**
**Expense Ratio (0.25%)    Holdings (24 December 2009) (cont.)**

| Ticker Symbol | Name | Weight | Sector |
|---|---|---|---|
| HCN | Health Care REIT Inc. | 2.59% | Healthcare |
| KIM | Kimco Realty Corp. | 2.56% | Strip Centers |
| FRT | Federal Realty Invt. Tr. | 1.95% | Strip Centers |
| SLG | SL Green Rlty Corp. | 1.83% | Office |
| NHP | Nationwide Health Pptys. Inc. | 1.80% | Healthcare |
| AMB | AMB Property Corp. | 1.79% | Industrial |
| LRY | Liberty Ppty. Tr. | 1.68% | Mixed Industrial/Office |
| MAC | Macerich Co. | 1.60% | Regional Malls |
| DLR | Digital Rlty. Tr. Inc. | 1.58% | Industrial |
| REG | Regency Ctrs. Corp. | 1.44% | Strip Centers |
| ARE | Alexandria Real Estate Eq. I. | 1.32% | Office |
| HPT | Hospitality Pptys. Tr. | 1.31% | Hotels |
| SNH | Senior Hsg. Pptys. Tr. | 1.30% | Healthcare |
| DRE | Duke Realty Corp. | 1.28% | Mixed Industrial/Office |
| CLI | Mack Cali Rlty Corp. | 1.27% | Office |
| UDR | UDR Inc. | 1.18% | Apartments |
| ESS | Essex Ppty. Tr. Inc. | 1.16% | Apartments |
| WRI | Weingarten Rlty. Invs. | 1.12% | Strip Centers |
| HIW | Highwoods Pptys. Inc. | 1.12% | Office |
| 85749P9A | State Str. Instl. Liquid Resvs. | 1.05% | Unassigned |
| OFC | Corporate Office Pptys. Tr. | 1.00% | Office |
| TCO | Taubman Ctrs. Inc. | 0.90% | Regional Malls |
| AIV | Apartment Invt. & Mgmt. Co. | 0.89% | Apartments |
| BRE | BRE Properties Inc. | 0.85% | Apartments |
| DEI | Douglas Emmett Inc. | 0.82% | Office |

**TABLE C.18  SPDR Dow Jones REIT ETF (RWR)**
**Expense Ratio (0.25%)   Holdings (24 December 2009) (cont.)**

| Ticker Symbol | Name | Weight | Sector |
|---|---|---|---|
| WRE | Washington Real Estate Invt. | 0.77% | Diversified |
| HME | Home Properties Inc. | 0.73% | Apartments |
| SKT | Tanger Factory Outlet Ctrs. | 0.73% | Factory Outlets |
| BMR | Biomed Realty Trust Inc. | 0.72% | Office |
| BDN | Brandywine Rlty. Tr. | 0.69% | Mixed Industrial/Office |
| ELS | Equity Lifestyle Pptys. Inc. | 0.69% | Manufactured Homes |
| ACC | American Campus Cmntys. Inc. | 0.68% | Apartments |
| HRP | HRPT Pptys .Tr. | 0.68% | Office |
| CBL | CBL & Assoc Pptys. Inc. | 0.66% | Regional Malls |
| MAA | Mid-Amer Apt. Cmntys. Inc. | 0.64% | Apartments |
| LHO | Lasalle Hotel Pptys. | 0.64% | Hotels |
| KRC | Kilroy Rlty. Corp. | 0.63% | Mixed Industrial/Office |
| HR | Healthcare Rlty. Tr. | 0.58% | Healthcare |
| DDR | Developers Diversified Rlty. | 0.53% | Strip Centers |
| DCT | DCT Industrial Trust Inc. | 0.49% | Industrial |
| FSP | Franklin Street Pptys. Corp. | 0.49% | Unassigned |
| EXR | Extra Space Storage Inc. | 0.48% | Self-Storage |
| DRH | DiamondRock Hospitality Co. | 0.46% | Hotels |
| SSS | Sovran Self Storage Inc. | 0.46% | Self-Storage |
| EGP | EastGroup Ppty. Inc. | 0.45% | Industrial |
| PSB | PS Business Pks. Inc. Calif. | 0.44% | Mixed Industrial/Office |
| PPS | Post Pptys. Inc. | 0.43% | Apartments |
| SHO | Sunstone Hotel Invs. Inc. | 0.39% | Hotels |
| CLP | Colonial Pptys. Tr. | 0.36% | Diversified |
| DFT | DuPont Fabros Technology In. | 0.34% | Industrial |

**TABLE C.18    SPDR Dow Jones REIT ETF (RWR)
Expense Ratio (0.25%)    Holdings (24 December 2009) (cont.)**

| Ticker Symbol | Name | Weight | Sector |
|---|---|---|---|
| ALX | Alexanders Inc. | 0.33% | Regional Malls |
| AKR | Acadia Rlty. Tr. | 0.31% | Strip Centers |
| CUZ | Cousins Pptys. Inc. | 0.30% | Diversified |
| EQY | Equity One | 0.29% | Strip Centers |
| IRC | Inland Real Estate Corp. | 0.27% | Strip Centers |
| YSI | U Store It Tr. | 0.27% | Self-Storage |
| PKY | Parkway Pptys Inc. | 0.21% | Office |
| PEI | Pennsylvania Real Estate Invt. | 0.18% | Regional Malls |
| FPO | First Potomac Rlty. Tr. | 0.17% | Mixed Industrial/Office |
| CDR | Cedar Shopping Ctrs. Inc. | 0.16% | Strip Centers |
| SUI | Sun Communities Inc. | 0.16% | Manufactured Homes |
| UHT | Universal Health Rlty. Incm. | 0.16% | Healthcare |
| AHT | Ashford Hospitality Tr. Inc. | 0.13% | Hotels |
| RPT | Ramco-Gershenson Pptys Tr. | 0.13% | Strip Centers |
| FR | First Industrial Realty Tru. | 0.13% | Industrial |
| KRG | Kite Rlty Group Tr. | 0.12% | Strip Centers |
| EDR | Education Rlty. Tr. Inc. | 0.12% | Apartments |
| FCH | FelCor Lodging Tr. Inc. | 0.11% | Hotels |
| BFS | Saul Ctrs. Inc. | 0.11% | Strip Centers |
| HT | Hersha Hospitality Tr. | 0.08% | Hotels |
| CASH_USD | U.S. Dollar | -1.03% | Unassigned |

**TABLE C.19  SPDR Dow Jones REIT ETF (VNQ)
Expense Ratio (0.11%)  Holdings (30 September 2009)**

| Ticker Symbol | Name | Weight | Sector |
|---|---|---|---|
| SPG | Simon Property Group Inc. | 9.60% | Regional Malls |
| VNO | Vornado Realty Trust | 5.00% | Diversified |
| PSA | Public Storage | 4.60% | Self-Storage |
| BXP | Boston Properties Inc. | 4.30% | Office |
| EQR | Equity Residential | 4.10% | Apartments |
| HCP | HCP Inc. | 4.10% | Healthcare |
| HST | Host Hotels & Resorts Inc. | 3.40% | Hotels |
| VTR | Ventas Inc. | 2.90% | Healthcare |
| AVB | Avalon Bay Communities | 2.80% | Apartments |
| PLD | Prologis | 2.60% | Industrial |
| HCN | Health Care REIT Inc. | 2.40% | Healthcare |
| KIM | Kimco Realty Corp. | 2.30% | Strip Centers |
| FRT | Federal Realty Investment Trust | 1.80% | Strip Centers |
| AMB | AMB Property Corp. | 1.60% | Industrial |
| LRY | Liberty Property Trust | 1.60% | Mixed Industrial/Office |
| DLR | Digital Realty Trust Inc. | 1.60% | Industrial |
| SLG | SL Green Realty Corp. | 1.60% | Office |
| NHP | Nationwide Health Properties Inc. | 1.60% | Healthcare |
| REG | Regency Centers Corp. | 1.40% | Strip Centers |
| DRE | Duke Realty Corp. | 1.30% | Mixed Industrial/Office |
| O | Realty Income Corp. | 1.30% | Single Tenant Retail |
| CPT | Camden Property Trust | 1.30% | Apartments |
| HPT | Hospitality Properties Trust | 1.20% | Hotels |
| CLI | Mack-Cali Realty Corp. | 1.20% | Office |
| MAC | Macerich Co. | 1.20% | Regional Malls |

**TABLE C.19   SPDR Dow Jones REIT ETF (VNQ)**
**Expense Ratio (0.11%)   Holdings (30 September 2009) (cont.)**

| Ticker Symbol | Name | Weight | Sector |
|---|---|---|---|
| SNH | Senior Housing Properties Trust | 1.20% | Healthcare |
| UDR | UDR Inc. | 1.20% | Apartments |
| ARE | Alexandria Real Estate Equities Inc. | 1.10% | Office |
| WRI | Weingarten Realty Investors | 1.10% | Strip Centers |
| HIW | Highwoods Properties Inc. | 1.10% | Offices |
| ESS | Essex Property Trust Inc. | 1.10% | Apartments |
| OEC | Corporate Office Properties Trust SBI MD | 1.00% | Office |
| TCO | Taubman Centers Inc. | 0.90% | Regional Malls |
| AIV | Apartment Investment & Management Co. | 0.80% | Apartments |
| NNN | National Retail Properties Inc. | 0.80% | Single Tenant Retail |
| HRP | HRPT Properties Trust | 0.80% | Office |
| WRE | Washington Real Estate Investment Trust | 0.80% | Diversified |
| BRE | BRE Properties Inc. | 0.80% | Apartments |
| SKT | Tanger Factory Outlet Centers | 0.70% | Factory Outlets |
| HME | Home Properties Inc. | 0.70% | Apartments |
| ACC | American Campus Communities Inc. | 0.70% | Apartments |
| BCN | Brandywine Realty Trust | 0.70% | Mixed Industrial/Office |
| BMR | BioMed Realty Trust Inc. | 0.70% | Office |
| OHI | Omega Healthcare Investors Inc. | 0.60% | Healthcare |
| MAA | Mid-America Apartment Communities Inc. | 0.60% | Apartments |
| DDR | Developers Diversified Realty Corp. | 0.60% | Strip Centers |

**TABLE C.19  SPDR Dow Jones REIT ETF (VNQ)
Expense Ratio (0.11%)   Holdings (30 September 2009) (cont.)**

| Ticker Symbol | Name | Weight | Sector |
|---|---|---|---|
| HR | Healthcare Realty Trust Inc. | 0.60% | Healthcare |
| LHO | LaSalle Hotel Properties | 0.60% | Hotels |
| ELS | Equity Lifestyle Properties Inc. | 0.60% | Manufactured Homes |
| CBL | CBL & Associates Properties Inc. | 0.60% | Regional Malls |
| EPR | Entertainment Properties Trust | 0.60% | Diversified |
| DEI | Douglas Emmett Inc. | 0.60% | Office |
| KRC | Kilroy Realty Corp. | 0.60% | Mixed Industrial/Office |
| DCT | DCT Industrial Trust Inc. | 0.50% | Industrial |
| PSB | PS Business Parks Inc. | 0.50% | Mixed Industrial/Office |
| EGP | EastGroup Properties Inc. | 0.50% | Industrial |
| FSP | Franklin Street Properties Corp. | 0.50% | Office |
| DRH | DiamondRock Hospitality Co. | 0.40% | Hotels |
| EXR | Extra Space Storage Inc. | 0.40% | Self-Storage |
| PPS | Post Properties Inc. | 0.40% | Apartments |
| SSS | Sovran Self Storage Inc. | 0.40% | Self-Storage |
| NHI | National Health Investors Inc. | 0.40% | Healthcare |
| CUZ | Cousins Properties Inc. | 0.30% | Diversified |
| EQY | Equity One Inc. | 0.30% | Strip Centers |
| IRC | Inland Real Estate Corp. | 0.30% | Strip Centers |
| MPT | Medical Properties Trust Inc. | 0.30% | Healthcare |
| ALX | Alexander's Inc. | 0.30% | Regional Malls |
| IRET | Investors Real Estate Trust | 0.30% | Diversified |
| AKR | Acadia Realty Trust | 0.30% | Strip Centers |
| DFT | DuPont Fabros Technology Inc. | 0.30% | Industrial |
| SHO | Sunstone Hotel Investors Inc. | 0.30% | Hotels |

**TABLE C.19   SPDR Dow Jones REIT ETF (VNQ)**
**Expense Ratio (0.11%)   Holdings (30 September 2009) (cont.)**

| Ticker Symbol | Name | Weight | Sector |
|---|---|---|---|
| LTC | LTC Properties Inc. | 0.20% | Healthcare |
| YSI | U-Store-It Trust | 0.20% | Self-Storage |
| GTY | Getty Realty Corp. | 0.20% | Single Tenant Retail |
| CLP | Colonial Properties Trust | 0.20% | Diversified |
| LXP | Lexington Realty Trust | 0.20% | Diversified |
| BFS | Saul Centers Inc. | 0.20% | Strip Centers |
| PKY | Parkway Properties Inc. | 0.20% | Office |
| SUI | Sun Communities Inc. | 0.20% | Manufactured Homes |
| UHT | Universal Health Realty Income Trust | 0.20% | Healthcare |
| FPO | First Potomac Realty Trust | 0.20% | Mixed Industrial/Office |
| EDR | Education Realty Trust Inc. | 0.20% | Apartments |
| AHT | Ashford Hospitality Trust Inc. | 0.10% | Hotels |
| FCH | FelCor Lodging Trust Inc. | 0.10% | Hotels |
| FR | First Industrial Realty Trust Inc. | 0.10% | Industrial |
| CDR | Cedar Shopping Centers Inc. | 0.10% | Strip Centers |
| PEI | Pennsylvania Real Estate Investment Trust | 0.10% | Regional Malls |
| UBA | Urstadt Biddle Properties Inc. Class A | 0.10% | Shopping Centers |
| RPT | Ramco-Gershenson Properties Trust | 0.10% | Strip Centers |
| KRG | Kite Realty Group Trust | 0.10% | Strip Centers |
| GRT | Glimcher Realty Trust | 0.10% | Regional Malls |
| BEE | Strategic Hotels & Resorts Inc. | 0.10% | Hotels |
| LSE | CapLease Inc.. | 0.10% | Diversified |
| HT | Hersha Hospitality Trust | 0.10% | Hotels |

**TABLE C.19   SPDR Dow Jones REIT ETF (VNQ)**
**Expense Ratio (0.11%)   Holdings (30 September 2009) (cont.)**

| Ticker Symbol | Name | Weight | Sector |
|---|---|---|---|
| FUR | Winthrop Realty Trust | 0.10% | Diversified |
| GKK | Gramercy Capital Corp. | 0.10% | Mortgage |
| UBP | Urstadt Biddle Properties Inc. | 0.00% | Shopping Centers |

# INDEX